ECONOMIC COMMISSION FOR EUROPE
Committee on Environmental Policy

ENVIRONMENTAL PERFORMANCE REVIEWS

ALBANIA

UNITED NATIONS
New York and Geneva, 2002

Environmental Performance Reviews Series No. 16

NOTE

Symbols of United Nations documents are composed of capital letters combined with figures. Mention of such a symbol indicates a reference to a United Nations document.

The designations employed and the presentation of the material in this publication do not imply the expression of any opinion whatsoever on the part of the Secretariat of the United Nations concerning the legal status of any country, territory, city or area, or of its authorities, or concerning the delimitation of its frontiers or boundaries.

UNITED NATIONS PUBLICATION
Sales No. E.03.II.E.23
ISBN 92-1-116838-4
ISSN 1020-4563

Foreword

The Environmental Performance Reviews are intended to assist countries in transition to improve their management of the environment by establishing baseline conditions and making concrete recommendations for better policy implementation and performance and to integrate environmental policies into sectoral policies at the national level. Through the Peer Review process, they also promote dialogue among UNECE member countries and harmonization of environmental conditions and policies throughout the region.

This work was initiated by ministers at the second Ministerial Conference "Environment for Europe," in Lucerne, in 1993. Acting on the request of the ministers, the UNECE Committee on Environmental Policy, meeting in special session in January 1994, decided to make the Environmental Performance Reviews a part of its regular programme. As a voluntary exercise, the Environmental Performance Review is undertaken only at the request of the country itself at the ministerial level.

The studies are carried out by international teams of experts from the region, working closely with national experts from the reviewed country. Through a process of broad consultations, the experts carry out a comprehensive assessment of a wide range of issues related to the environment, covering three broad themes: the framework for environmental policy and management, management of pollution and natural resources and economic and sectoral integration. The team's final report contains recommendations for further improvement, taking into consideration the country's progress in the current transition period.

The teams also benefit from close cooperation with other organizations in the United Nations system, including the United Nations Development Programme, the United Nations Environment Programme, the World Bank and the World Health Organization.

This Environmental Performance Review is the sixteenth in the series published by the United Nations Economic Commission. I hope that this Review will be useful to all countries in the region, to intergovernmental and non-governmental organization and, especially, to Albania, to its Government, all national stakeholders, to its people.

Brigita Schmögnerova
Executive Secretary

Preface

In September 2001, the UNECE Committee on Environmental Policy agreed to the Albanian request for an Environmental Performance Review (EPR).

During the preparatory mission in July 2001, final decisions were reached on both the structure and the organizational details of the project, taking into account the considerable changes that made by the country after the ten-year isolation.

The review mission took place in October 2001. The review team included experts from Bulgaria, Croatia, Norway, the Russian Federation, Switzerland, together with experts from the secretariat of the United Nations Economic Commission for Europe (UNECE), the United Nations Environment Programme (UNEP) and the European Centre for Environment and Health of the World Health Organization (WHO).

In October 2002, the draft was submitted for consideration to the Ad Hoc Expert Group on Environmental Performance Reviews. During this meeting, the Expert Group discussed the report in detail with representatives of the Albanian Government, focusing in particular on the conclusions and recommendations. The EPR report, as amended by the Expert Group, was then submitted for peer review to the UNECE Committee on Environmental Policy at its annual session in Geneva on 4 to 6 November 2002. A high-level delegation from the Government of Albania, led by the Minister of Environment, assisted the Committee in its deliberations. The Committee adopted the recommendations as set out in this report.

Between the date of the review mission and that of the Expert and Peer Reviews, Albania had already made significant progress, necessitating a number of changes to the draft text. Of particular importance was the adoption of both a new comprehensive framework Law on Environmental Protection and an updated National Environmental Action Plan (2002-2007). This is clear evidence of the increasing support that the Government and the people of Albania are giving to environmental matters within the country. The report also notes a number of key areas that continue to need urgent attention, including, for example, waste management, coastal zone management and tourism, and agriculture and soil protection.

The UNECE Committee on Environmental Policy and the UNECE review team would like to thank both the Government of Albania for its invitation to carry out this review and the many excellent national experts who worked with the international experts and contributed with their knowledge and assistance. UNECE wishes Albania success in carrying out the tasks before it to meet its environmental objectives, including implementation of the recommendations contained in the present report.

UNECE would also like to express its appreciation to the Governments of Denmark, Germany, the Netherlands, Norway and Switzerland for their support, and to the United Nations Development Programme (UNDP) office in Tirana, the UNEP Regional Office in Europe, the WHO European Centre for Environment and Health (ECEH), and UNEP/Grid-Arendal for participating in this Environmental Performance Review and contributing to the report.

LIST OF TEAM MEMBERS

Ms. Mary Pat SILVEIRA	(ECE secretariat)	Team Leader
Ms. Catherine MASSON	(ECE secretariat)	Project Coordinator
Ms. Mijke HERTOGHS	(ECE secretariat)	Asst. Coordinator
Mr. Jyrki HIRVONEN	(ECE secretariat)	Introduction
Ms. Vanya GRIGOROVA	(BULGARIA)	Chapter 1
Ms. Mijke HERTOGHS	(ECE secretariat)	Chapter 2
Mrs. Irina KRASNOVA	(RUSSIAN FEDERATION)	Chapter 3
Ms. Ieva RUCEVSKA	(UNEP/GRID-Arendal)	Chapter 4
Ms. Eli Marie ASEN	(NORWAY)	Chapter 5
Ms. Catherine MASSON	(ECE secretariat)	Chapter 6
Mr. Ivan NARKEVITCH	(ECE secretariat)	Chapter 7
Ms. Stella SATALIC	(CROATIA)	Chapter 8
Mr. René NIJENHUIS	(ECE secretariat)	Chapter 9
Ms. Elisabeth CLÉMENT-ARNOLD	(SWITZERLAND)	Chapter 10
Mr. Ivica TRUMBIC	(UNEP/PAP/RAC)	Chapter 11
Ms. Bettina MENNE	(WHO/ECEH)	Chapter 12

The preparatory mission for the project took place from 26 to 27 July 2001. The review mission was organized from 16 to 24 October 2001.

LIST OF NATIONAL CONTRIBUTORS

<u>Albania</u>

Tatjana Hema	Ministry of Environment
Narin Panariti	Ministry of Environment
Elvana Ramaj	Ministry of Environment
Diana Jaho	Ministry of Environment
Daniela Godo	Ministry of Environment
Madalena Rroço	Ministry of Environment
Bajram Mejdiaj	Ministry of Environment
Alma Bako	Ministry of Environment
Trajan Vasili	Ministry of Environment
Xhaferr Baloshi	Ministry of Environment
Bashkim Saliasi	Ministry of Environment
Mirela Kamberi	Ministry of Environment
Zamir Dedej	Ministry of Environment
Shkelqim Mema	Ministry of Environment
Spartak Sinoimeri	Ministry of Environment
Klodiana Agolli	Ministry of Environment
Eno Dodbiba	Ministry of Environment
Ermira Fida	Ministry of Environment
Bujar Reme	Ministry of Environment
Margarita Lutaj	Ministry of Environment
Aurela Binjaku	Ministry of Environment
Kujtim Biçaku	Ministry of Environment
Arben Luzati	Ministry of Environment
Astrit Avdyli	Ministry of Environment
Arjan Gaçe	Ministry of Environment
Arben Pustina	Ministry of Environment
Marieta Mima	Ministry of Environment
Ermal Halimi	Ministry of Environment
Sherif Lushaj	Ministry of Environment
Valentina Suljoti	Ministry of Environment
Shpresa Leka	Ministry of Environment
Marita Selfo	Ministry of Environment
Petrit Vasili	Ministry of Environment
Silva Bino	Ministry of Environment
Arjana Koça	Ministry of Environment

TABLE OF CONTENTS

ANNEXES

LIST OF FIGURES

LIST OF TABLES

LIST OF BOXES

ACRONYMS AND ABBREVIATIONS

BaP	Benzo(a)pyrene
BOD	Biological oxygen demand
CARDS	Community Assistance for Reconstruction
CFCs	Chlorofluorocarbons
CITES	Convention on International Trade in Endangered Species of Wild Fauna and Flora
COD	Chemical oxygen demand
CPI	Consumer price index
EBRD	European Bank for Reconstruction and Development
EC	European Commission
ECAT	Environmental Centre for Administration and Technology
ECE	Economic Commission for Europe
ECEH	European Centre for Environment and Health
ECU	European currency unit
EIA	Environmental impact assessment
EIONET	European Environment Information and Observation Network
EMEP	Cooperative Programme for Monitoring and Evaluation of the Long-range Transmission of Air Pollutants in Europe
EPR	Environmental Performance Review
EU	European Union
GDP	Gross domestic product
GEF	Global Environment Facility
HCFCs	Hydrochlorofluorocarbons
IMF	International Monetary Fund
IUCN	World Conservation Union
MAC	Maximum allowable concentration
MAP	Mediterranean Action Plan
MED POL	Mediterranean Pollution Monitoring and Research Programme
MTEF	Medium-Term Expenditure Framework
NATO	North Atlantic Treaty Organisation
NEAP	National Environmental Action Plan
NEHAP	National Environmental Health Action Plan
NGO	Non-governmental organization
NWC	National Water Council
OECD	Organisation for Economic Co-operation and Development
OSCE	Organization for Security and Co-operation in Europe
PAP/RAC	Priorities Action Programme / Regional Activity Centre
PHARE	Assistance for Economic Restructuring in the countries of Central and Eastern Europe
PM	Particulate matter
POP	Persistent organic pollutant
REMPEC	Regional Marine Pollution Emergency Response Centre
REReP	Regional Environmental Reconstruction Programme
SECI	Southeast European Cooperation Initiative
SEECP	South-East European Cooperation Process
SoE	State of the Environment
SP	Suspended particulates
UNDP	United Nations Development Programme
UNECE	United Nations Economic Commission for Europe
UNEP	United Nations Environment Programme
UNESCO	United Nations Educational, Scientific and Cultural Organization
UNIDO	United Nations Organization for Industrial Development

USAID	United States Agency for International Development
VAT	Value-added tax
VOC	Volatile organic compound
WHO	World Health Organization
WTO	World Trade Organization

SIGNS AND MEASURES

..	not available
-	nil or negligible
.	decimal point
ha	hectare
kt	kiloton
g	gram
kg	kilogram
mg	milligram
mm	millimetre
cm²	square centimetre
m³	cubic metre
km	kilometre
km²	square kilometre
toe	ton oil equivalent
l	litre
ml	millilitre
min	minute
s	second
m	metre
°C	degree Celsius
GJ	gigajoule
kW$_{el}$	kilowatt (electric)
kW$_{th}$	kilowatt (thermal)
MW$_{el}$	megawatt (electric)
MW$_{th}$	megawatt (thermal)
MWh	megawatt-hour
GWh	gigawatt-hour
TWh	terawatt-hour
Bq	becquerel
Ci	curie
MSv	millisievert
Cap	capita
Eq	equivalent
H	hour
kv	kilovolt
MW	megawatt
Gcal	gigacalorie
Hz	hertz

Currency

Monetary unit: Albanian Lek

Exchange rates: IMF does not provide exchange rate for the Lek prior to the 1992.

Year	Lek/US$	Lek/Euro
1992	75.03	97.30
1993	102.06	119.64
1994	94.62	112.47
1995	92.70	121.26
1996	104.50	132.51
1997	148.93	168.90
1998	150.63	168.71
1999	137.69	146.89
2000	143.71	132.79
2001	143.48	128.50

Source: IMF. International Financial Statistics, May 2002

Note: Values are annual averages

INTRODUCTION

I.1 The physical context

Albania is situated on the western edge of the Balkan Peninsula. With 28,748 km², Albania is one of the smallest countries in Europe. It has a 476-km-long coastline on the Adriatic and Ionian Seas to the west, and it is bounded by Yugoslavia to the north and northeast (Republics of Serbia and Montenegro, respectively), by the former Yugoslav Republic of Macedonia to the east, and by Greece on the southeast and south. The lowlands of the west face the Adriatic Sea. Fewer than 100 km over the strategically important Strait of Otranto separate Albania and the Italian peninsula.

Albania is a mountainous country. Approximately three fourths of its territory consists of highlands above 300 m (1,000 ft). The mountains, which form a generally north-south backbone running parallel to the Adriatic coast, are a southern continuation of the Dinaric Alps. The North Albanian Alps, a glaciated limestone range in the extreme north, are among the most rugged and inaccessible regions in the country. The highest peak, Maja e Korabit (2,753 m), is in the Korab Mountains on the border with the former Yugoslav Republic of Macedonia. The rest consists of coastal flat plains or low hills.

The climate varies with the topography. The coastal plains have a Mediterranean climate with hot and dry summers, and frequent thunderstorms. Winters are wet and mild; freezing temperatures are rare. In the mountains the summer precipitation is higher than on the lowlands, daytime temperatures in the mountains soar but nights are much cooler. The winters can be quite severe in the mountains with heavy snowfall, thunderstorms and snow cover lasting for long periods of time. December, the wettest month, has an average rainfall of 211 mm, while the driest months, July and August, receive only 32 mm of rain. On the coast annual rainfall averages 1,000 mm, but in the mountains it may be as high as 3,000 mm. The average temperatures in August, the hottest month, range from 17° to 31°C. In January, the coldest month, they range from 2° to 12°C.

Most of the precipitation drains into the rivers and flows into the Adriatic Sea. Since the topographical water divide is east of Albania, a considerable amount of water from neighbouring countries drains through Albania.

Nearly all the country's rivers have highly irregular seasonal flow patterns. In the summer, most carry less than a tenth of their winter averages, if they are not altogether dry. This seasonal flow pattern makes rivers difficult to control and unnavigable. The exception is the Bunë, which can be navigated by small ships.

The river Drini (282 km) is the longest river with a stable, constant stream. Fed by melting snows from the northern and eastern mountains and by the more evenly distributed seasonal precipitation of that area, its normal flow varies seasonally by only about one third. Its drainage area within Albania is 5,957 km², but, as it also collects water from the Adriatic portion of the Kosovo watershed and from the three border lakes (Shkodra, Prespa and Ohrid), its total catchment basin covers 15,540 km².

Albania's borders divide the country's three major lakes: Ohrid (the largest, with 358.2 km²), Shkodra and Prespa. There are also many lagoon lakes in the lowlands as well as small glacial lakes in the uplands.

Most of the land is difficult to farm because of drainage and water-supply problems. The beds of the streams rise as silt is deposited in them and eventually streams break out of their riverbeds and change channel on the lower plains. Old channels become barriers to proper drainage and create swamps or marshlands. Shifting of the water channels hinders development and use of the land in many areas.

Since less than 21 per cent of annual rainfall occurs between April and September, the period of maximum evapo-transpiration, irrigation is necessary, especially in the coastal areas, where most of the highly productive land is located.

Irrigation works have existed for a long time, but the largest irrigation projects were completed after the Second World War, including the Vjosë-Levan-Fier irrigation canal, with an irrigation capacity of 15,000 hectares, and the reservoir at Thanë, in Lushnjë District, with an irrigation capacity of 35,100 hectares. In 1986 nearly 400,000 hectares of land, or 56 per cent of the total cultivated area, were under irrigation, compared with 29,000 hectares, or 10 per cent of the total cultivated area, in 1938.

Forest and woodland cover 38 per cent of Albania; 21 per cent is arable land; 5 per cent is under permanent crops; and 15 per cent is permanent pasture.

The most important crops are wheat, corn, sugar beet, sunflower seeds, tobacco, fruit and potatoes. Albanian farmers have shifted away from industrial crops like cotton, partly because the country's textile industry is declining.

Albania's mineral resources include large reserves of chromium, copper and iron-nickel. There are smaller deposits of gold, silver, bauxite, magnesite and zinc. In 1994, chrome accounted for 18 per cent of Albania's exports and was the country's biggest earner of foreign currency. Albania is the world's third largest producer of chromium per capita and the only country in Europe with significant reserves, estimated at more than 33 million metric tons of recoverable ore (5 per cent of the world's known deposits). Mining activity is now concentrated on chrome and copper, with enough reserves to support production until about 2025. In recent years extraction has become more difficult because of a lack of ore suitable for opencast mining. Most reserves lie in deep deposits in remote and mountainous areas of Albania's north and east, making exploitation more expensive.

Albania could be self-sufficient in electric energy owing to the abundance of streams and gorges suitable for huge dams that provides the country with cheap hydroelectric power. Hydroelectric plants, mostly on the Drin, Mati, and Bistricë rivers, generate 97 per cent of the country's electricity. In 2000 Albania exported 10 per cent of the generated electricity. In recent years electricity demand from the household sector has surged as people use more electrical appliances and individual electric heaters.

Figure I.1: Land use, 1997

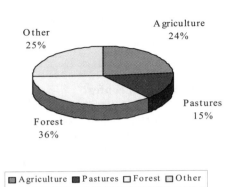

Source: Ministry of Agriculture, Food and Forests (Department of Statistics), 2002.

Moderate oil reserves are located near the central Albanian town of Berat (Patos-Marinza oilfield). Of the estimated 490-million-metric-ton reserves, about 10 per cent have been extracted. The production of natural gas declined from 200-250 million m^3 per year (equivalent to 0.2-0.25 million ton oil equivalent (toe)) in 1989-90 to 20-25 million m^3 in recent years, mainly due to a lack of investment. Until 1991 the combined oil and gas output remained relatively constant between 1.3 and 1.5 million toe but after 1997 it declined to less than 0.4 million toe. The country's coal reserves are substantial. In the late 1980s during a period of high production (2.2 million tons per year or 0.5 million toe) Albania's coal reserves would have lasted for 300 years. Since then, together with industrial production, coal extraction has collapsed to approximately 0.03 million toe annually, but its potential is enormous.

I.2   Demography

Albanians are believed to be descendants of the ancient Illyrians. Depending on the information source, 92 to 98 per cent of the population of the country is ethnic Albanian. This homogeneous ethnic composition, atypical of Balkan populations, has preserved the national identity and language well. Albania's ethnic minorities include Macedonians, Vlachs, Bulgarians, Gypsies, Serbs and Greeks in the south. The main religions are Islam, Orthodox Christianity and Catholicism.

Albania has Europe's highest total fertility rate (2.8), double the European average (1.4). Its birth rate (17.2/1000 in 1999) is also one of the highest in Europe (Western Europe 11.3/1000 in 1998). During the 1945-1990 period the population tripled from little over 1 million to the current total of 3,411,000. Although the country's total fertility and birth rates are high, the rate of population increase is declining due to massive emigration since 1990. There are also many ethnic Albanians living in adjoining areas of Yugoslavia (Kosovo) and the former Yugoslav Republic of Macedonia.

The average population density is 111 inhabitants/km^2 (EU average: 114 inhabitants/km^2). More than 60 per cent of the population is concentrated on the Western Lowland, especially in areas in and around the main cities. The urban population is growing fast. In 1989 it was 36 per cent of the total population, by 1999 it had risen to 41 per cent. This urbanization with substantial population movements started after 1990, when the law banning free movement was abolished.

Population density varies considerably within the country. In the most populated regions, the lowland between Tirana (445,976 inh.) and Durrës (157,339 inh.), it is over 300 inhabitants/km^2. In the mountainous northern region it is much lower at 40 inhabitants/km^2.

The infant mortality rate is a good indicator of the general well being of the population. Albania's infant mortality rate was 12.2 per 1000 live births in 1999 (West European average is 3 to 7 per 1000), significantly lower than the 60 per 1000 recorded from 1970 to 1975. In 1998 life expectancy at birth for men was 71.5 and for women 78.7 years.

At 93 per cent, Albania's literacy rate is quite high. Measured by the UNDP *Human Development Index*, Albania has made progress since 1995, when it ranked 105th among 174 reviewed countries. In 1999, it was 85th out of 162 countries.

Figure I.2: GDP – composition by sector: 1990 and 1999 (per cent of the total)

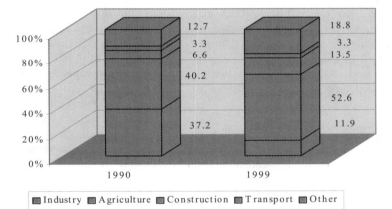

Source: UNECE common statistical database, 2002.

Table I.1: Living standard indicators, 1990-1999

	1990	1991	1992	1993	1994	1995	1996	1997	1998	1999
Passenger cars (per 1000 inhabitants)	..	..	11	18	21	18	20	23	27	29*
Basic telephone lines (per 1000 inhabitants)	12.3	12.7	13.3	12.4	11.7	11.7	17.4	23.3	30.5	36.5
Private telephone lines (per 1000 inhabitants)	..	..	..	..	..	..	..	..	..	..
Mobile telephone subscribers (per 1000 inhabitants	..	..	..	..	..	..	0.6	0.9	1.5	2.9
Internet hosts	..	..	..	..	..	35	79	117	142	215
Estimated Internet users	..	..	..	..	..	350	1000	1500	2000	2500

Source: ITU. Yearbook of Statistics 2001 and Social Indicators Yearbook, 2000.

Note: * 9 month figure

Table I.2: Demography and health indices, 1990-2001

	1990	1991	1992	1993	1994	1995	1996	1997	1998	1999	2000	2001
Birth rate (per 1000)	25.0	23.7	23.6	21.4	22.5	22.2	20.8	18.6	17.9	17.2	..	..
Fertility rate check this	3.0	2.8	2.8	2.6	2.8	2.7	2.6	2.3	2.2	2.1	..	..
Mortality rate (per 1000)	5.5	5.4	5.4	5.7	5.7	5.6	5.4	5.5	5.4	5.0	..	..
Infant mortality rate (per 1000)	28.5	33.1	33.8	35.7	36.0	30.5	26.3	22.9	15.5	12.2	..	..
Female life expectancy at birth (years)	75.9	..	76.7	77.2	79.2	78.3	78.2	79.5	78.7	..	72.9*	74.9**
Male life expectancy at birth (years)	69.6	..	69.8	70.3	71.9	71.5	71.3	70.8	71.6	..	64.3*	69.0**
Life expectancy at birth (years)	72.6	..	73.2	73.7	75.4	74.9	74.6	75.0	75.1	..	..	71.8**
Population aged 1-14 in total (%)	32.5	32.8	33.5	33.7	33.4	33.0	33.0	33.0	32.6	32.4	..	..
Population aged 65 and over in total (%)	5.3	5.5	5.7	5.9	6.0	6.1	6.1	6.1	6.1	5.9		
Basic school enrolment rate (%)	102.0	97.9	94.5	95.3	96.6	96.8	96.1	94.6	92.6	90.0	..	..
Tertiary education attainment rate (%)	..	..	..	..	..	..	..	..	..	..	..	..

Sources : UNECE PAU, 2002; World Bank, 2001; *WHO Health for all Database; **CIA Factbook, 2001.

I.3 The economic context and the transition to a market economy

Since the Second World War, Albanian economic policy, performance and development have been erratic and dependent on the political situation. Albania formed political and economic relationships with Yugoslavia, the Soviet Union and China then cut all ties with them one by one. The reasons varied from Albania's fear of being dominated to disagreements over Albania's industrial policy.

At the end of the 1960s it became clear that Albania's development strategy could not provide growth without substantial aid and credits from abroad. China, which had given Albania about US$ 900 million in aid and provided extensive credits for industrialization, changed its policy by reducing its aid substantially in 1972 and ending it completely in 1978.

After the break with China, Albania chose a policy of strict autarky. The Government's response to the loss of Chinese aid was a rapid increase in the production and export of the main sources of hard currency income: oil, chromite, copper and electric power. This self-imposed autarky, however, proved unsuccessful. Between 1981 and 1988, average net material product growth was 1.7 per cent, which was not sufficient to keep pace with the country's annual population growth of 2 per cent. A drought between 1983 and 1988 set back agriculture and hydroelectric power production. Output declined, hard currency income fell and investments contracted, causing productivity to drop.

In 1989, the Government initiated reform measures, which came too late and were never fully implemented. By the summer of 1990, unemployment was evident. Again a drought reduced electricity supplies and plants were forced to shut down. Anti-government riots broke out in Tirana and Shkodër in April 1991 and thousands of Albanians fled to Italy, Germany and Greece. In the summer of 1991 only a quarter of Albania's production capacity was functioning. Inflation was fed by the Government's decision to pay idle workers 80 per cent of their salaries. The prolonged shutdown of the production lines caused damage to the equipment, and the breakdown of the rule of law caused widespread theft of private and State-owned property.

In this chaos a coalition Government took office in June 1991 and announced its intention to carry out radical economic reforms. The coalition fell a few months later and, in 1992, the Albanian Democratic Party took over and started to implement badly needed reforms.

New beginning: transition to a market economy

Albania started its transition towards a market economy from a difficult economic situation. All production sectors except agriculture were at a standstill. In 1992 inflation was 226 per cent and almost 30 per cent of the workforce was unemployed. According to the International Monetary Fund (IMF), the country's real GDP fell by 10 per cent in 1990, 28 per cent in 1991 and 7.2 per cent in 1992.

Table I.3: Selected economic indicators, 1990-2000

	1990	1991	1992	1993	1994	1995	1996	1997	1998	1999	2000
GDP in current prices (Lek billion)	16.8	16.4	50.7	125.3	184.4	229.8	281.0	341.7	460.6	506.2	536.4
GDP in current prices ($US, billion)	1.9	0.7	0.7	1.2	1.9	2.5	2.7	2.3	3.1	3.7	3.7
GDP per capita ($US PPP per capita)	2,401	1,775	1,781	2,036	2,233	2,571	2,861	2,683	2,912	3,148	3,439
GDP (change, 1989=100)	90	65	60	66	71	81	88	82	89	95	102
GDP (% change over previous year)	-10.0	-28.0	-7.2	9.6	8.3	13.3	9.1	-7.0	8.0	7.3	7.8
Share of agriculture in GDP (%)	40.2	42.5	54.2	54.6	54.6	54.6	52.8	56.0	54.4	52.6	..
Industrial output (% change over previous year)	-13.3	-41.9	-30.1	-10.0	-18.6	-7.2	-24.4	2.8	21.8	16.0	12.0
Agricultural output (% change over previous year)	..	..	..	..	..	..	..	..	..	..	..
Labour productivity in industry (% change over previous year)	..	..	..	..	..	8.5	-15.8	-0.7	27.9	18.5	57.0
CPI (% change over the preceding year, annual average)	..	35.5	226.0	85.0	22.5	8.0	12.7	33.2	20.6	0.4	0.0
PPI (% change over the preceding year, annual average)	..	..	..	..	..	..	..	..	..	..	..
Registered unemployment (% of labour force, end of period)	9.5	9.2	27.0	22.0	18.0	12.9	12.3	14.9	17.6	18.2	16.9
Balance of trade in goods and non-factor services (million US$)	-134.0	-208.0	-471.0	-490.0	-459.6	-475.0	-678.3	-534.9	-603.7	-662.8	-821.0
Current account balance (million US$)	-118.0	-168.0	-51.0	14.0	-42.5	-14.5	-62.3	-254.1	-45.2	-132.9	-163.1
" (as % of GDP)	-6.3	-24.8	-7.5	12.0	-2.2	-0.6	-2.3	-11.1	-1.5	-3.6	-4.4
Net FDI inflows (million US$)	..	..	20	58	53	70	90	48	45	41	143
Net FDI flows (as % of GDP)	..	..	3.0	4.7	2.7	2.8	3.3	2.1	1.5	1.1	3.8
Cumulative FDI (million US$)	..	..	20	78	131	201	291	339	384	425	568
Foreign exchange reserves (million US$)	199	9	72	147	205	241	281	309	349	369	352
Total net external debt (million US$)	178	733	739	789	800	441	453	450	533	606	681
Exports of goods (million US$)	322	73	70	112	141	205	244	159	208	275	255
Imports of goods (million US$)	456	281	541	601	601	680	922	694	812	938	1076
Ratio of net debt to exports (%) (calc)	55.3	1004.1	1055.7	704.5	565.8	215.3	185.9	283.7	256.4	220.3	266.7
Ratio of gross debt to GDP (%)	20.0	109.0	120.0	76.0	52.0	28.0	27.0	33.0	29.0	27.0	28.0
Exchange rates: annual averages (NC/US$)	8.9	24.2	75.0	102.1	94.6	93.1	104.3	148.9	150.6	137.7	143.7
Population (1000)	3,273	3,225	3,179	3,185	3,225	3,266	3,304	3,339	3,364	3,387	3,411

Source: UNECE Common statistical database and National Statistics.
Note: NC stands for the National Currency

Introduction

Figure I.3: Map of Albania (administrative and main cities)

Source: Department of Public Information of the United Nations (UNDPI), Cartographic Section, New York, Post-Conflict "Environmental Assessment-Albania", United Nations Environment Programme (UNEP).

"The boundaries and names shown on this map do not imply official endorsement or acceptance by the United Nations"

After the economy bottomed out, Albania had an impressive record of recovery from 1993 to 1996. During this period annual real GDP growth was between 8.3 and 13.3 per cent. Inflation measured by the consumer price index (CPI) dropped from 226 per cent in 1992 to 8.0 per cent in 1995, but rose again to 12.7 per cent in 1996. Surprisingly, the national currency, the lek, remained stable against the United States dollar until 1996. Unemployment contracted from 22 per cent in 1993 to 12.3 per cent in 1996, but this was largely due to the huge emigration of Albanians of working age.

The agricultural sector and small and medium-sized enterprises were privatized, and structural reforms, including price and trade liberalization, were started. The steady economic development came to an abrupt end at the beginning of 1997, however, when the pyramid schemes collapsed. These investment schemes had enticed one in six Albanians by promising huge returns. The first scheme's bankruptcy in January 1997 instigated riots. Other bankruptcies followed and, by March, Albania was in turmoil. Widespread rioting and looting led the country into near anarchy and caused a virtual collapse of the State. Over 1500 people were killed and rioting damaged the country's infrastructure.

The economic consequence was severe. GDP contracted by 7 per cent in 1997. Inflation jumped to 33.2 per cent. Exports decreased by 27 per cent and imports by 25 per cent. Remittances from abroad dropped from US$ 425 million to US$ 250 million. External debt rose from 27 to 33 per cent of GDP. Even foreign aid and investment flows came to a halt. Thousands of people were impoverished either by the loss of their investments or by the destruction of their property during the subsequent violence. The new Government that took office after the July 1997 election re-established macroeconomic and fiscal controls.

In 1998, the Government embarked on a recovery programme with fundamental reforms in the administration and the financial sector. In June 1998, it launched a major anti-corruption programme focused on strengthening the judiciary system. In September 1998, a new Government was formed and a month later a new Constitution, laying the foundation for democratic institutions, was approved.

The economy returned back to its 1996 growth trend. The CPI fell to 8.7 per cent. Remittances from abroad returned to an annual US$ 440 million.

Real GDP growth returned to 8 per cent a year and the lek appreciated against the US dollar.

In early 1999, the Kosovo conflict created a new crisis for the Government. The conflict threatened internal security and stretched Albania's administrative capacity. The Kosovar refugees swelled Albania's population by 14 per cent, but Albania also got much-needed international financial assistance. In spite of the human tragedy the macroeconomic performance of the country remained good. GDP continued to grow at a fast 7.3 per cent in 1999 and an even faster 7.8 per cent in 2000. Tight monetary policies and large humanitarian aid imports brought inflation to zero and strengthened the lek's exchange rate. With a steady currency and growing GDP, Albania's economic development has stabilized after the turmoil of the past decade, but the country is still dependent on international aid.

Albania succeeded in managing a privatization process during this difficult time. The process started in 1991 with the privatization of small service and production units. This was relatively simple and the former employees took over 19,000 units in 1991-1992. The privatization of agricultural land and housing moved quickly and, by the end of 1993, 94 per cent of the agricultural land was distributed to 450,000 households and former tenants owned 97 per cent of the flats. During 1993-1995, 8,900 small and medium-size enterprises (SMEs) were privatized. The lack of foreign investors and very low savings prevented the privatization of the big enterprises. The mass privatization programme started in 1995 with the distribution of privatization vouchers to the citizens. This voucher could be used to buy stocks and so transform enterprises into joint-stock companies. The programme was not a success, but 17 of the 97 big enterprises were partially privatized. Privatization is still continuing in the banking, oil and gas and telecommunications sectors.

I.4 Institutions

Albania is a parliamentary republic with a unicameral parliament, the Assembly of Albania, to which 140 deputies are elected by universal suffrage for a four-year term. In the past parliamentary elections on 24 June 2001, the Socialist Party of Albania won 71 seats. The Assembly elects the President with a two-third majority for a five-year term and with the right to be re-elected. The last presidential election was held on 24 July 1997, the next is scheduled to take place in 2002. The President appoints the Prime Minister to lead the Council of Ministers (currently 19 members). The Council of Ministers is the executive organ, nominated by the Prime Minister and approved by the President. The Council must have a vote of confidence from the Assembly of Albania.

The judiciary consists of the Constitutional Court, the Supreme Court, appeals courts, and district courts. For the first time in Albanian history a Constitutional Court, which interprets the Constitution, determines the constitutionality of laws, and resolves disagreements between local and federal authorities, is included in the judicial system. The other courts are each divided into three jurisdictions: criminal, civil and military. The Supreme Court is the highest court of appeal and consists of 11 members appointed by the Assembly of Albania.

Albania is divided into 12 regions (qark), which are further divided into 65 municipalities and 309 communes. Each region has its own Head of the Region, which is elected by the Council of the Region. The Councils of the Regions are selected from party lists on the basis of proportional representation. City mayors are elected by direct vote, while city councils are chosen by proportional representation.

I.5   The environmental context

The impact of the centralized economic system on the environment became apparent with the beginning of Albania's transition period. Even though Albania was facing other severe problems, environmental concerns were taken seriously and the Committee for Environmental Protection was established (1991) and new environmental legislation was enacted (including the 1993 Law on Environmental Protection). Several environmental studies and projects were carried out and the National Environmental Action Plan was prepared (1994).

Political problems and economic difficulties around the country diverted the Government's attention to other, more pressing, issues than the environment.

Recently, however, the environment has again become one of the Government's priorities. In 1998 the Committee for Environmental Protection became the National Environmental Agency and its position was strengthened by placing it under the Council of Ministers. This laid the seeds for the Ministry of Environment into which the Agency was transformed in September 2001. The role of the NGOs has increased steadily over the years, although environmental awareness among the general public and the business community is low and NGOs do not yet have an impact on the public and political life of the country.

Albania has to tackle a wide range of environmental problems. The latest NEAP of 2001 points out some problems that have been identified as the key environmental issues in Albania.

Industries using obsolete technology and the fleet of old vehicles with diesel engines are generating much air pollution. Groundwater resources are polluted by industrial discharges although the condition of the surface water appears better than in the 1980s, mainly due to the closure of factories and the limited use of chemicals in agriculture.

Urban waste and industrial discharges are polluting the soil. Decades of inappropriate land use and unsustainable agricultural and animal farming practices have caused soil erosion and the salinization of arable land.

Polluted "hot spots", often abandoned industrial sites, have very high concentrations of toxic and carcinogenic substances, exposing the local population to health risks and contaminating the surrounding environment.

The lack of organizational measures and a long-term systematic over-exploitation of forest resources are causing deforestation. Biodiversity is affected by deforestation and by the fragmentation of the habitats and the degradation of the ecosystems.

All these problems and others, together with an analysis of their causes, are reviewed in more detail in the present Environmental Performance Review of Albania.

PART I: THE FRAMEWORK FOR ENVIRONMENTAL POLICY AND MANAGEMENT

Chapter 1

POLICY FRAMEWORK, LEGAL INSTRUMENTS AND INSTITUTIONAL ARRANGEMENTS

1.1 The context

After the Second World War, Albania went through dramatic political developments that impacted greatly on the country for several decades. The communist leaders of the Albanian Labour Party isolated the country politically, and this led to restrictions on trade and foreign investments. Industrial activities were mostly focused on heavy industry. Industrial technology (smelting, metallurgy, chemical production, oil refinery) was imported primarily from the Soviet Union and China. Few factories had clean-up facilities (for emissions in the air, for waste-water treatment).

In March 1992, with the electoral victory of the opposition, Albania began its transition to a free market economy, and the country proceeded during the next three years to develop its new environmental policies and strategies. The first of these was the National Environmental Action Plan (NEAP), developed in 1993 with support from the World Bank and, subsequently, the European Union's PHARE Programme. The Government approved the NEAP in 1994. It has lately been followed by a series of measures as expressed in the report Immediate Measures for the Implementation of the NEAP, which was adopted in 2001. Since the mid-90s, several additional environmental strategies have been adopted. These include the National Waste Management Plan adopted in 1998, and the National Environmental Health Action Plan (NEHAP) and the National Biodiversity Strategy and Action Plan, both adopted in 1999. The Coastal Zone Management Plan prepared in 1996 was approved in 2002. The National Water Strategy developed in 1997 has not yet been adopted.

The reasons for the failure to adopt them are complex, but among them was the acute social-economic disruption caused by the collapse of popular pyramid savings schemes in early 1997, which brought down the Government (see the Introductory Chapter) and greatly weakened the authority of the State. The State has been gradually reasserting itself, but a number of policies and laws drafted prior to or during 1997 remain in draft form only.

1.2 Institutional arrangements

Ministry of Environment

Albania established its first Ministry of Environment in September 2001. The institutional history for environmental protection dates back to 1991, when the Committee for Environmental Protection and Preservation was established within the Ministry of Health. This was followed, in 1991, by the establishment of the Committee on Environmental Protection, within the Ministry of Health and Environment. In 1998, the Albanian Parliament, through Law No. 8364, transformed the National Environmental Agency into an independent institution reporting directly to the Prime Minister. The creation of the Ministry in 2001 continued the trend toward giving greater importance and authority to the environmental protection authorities.

According to the 2002 Law on Environmental Protection, the main responsibilities of the Ministry of Environment are:

- To cooperate and coordinate with central and local government institutions, the public and non-profit organizations to increase the level of enforcement of environmental legislation;
- To prepare draft agreements, conventions, protocols, projects and programs that are carried out in the framework of bilateral and multilateral cooperation, including with international environmental organizations, and to follow their implementation when they are finalized;
- To study the country's needs for specialists and to coordinate the qualification and specialization activities of the personnel dealing with environmental protection;
- To support projects on scientific research, improvement of the state of the environment,

introduction of clean technologies and promotion of activities of non-profit organizations; and

- To assist the local government bodies on environmental protection and in the preparation of local environmental action plans.

In addition, the Minister has authority under the new law, inter alia, to request the Prime Minister to suspend approval of sectoral strategies and plans that do not comply with the environmental statement and to consult the relevant ministries on the determination and rational use of environmental funds

The Ministry of Environment inherited the staff and the structure of the National Environmental Agency. The Ministry has 40 employees working in six Directorates: the Directorate for Pollution Control and Prevention; the Directorate for Natural Resources and Biodiversity Management; the Directorate for Environmental Impact Assessment and Information; the Directorate for Environmental Policy and Project Implementation; the Directorate for Environmental Legislation and Foreign Relations; and the Directorate for Personnel, Organization and Services. There is also a small unit for information services and public relations. The unit is placed within the Ministry, but it is subordinate to the Environmental Centre for Administration and Technology-Tirana.

The functions and substructures of some of the Directorates are still not well-defined. For example, the Directorate for Pollution Control and Prevention may need to reorganize in order to support pollution control and prevention, respond to emergencies and coordinate the Regional Environmental Agencies. The same is true of the Directorate for Environmental Impact Assessment, which has been given the task of reviewing all environmental impact statements prepared in the country and for collecting operational information from the Regional Environmental Agencies.

The new, stronger position of the environmental authority within the Government puts more ambitious tasks before the Minister to strengthen the administrative capacity and to design the most appropriate institution responsible for environmental management. Major efforts will be made to establish a monitoring centre within the Ministry. The specialized Directorates do not have sufficient staff to do all these tasks.

The Ministry has 12 Regional Environmental Agencies with a total staff of 30 specialists. Their responsibilities are implementing and enforcing legislation; carrying out site inspections; controlling operating facilities and the use of natural resources within their regions; taking part in environmental permitting for new activities; and supporting environmental monitoring and assessments. They meet once a month with the Ministry staff (the Directorate for Environmental Impact Assessment and Information) to report on their current tasks, review environmental impact statements and share experience. The Directorate for Environmental Impact Assessment and Information coordinates their work and collects their reports.

Other authorities with environmental responsibilities at the central level

The Permanent Commission on Health and Environment works for Parliament and reviews the drafts of laws prepared by the Ministry of Environment, approves international environmental agreements and approves debates on environmental issues. Its mandate is determined by Parliament and its members are representatives from all parliamentary groups. The Commission reviews and prepares legal acts for adoption by Parliament. It has the right to oversee the activities of the Ministry of Health and the Ministry of Environment case by case when there is a special public interest.

There are a number of ministries and institutions that undertake tasks important to environmental protection and management. Some of these ministries have special environmental units with staff delegated by the Ministry of Environment (see Chapter 9). This is an important institutional arrangement aimed at facilitating inter-relationships with the other ministries. At the moment, the staff of these environmental units does not seem to play a significant role in decision-making in the sectoral ministries.

Regional and local levels

At the regional level, there are environmental protection arrangements between the Regional Environmental Agencies, the regional inspectorates of the Ministry of Agriculture and Food and the Health Inspectorate of the Ministry of Health.

At the local level, the municipalities are responsible for environmental protection, although there are no specialized environmental units except in the municipality of Tirana. According to the new Law on the Organization and Functioning of Local Government (No. 8652/2000), local authorities assumed responsibility for the management of water supplies, municipal waste, transport infrastructure and urban green areas at the beginning of 2001. The municipalities are also responsible for the closed and abandoned industrial sites that are within their territory.

Before the adoption of Law No. 8652/2000, municipalities had very little autonomy. The new Law regulates not only the powers and responsibilities but also the financial basis of the activities of local authorities in Albania. It provides for the decentralization of powers through the delegation of duties and rights from the central to the local governments. Article 11 of this Law states that the protection of the environment is an area where local government can be involved. Funds may be provided by the central Government or raised through local charges and taxes.

Local authorities lack adequate training on environmental matters to manage their new environmental responsibilities. Such training could begin with a wide public awareness campaign organized jointly by the Ministry of Environment, the relevant Regional Environmental Agency and the concerned municipality on the most serious and urgent urban development problems that are also linked to significant negative impacts on the environment, such as transport-caused air pollution, lack of municipal waste management, illegal connection to water supply pipes, illegal construction and the reduction of urban green areas.

1.3 Policies and strategies

The 1994 National Environmental Action Plan identified six priorities:

- Monitoring industrial and urban pollution;
- Establishing admissible pollution standards;
- Halting illegal tree cutting and investing in soil erosion prevention;
- Assessing the environmental protection needs of the Albanian coastline;
- Regenerating severely polluted zones; and
- Implementing European-level environmental mechanisms.

The EU PHARE Programme and the World Bank have assisted Albania in updating the 1994 NEAP. Ten priorities have been identified:

- Improving cooperation among ministries, departments and local authorities;
- Developing suitable environmental policies;
- Promoting the sustainable use of natural resources;
- Improving the country's environmental inspection structure;
- Establishing an information system;
- Improving environmental information available to NGOs and the public;
- Developing an adequate strategy with business on the environmental issues;
- Strengthening the environmental impact assessment system;
- Completing the country's environmental legal framework; and
- Drafting local environmental action plans (LEAPs).

Among the objectives is the creation of conditions for future membership of the European Union (EU).

The updated NEAP, which was adopted by the Government in January 2002, will be implemented over a period of five years. Public participation in developing the new NEAP has been facilitated through the organization of two workshops.

The new NEAP also takes into account the need to integrate environment into other sectors. For example, it envisages the development of a strategy and action plan for the development of sustainable transport, a sustainable and integrated rural strategy, a strategy for sustainable tourism, and a strategy and action plan for land protection against erosion. An inter-ministerial group led by the Deputy Chair of the Council of Ministers monitored the coordination of the NEAP preparation.

The Government has also decided to prepare local environmental action plans as a follow-up to the 1994 NEAP. The development of local action plans is in conformity with the strategy of decentralizing power to local governments. The LEAPs will provide for environmental assessment at the local level, the identification of priorities, the establishment of training programmes and the development of partnerships with NGOs. They will also set up local intersectoral coordination structures. The process has begun with the drafting of LEAPs for three towns (Korçe, Fier and Peshkopi) with support from the Regional Environmental Center (REC).

The 1998 National Waste Management Plan includes measures for solid, urban, industrial and hospital waste management, and for the rehabilitation of existing uncontrolled dumpsites. The Plan also contains a budget for finding appropriate solutions for the landfills (see Chapter 7).

The National Water Strategy was drafted in 1997, but it has not yet been adopted because of a lack of agreement among the authorities with competencies in water policy (see Chapter 6).

From 1993 to 1996 a programme for coastal zone management in Albania was initiated in cooperation with the United Nations Environment Programme, the World Bank and the European Union. In 1996, Albania drafted its Coastal Zone Management Plan, focusing on the development of tourism and biodiversity protection in the coastal area development of recreational activities, and institutional strengthening of the institutions responsible for coastal management. The Coastal Zone Management Plan was approved in 2002.

In 1999 the Government approved the National Environmental Health Action Plan (NEHAP) that had been proposed by the Ministry of Health. The NEHAP identifies a number of specific objectives such as assessing environmental hazards related to health, establishing economic and financial instruments that promote environmental health improvement, and strengthening environmental health services and public information (see Chapter 12).

In 1999, the Council of Ministers approved the National Biodiversity Strategy and Action Plan, prepared under the Global Environment Facility (GEF). The main goal was to fulfil the requirements of the Convention on Biological Diversity, signed by Albania in 1994, and the provisions of the Pan-European Strategy on Biological and Landscape Diversity. The document defines national priorities and necessary institutional changes for the implementation of the Convention (see Chapter 8).

In 2001 the Albanian Government, in collaboration with the World Bank, prepared its Strategy on Growth and Poverty Reduction, which is the country's first comprehensive economic development strategy with a focus on sustainable development. The Strategy should help the Government improve the effectiveness of its policies by identifying priorities and the measures needed to solve poverty problems. It also serves as a framework for identifying projects for international funding.

The Strategy on Growth and Poverty Reduction ("National Strategy for Socio-Economic Development") contains a chapter entitled "Environment, Growth and Poverty Reduction", which presents the long- and medium-term objectives for the environment. In the longer term, Albania would like to "achieve gradually appropriate environmental standards, in accordance with Albania's commitments stemming from its association process with the EU". The medium-term objectives are oriented in three main directions: (i) to stop environmental degradation; (ii) to create conditions for the rehabilitation of polluted areas and bring them within minimum safety standards; and (iii) to make the use of natural resources more sustainable. These objectives are consistent with those contained in the new NEAP, but they are placed in a broader, multisectoral context and explicitly linked to poverty reduction and sustainable growth.

1.4   Legal framework and implementation of environmental legislation

Environmental legislation

The legal system is based on the following hierarchy: Constitution, primary legislation (laws) and supporting normative acts, such as by-laws, government decisions, decrees, ministerial orders, regulations, instructions and standards. The Constitution, approved in 1998, calls upon the Albanian authorities to preserve a healthy environment, ecologically suitable for present and future generations (Chapter V on social objectives). To achieve this, the Government must further improve and complete the legal and institutional framework covering the environment, nature and biodiversity protection.

Albania is in the process of establishing its legal framework for the environment. Although the first basic law on the environment was approved in 1967, the development of a modern environmental legal system based on democratic principles began only in 1991. Most laws are drafted by the technical directorates of the Ministry of Environment in close cooperation with the Directorate for Environmental Legislation and Foreign Relations. The Government is paying special attention to begin harmonizing its laws with the environmental legislation of the European Union. The basic environmental laws that have been approved since 1991 are given in Box 1.1.

The 2002 Law on Environmental Protection is a comprehensive framework law with the following objectives:

- Rational use of the environment and reduction of discharges into and pollution of the environment, prevention of its damage, rehabilitation and restoration of the damages environment;

- Improvement of environmental conditions, related to the quality of life and protection of public health;

- Preservation and maintenance of natural resources, renewable and non-renewable, rational and efficient management by ensuring their regeneration;

- Coordination of the state activities to meet the environmental protection requirements;

- International cooperation in the field of environmental protection;

- Promotion of public participation in environmental protection activities;

- Coordination of the economic and social development of the country with the requirements of environmental protection and sustainable development.

- Establishment and strengthening of the institutional system of environmental protection on national and local level.

The framework law covers a broad range of issues, including, environmental policies, strategies and programmes; use and protection of soil, the humus layer, water, air, human building environment, waste, including hazardous waste, and environmental charges and taxes; EIA and SEA; permitting; prevention and reduction of environmental pollution, including establishing norms; monitoring and information; control of the state of the environment; duties of State Bodies for the environment; the role of the public; sanctions; and (12) environmental funds.

The political development that led to the establishment of the Ministry of Environment raised as a priority the formulation of a new Law on Environmental Protection. This law was prepared by the Ministry of Environment and adopted by the Parliament in September 2002.

There are also a number of new draft laws that promote environmental management. Some of these are under review by the authorities; others are still being prepared. (Box 1.2)

Most of the new laws and draft laws address an area of environmental protection not previously covered by legislation. These include air protection, gaseous emission standards, monitoring systems, nature protection areas and biodiversity protection. Some of the draft laws amend existing sectoral laws; these include legislation on water and soil management. Another group amends horizontal legislation, including on environmental impact assessment and environmental information, so that these important tools of environmental management comply with EU legislation.

Despite these efforts, gaps remain, so the existing legal framework needs to be further developed, particularly regarding waste management, including hazardous waste, chemicals, industrial accidents, permits and environmental auditing. Also, in order to fill the gaps, there is a tendency to draw up new additional laws that have a narrow scope, resulting in a complicated legal system. For instance, the two laws regulating the management of water resources (i.e. Law on Water Resources, No. 8093/1996 and Law on Water Supply and Sanitation Sector Regulation, No. 8102/1996) will be complemented with two laws currently in draft form (draft law on rules on water intended for human consumption and draft law on water protection).

Albania's environmental laws are implemented through by-laws, regulations and decisions. Implementation may be the responsibility not only of the Ministry of Environment but also of other ministries or authorities with environmental protection responsibilities, such as the Ministry of Health, the Ministry of Agriculture and Food, the Ministry of Territorial Adjustment and Tourism, and the National Water Council. These include, for example, a regulation on cooperation among environmental inspectors, forestry inspectors and the police as well as regulations concerning sanitary conditions and urban planning.

Other laws with environmental provisions

There are other laws of a general character that contain provisions for the rights of non-governmental organizations (NGOs) in environmental decision-making; for penalties for violations of environmental legislation; and for environmental liability and the right to information.

One important provision for the right of citizens is the issue of standing during administrative procedures following the Code of Administrative Procedures (Law No. 8485/1999). Article 45 of the Code recognizes the right of environmental NGOs to be parties to the appeal procedure with a legitimate interest, due to the fact that they act in the broad interest of the public. In order to stimulate the participation of different pressure groups in environmental policy-making, the possibility for environmental NGOs to be given standing during administrative proceedings may prove to be of great importance.

The Albanian Penal Code, Law No. 7895/1995, has dedicated some provisions to environmental crimes. Articles 201 to 207 provide for different penal sanctions ranging from fines to imprisonment for up to 15 years (article 202, for example, deals with the transport of toxic waste). At first glance, criminal law would seem to offer an effective means to solve pollution-related problems. However, the essential nature of criminal law precludes its effectiveness. For example, a definition would be needed for a particular crime.

Although these are indeed provided in the Albanian Penal Code, it is unclear what would qualify as a criminal act as opposed to an infringement of administrative rules. The Albanian Civil Code, Law No. 7850/1994, also addresses environmental liability, in article 624. Persons that have wrongfully inflicted environmental damage or harm are liable for the full payment of the damage. However, to date, no case law exists. This seems to suggest that the Albania legislature may need to provide more specific rules of implementation for article 624.

Law No. 8503/1999 on the Right to Information gives all persons the right to ask for official documents. Public authorities are required to make available any information relating to an official document, except where the law forbids it.

International legislation

Albania has signed and ratified a number of international environmental conventions (see Annex III and Chapter 3). The international agreements are reflected in national legislation through the adoption of laws, e.g. Law No. 8216/1997, which provides for adherence to the Basel Convention; Law No. 8463/1999, to the Vienna Convention and the Montreal Protocol; Law No. 8556/1999, to the United Nations Convention to Combat Desertification; and Law No. 8672/2000, to the Aarhus Convention.

Box 1.1:   Selected national legislation related to environmental management and protection

- Laws on Land and its Distribution (No. 7491 and No. 7501, 19 July 1991)
- Law on City Planning (No. 7693, 20 April 1993, amended 1998)
- Law on Forestry and the Forestry Police Service (No. 7223, 13 October 1992; amended in 1994)
- Law on Environmental Protection (No. 7664, 1993; amended by Law No. 8364, 2 July 1998)
- Law on the Plant Protection Service (No. 7662, 19 July 1993; amended by Law No. 8531, 23 September 1999)
- Law on Hunting and Wildlife Protection (No. 7875, 23 November 1994)
- Law on Fishing and Fish Farming (No. 7908, 5 April 1995)
- Law on Radioactive, Nuclear and Atomic Waste (No. 8025, 9 November 1995)
- Law on Water Resources (No. 8093, 21 March 1996)
- Law on Public Waste Disposal (No. 8094, 21 March 1996)
- Law on Public Waste Disposal Taxation (No. 8108, 28 March 1996)
- Law on Water Supply and Sanitation Sector Regulation (No. 8102, 28 March 1996)
- Law on the Construction Police (No. 8408, 17 September 1998)
- Law on the Organization and Functioning of Local Government (No. 8652, 31 July 2000)
- Law on the Establishment and Operation of Soil Administration and Protection Structures (No. 8752, 26 March 2001)
- Law on Air Protection (No. 8897, 16 May 2002)
- Law on Protected Areas (No. 8906, 6 June 2002)
- Law on Environmental Protection (No. 9834, 5 September 2002)
- Decision on Gaseous Emission Standards (12 September, 2002)

```
┌──────────────────────────────────────────────────────────────────────────────────┐
│         Box 1.2:       Environmental legislation currently in draft form           │
│                                                                                    │
│ Draft laws being prepared                                                          │
│   •   Draft law on water protection                                                │
│   •   Draft law on soil protection                                                 │
│                                                                                    │
│ Draft laws under review                                                            │
│   •   Draft law on environmental impact assessment                                 │
│   •   Draft law on biodiversity protection and conservation                        │
│   •   Draft law on sea and coastal defence and protection                          │
│   •   Draft law on natural resources preservation, protected areas and national parks │
│   •   Draft law on public access to environmental information                      │
│   •   Draft law on the handling of chemicals                                       │
│   •   Draft law on waste management                                                │
│   •   Draft law on waste water treatment                                           │
└──────────────────────────────────────────────────────────────────────────────────┘
```

Real transposition and implementation of the requirements of the conventions in national legislation started recently with the amendments to the Law on Environmental Protection from 1998 (art. 2) and the 2002 Law on Environmental Protection, referring to basic provisions in the Aarhus Convention and with the draft law on environmental impact assessment, which substantially transposes the requirements of the Espoo Convention on Environmental Impact Assessment in a Transboundary Context.

Implementation and enforcement of the legislation

The biggest problem with Albania's legal framework, however, is not the development of the laws but their lack of implementation and enforcement. Poor implementation stems from a number of sources: lack of respect for the law, rooted in the years Albania suffered under a repressive dictatorship; absence of an ability to measure and monitor compliance; weak enforcement procedures; lack of institutional and administrative capacity, and a dysfunctional distribution of competencies among ministries. Poor implementation and weak enforcement are also due to the absence of information and education campaigns that would increase public awareness and sense of responsibility.

Standards for air emissions, surface and groundwater quality, drinking-water quality and soil pollution have existed since 1974. However, there are no sampling methodologies and no guidelines for environmental monitoring. The 1995 Decree of the Council of Ministers on the Tasks that Ministries, Research Institutes and Physical and Legal Persons Have in Regard to Environmental Monitoring obliges some central specialized institutes to monitor air, water and soil and to supply the National Environmental Agency (now the Ministry of Environment) with relevant data every three months (see Chapter 4).

Practical mechanisms for enforcement are incomplete and inadequate, and in need of simplification. The principal enforcement instruments are fines, suspending or closing operations, withdrawing permits (issued through EIA) and prosecution under one of the seven environmental crimes in the Penal Code. Only a small percentage of fines imposed for violating the law are actually paid, because the penalty for non-payment, confiscation, is a very slow and complicated procedure. The 1998 amendments to the Law on Environmental Protection increased fines to a maximum of half a million leks (i.e. about US$ 3,500); the 2002 Law on Environmental Protection has doubled the this amount.

Enforcement of the country's environmental laws is also complicated by the fact that the environmental authority (i.e. now the Ministry of Environment) is not in charge of resource management (e.g. water, forest, fish and mineral resources). These competencies have been assigned to ministries or institutions, such as the National Water Council, the Ministry of Territorial Adjustment and Tourism, the Ministry of Agriculture and Food, and the Ministry of Industry and Energy, which are focused more on resource use than resource protection. Government awareness of the need for sustainable resource management is evolving slowly due to severe economic and social constraints.

Environmental impact assessment

Environmental impact assessment (EIA) was introduced in the 1993 framework Law on

Environmental Protection. According to this Law, EIA is required for:

- National and local programmes;
- Spatial planning and urban development plans and their amendments;
- Projects and activities that may have a strong impact on the environment and be particularly dangerous to human health, as well as projects for the reconstruction and expansion of activities;
- Projects of local activities according to the judgment and definitions of the local authority.

Environmental impact statements have to be prepared by experts or institutions nominated by the Ministry. The project developer then submits this statement to the Regional Environmental Agency for a first review. The Agency sends it, together with its written opinion, to the Ministry of Environment for its approval. Final decisions on major cases are taken by a panel that includes experts from all the specialized units in the Ministry of Environment. There is no public participation envisaged in this process; no public access to the environmental impact documentation; and no public discussion.

The 2002 Law on Environmental Protection also includes EIA, but the projects that are subject to this process, the criteria for their selection, the procedures for asking and undertaking the process of EIA, the review, decision-making and follow-up, as well as public participation in this process, still need to be defined in a special law. This law currently exists as a draft.

At the moment, there is no clear distinction in the subject, methodology or administrative procedure between an environmental impact statement and environmental licences or permits (see Chapter 2). In the absence of a regulation on the procedure for granting licences, effective implementation is questionable. Similarly, there is no auditing procedure to assess the situation of an existing enterprise and its environmental impacts.

Unfortunately, Albania has not passed the necessary decree or regulation that would define further the steps of the EIA process, or provide the required details about the different tasks and responsibilities of all parties in this complex process. It is not sufficiently clear when an EIA should be carried out and how the public may participate in the process. There is no list of projects that require EIA and no procedural

differentiation between small and big projects or between local and national-level activities.

A new law on EIA has been drafted, but it is still under review. This law would establish provisions for all of the steps necessary to implement the EIA procedure: presentation of the application, initial review, selection and classification, consultation, access to information, duties and rights of other bodies, decision-making, public participation, monitoring and control. Requirements for the implementation of transboundary EIA are included too, as Albania has ratified the Espoo Convention on Transboundary Impact Assessment (see Chapter 3).

1.5   Conclusions and Recommendations

The drawing-up of the basic environmental policy documents began in 1992, immediately after the democratic changes in Albania. Since then, efforts have been made to define the needs and to set primary goals for the improvement of Albania's environmental conditions.

Most policies and strategies concerning environmental protection were drawn up between 1993 and 1997 with financial and technical assistance from the PHARE Programme and the World Bank (GEF included). Special attention was given to policies for both coastal zone management and water management. However, while the Coastal Zone Management Plan has been adopted, there is no new management plan for water.

The updated NEAP 2001 should close all of the gaps left by the previous National Environmental Action Plan, and it should increase attention to implementation.

Recommendation 1.1:
The relevant authorities, with the cooperation of the Ministry of Environment, should review and update all environmental policy documents. In undertaking these reviews, they should organize preparatory meetings with interested institutions to facilitate the adoption of these policies. An information campaign about their purpose and benefits should be considered.

Albanian legislation on environmental protection has been partially inspired by the standards of the European Union. The NEAP of 1994 noted that a short-term objective was "implementing European-level environmental mechanisms". The NEAP 2001 is concerned with creating the "conditions for the country's membership of the European Union". The main principles of the EU environmental laws are to be found in Albanian legislation, although only indirectly. These principles are not sufficiently elaborated and do not include implementing mechanisms.

Fundamental to needed legal reform of environmental policy was the recent adoption of a new Law on Environmental Protection (No. 8934/2002). Equally important is the need to improve sectoral and issue-specific legislation. Taken individually, many of the laws are well written, but, taken together, they lack consistency and overall coherence. In some cases they are fragmented, overlapping or contradictory. Further, there are some critical areas where there is no legislation, for example, management of hazardous waste or protection from the adverse impact of chemicals.

Recommendation 1.2:
Efforts should be made to consolidate discrete legislation into coherent and comprehensive laws. For example, there should be a single water act instead of four separate laws (Law on Water Resources, Law on Water Supply and Sanitation Sector Regulation, draft law on water protection and draft law on rules on water intended for human consumption) and a single waste management act, including the management of all kind of waste (except radioactive waste). (see also recommendation 7.1)

Existing legislation on environmental impact assessment fails to address adequately a number of important procedural elements, including identifying which authorities are competent to carry out EIA; who should serve as independent experts; how best to report the results of the EIA; the responsibilities of the developer of the planned activity; the role of the concerned parties; and the manner in which the final decision is taken. In addition, a list of the proposed activities for which EIA is obligatory above certain thresholds is needed. The approach to be taken for the environmental assessment of plans and programmes should be set out, since this is not necessarily the same as that used for projects. The place of environmental assessment within the whole planning process should be defined. The law also needs to include detailed procedures for public involvement in the EIA process and the conditions for public access to the EIA report, for public discussion of the EIA results, for taking into account public concerns in the decision-making process and for ensuring access to justice.

Because the EIA process is strongly centralized, the Ministry is overloaded with applications to review and give final approval to environmental assessments for environmental permits. It is necessary to separate the competencies for EIA and environmental permits between the central and regional authorities, and this should also be foreseen in a new EIA law. The Ministry should be responsible for assessing projects of national importance, for activities with transboundary impact and for those to be developed in protected areas; the Regional Environmental Agencies should have competence for all other projects and be trained adequately for this purpose.

There is no environmental auditing system in place. Environmental impact assessment is used for new activities, but it cannot replace a mechanism for assessing the impacts of existing activities on the environment. Environmental permitting should be developed under the responsibility of the Ministry of Environment so as to bring industrial enterprises into compliance with the legislation. Environmental audit should be carried out also if new developments are proposed on existing industrial sites or in case of privatization.

Recommendation 1.3:
(a) The draft environmental impact assessment law should distinguish clearly between EIA for projects and environmental assessment for plans and programmes (strategic environmental assessment);

(b) A legally binding environmental audit should be the precondition for issuing environmental permits (licence) for operating facilities;

(c) Public participation in both EIA and environmental auditing should be developed, reflected in law and implemented; (see also recommendation 4.3)

(d) The respective competencies of the Ministry and the Regional Environmental Agencies should be clearly defined by the law.

The newly established Ministry of Environment is a significant step forward for environmental policy and environmental management in the country. It is evidence of the understanding and support of the Government for the important role that the environmental authorities have to play in Albania. At the same time, the current capacity of the Ministry remains unchanged from what was available to its predecessor, the National Environmental Agency.

Strengthening the new Ministry should be a national priority. This includes allocating sufficient numbers of competent staff to both the specialized Directorates of the central authority and the Regional Environmental Agencies to ensure national environmental monitoring, the implementation of policies and legislation, undertaking environmental impact assessment and managing the enforcement and compliance process.

In February 2001, the Directorate for Environmental Policy and Project Implementation was established for the first time. The implementation of the recently approved NEAP, the Strategy on Growth and Poverty Reduction, the Stabilization and Association Agreement, as well as the integration of environmental considerations into other sectoral policies, calls for the immediate strengthening of this Directorate.

Technical capacity also needs to be strengthened in order to maintain and properly use technical equipment. A corresponding and substantially increased budget is necessary to fulfil all these tasks.

Special attention should be given to the capacity of the Regional Environmental Agencies, particularly in view of the new responsibilities that they will assume with the development of full EIA procedures, environmental permitting and a national environmental monitoring system. It is of

crucial importance not only to expand the staff but also to provide the necessary training for the staff.

Recommendation 1.4:
(a) The structure of the Ministry of Environment, which is function- and management-oriented, needs to be expanded. Specifically, the following new sectors under the directorates should be created:

- *A section for hazardous waste management and a section for emergency situations within the Directorate for Pollution Control and Prevention;*
- *A section for environmental impact assessment and a separate section for environmental permitting within the Directorate for EIA and Information;*
- *A national centre for environmental monitoring as a matter of high priority; (see recommendation 4.1)*

(b) The Ministry of Environment should consider establishing a new department for coastal areas; (see recommendation 11.3)

(c) In addition, the following should be strengthened:

- *Directorate for Environmental Policy and Project Implementation;*
- *Directorate for Natural Resources Management and Biodiversity Management;*
- *The Information and Public Relations Unit.*

(d) The staff of both the Ministry and the Regional Environmental Agencies should have access to ongoing training in all of the areas that fall within their competence.

Chapter 2

ECONOMIC AND REGULATORY INSTRUMENTS FOR ENVIRONMENTAL PROTECTION

2.1   Background

Despite the setbacks of recent years, including the collapse of the pyramid schemes in 1997 and the influx of refugees from the war in neighbouring Kosovo in 1999, Albania has made substantial progress in achieving macroeconomic and financial stability. The country appears to be entering a period of political stability; national security has improved, and international moves to support regional integration are helping to restore infrastructure and boost trade. Nevertheless, Albania remains one of Europe's poorest countries and still faces some major challenges in the transition to a market economy. Gross domestic product (GDP) grew in 1998, 1999 and 2000 at a rate of 8 per cent, in part as a result of restructuring and economic reform. The GDP growth rate is projected to continue to grow by around 7 per cent annually with inflation remaining at around 3 per cent annually. However, unemployment, which peaked at 18.2 per cent in 1999, continues to be a major concern (see Introduction table I.3 for macroeconomic indicators).

As part of the transition process, the Government of Albania has started to develop environmental policy, with the principle of sustainable development included in the new Constitution of 1998. Still, the environment is not considered to be a priority, because of the country's difficult economic and financial situation. Therefore, when evaluating the status and impact of instruments for environmental protection, past and recent economic and social developments need to be taken into account.

2.2   Regulatory instruments for environmental protection

Environmental permits

According to the 2002 Law on Environmental Protection, economic and social activities that may have an impact on the environment require an environmental permit (also referred to as a

'licence') from the Ministry of Environment. These include various activities such as construction and the building of roads and industrial facilities; the exploration for, extraction, exploitation and technological processing of natural resources; the exploitation of forests, flora and fauna; and the transport and disposal of toxic and hazardous waste.

Environmental permits must be obtained prior to applying for other permits, such as a location permit, a building permit or an activity permit. According to Article 45 of the 2002 Law on Environmental Protection, activities of local character having an impact on the environment but not otherwise defined by the Council of Ministers, are approved by the Regional Environmental Agencies in cooperation with local government bodies. The Ministry of Environment receives approximately 450 permit requests of national interest a year. The Directorate within the Ministry of Environment that reviews permit applications consists of four persons and lacks sufficient capacity to do the job properly.

The permit is given no later than three months after the presentation of the request, and it remains valid so long as the conditions on which the permit is based do not change. Upon decision of the Ministry of Environment, the environmental permit is based on two different types of standards. New enterprises are required to apply European Union (EU) standards for the protection of the environment, while existing enterprises (particularly State-owned enterprises) are required to apply only the 1974 Albanian quality standards for a transitional period of several years, until the enterprise can make the necessary investments to comply with EU standards. Historically, Albania has followed the environmental quality approach for standard setting, imposing limits on levels of specific substances in the environment (air, water, soil), rather than limits on emissions to the environment. Currently, there are quality standards for air and water. The individual permits refer to these standards, but do not take into account specific enterprise conditions, such as production volume, operation methods, raw materials input or location specifications.

In the few cases where the environmental permit procedures have been enforced (for new applications and for State-owned industries that are being privatized), the permit is delivered on condition that the operators of pollution sources apply end-of-pipe or cleaner production technologies, monitor their gaseous, liquid and solid discharges and report them to the Regional Environmental Agencies. In general, operators do not self-monitor their pollution. In addition, Albania has not yet established a national or regional environmental database or registration system for emissions. Due to institutional and professional weaknesses, the environmental inspectorates cannot impose or promote efficient compliance with legal environmental standards, or the recording and provision of information.

Permits for water use and water discharges are not issued by the Ministry of Environment. There are inconsistencies between the Law on Environmental Protection and the Law on Water Resources (No. 8093/1996). The Ministry of Environment is responsible under the Law on Environmental Protection for issuing permits for effluent discharges and water use. According to the Law on Water Resources, the National Water Council and the water authorities also have this same responsibility. The National Water Council has not granted any permits over the past two years, a fact clearly indicating that the permit system does not function properly at the moment (see also Chapter 6).

Permits for the import, export, transport, processing or disposal of toxic and hazardous substances are issued by the Ministry of Health.

In 1999, Albania acceded to the Basel Convention on the Control of Transboundary Movements of Hazardous Wastes and Their Disposal. According to the Decision of the Council of Ministers (No. 26, 31 January 1994) on Hazardous Wastes and Residues, the import of hazardous waste and bulk waste and waste refined for disposal is prohibited. The import of waste is accepted only with an import permit granted by the Ministry of Environment and valid for one year. The Decision also regulates the procedures for transboundary movements of wastes. The Decision prohibits the export of hazardous waste unless the authorized

institution of the importing State provides the exporter with the relevant documentation.

Both the 1993 and the 2002 Laws on Environmental Protection stipulate that all projects and activities that have a significant impact on the environment or are particularly dangerous to human health are subject to environmental impact assessments (EIA). According to the Law, every permit application must be accompanied by an EIA (carried out by the applicant). However, there are no regulations on EIA procedures. In addition, there are no procedures for applying the results of an EIA before a project is given the go-ahead. Till now, only foreign companies with new activities in Albania have conducted full EIAs. A law on EIA was drafted in 1998 and is still under review. This draft law defines the types of projects that require EIA, the procedures that have to be followed and the process by which government officials make decisions on the implementation of a project (see also Chapters 1 and 9).

Standards

The General Directorate of Standardization approves Albanian standards and adjusts and adopts the European, ISO and other international standards. The main tasks of the Directorate are to coordinate standardization, to manage the accreditation system and to carry out certification for quality assurance. Its work is based on Law No. 8464 on Standardization (1999). In 1994 and 1995 technical committees of ministries adopted 200 technical standards relating to the environment.

In permits for existing (particularly State-owned) enterprises the Ministry of Environment refers only to the 1974 Albanian air quality and surface-water quality standards. These define maximum allowable concentrations (MAC) of certain substances in air, water and soil. The standards for drinking-water quality were revised and approved in 1998 by the Ministry of Health, on the basis of an EU directive and World Health Organization guidelines. The standards themselves are not specifically stated in the permit conditions, but reference is made to them.

In the 2002 Law on Environmental Protection, Article 50 states that the definition of the norm values will be based on EC Directives, objectives of the national environmental state policy and best available techniques. The law also provides for responsible bodies to amend an environmental permit under a number of conditions, including new information about the environment, the adoption of new environmental provisions, improvements in best available technologies, requirements of technical safety, essential changes to the activity or identification of pollution above admissible levels.

During 1998-1999, the environmental authorities prepared a draft law on air protection and a draft law on gaseous emission standards on the basis of EU directives. These laws have been recently approved by the Government and oblige polluters to self-monitor and submit periodic reports.

The Ministry of Environment approves, in cooperation with other ministries and institutions, emission limit values of gaseous, liquid and solid and radioactive pollutants to be discharged into water, air and soil, as well as admissible levels of harmful and toxic substances in hazardous waste, and adopts rules for the storage, disposal, conservation, transport and classification of hazardous waste and substances.

2.3 Enforcement

The enforcement of environmental legislation is the responsibility of the inspectors from the 12 Regional Environmental Agencies. Each month, the inspectors perform an average of ten inspections. They may impose fines, withdraw permits, suspend or close operations, and enforce the Penal Code with regard to the seven environmental crimes.

Because there is no polluter register, inspectors use their discretion to determine which companies to inspect. According to the 1993 Law on Environmental Protection, companies are required to provide information on their emissions and discharges to the Ministry of Environment and the public every three months. So far, companies have not complied with this duty, which complicates inspections. In addition, the inspectors are often refused access to the companies that they want to inspect.

The regional inspectors meet once a month at the Ministry of Environment in Tirana to share information, discuss problems and submit requests for new environmental permits. The local bodies do not have the right to decide without the approval of the central bodies (i.e. Ministry of Environment), which shows the extent to which the administrative system in Albania is still centralized. Even decisions relating to permit problems must be made by the Ministry of Environment.

The Regional Environmental Agencies do not have their own laboratories, and analyses are therefore conducted by laboratories of the regional Public Health Institutes. The Regional Environmental Agencies occasionally cooperate with the forestry and health inspectorates, which perform other environment-related inspections. In specific cases, the inspectors also cooperate with the construction police. Cooperation with other regional bodies responsible for environmental matters, however, is still non-existent.

If an enterprise does not comply with the relevant standards or permit, the inspector can impose an administrative fine. The level of the fine is prescribed in the 2002 Law on Environmental Protection is 1 million leks. Ultimately, non-compliance may result in a court decision or appeal. According to the legislation, enterprises need to take measures to improve and upgrade their operations to comply with regulations, otherwise they face closure. In practice, this rarely happens, and enforcement relies mainly on fines. Furthermore, corruption within the judicial system also complicates law enforcement.

The inspectors do not collect the fines. The fines imposed are paid into the account of the Ministry of Environment and are used as a secondary fund for environmental purposes (see paragraph 2.5 - Environmental financing and expenditures).

Enforcement of environmental laws is weak in Albania. Impacts on the environment have been exacerbated by poor enforcement of the law. The practical mechanisms for enforcement are incomplete and inadequate. Fines are rarely paid because collection procedures, confiscation and closure (as a consequence of non-payment), are slow and complicated. Another complicating factor is the fact that the granting of permits and their enforcement are the responsibility of the same institution (Ministry of Environment and Regional Environmental Agencies).

The situation is exacerbated by the inspectorates' lack of basic resources (e.g. cars to travel within their prefectures, computers, telephones) and technical capacity. The inspectors do not have access to reliable, up-to-date environmental information and this makes enforcement difficult. A related problem is the low status of the environmental inspectorate among local authorities and other institutions.

2.4 Economic instruments for environmental protection

Background and policy objectives

Economic instruments in environmental policy were not in use in Albania before 1990. Even today, command and control instruments dominate environmental policy. Permits, royalties and concessions for the use of natural resources, as well as penalties for law violations are widespread in Albania's environmental legislation. A first attempt to introduce economic instruments for environmental protection coincided with the beginning of the political reforms and the transition to a market economy. Environment-related taxes are conceived mainly as user charges to raise revenue. The taxes are incorporated in the Law on Taxation, which was introduced in 1991 (No. 7777/1991) and revised in 1998 (No. 8435/1998). Other forms of economic instruments have been introduced through the Law on Water Resources (No. 8093/1996), the Law on Mining (No. 7796/1994), the Law on Hunting and Wildlife Protection (No. 7875/1994), and the Law for the Management of Revenues Generated from State Forests and Pastures (No. 8302/1998).

The 1993 Law on Environmental Protection does not provide any basis for a system of pollution charges and charges for the use of natural resources. The Law only makes reference to some administrative penalties for environmental damage or violation of environmental legislation. The 2002 Law on Environmental Protection states that "physical and legal persons who use produce with high pollution potential and who discharge into the air, water and soil, are subject to environmental taxes." These taxes, including the procedures for collection, will be established with a special law.

Today, the economic instruments in force in Albania include:

- Taxes on environmental pollution, e.g. user charges for sewage treatment and industrial waste collection and disposal;
- Taxes on the extraction and use of natural resources, e.g. taxes on water, land, minerals, flora, fauna;
- User charges for municipal services, e.g. charges for water supply, sewage collection, and municipal waste collection and disposal;
- Product charges, e.g. charges on transport vehicles;

- Penalties and fines for non-compliance; and
- Financial incentives such as grants and soft loans.

The National Environmental Action Plan (NEAP) of 1994 constitutes a core document in setting the aims and directions of Albania's policy framework. The NEAP recommends a set of priority investment projects and a number of necessary institutional and regulatory measures. For instance, the NEAP points to the need to restructure economic incentives so as to encourage more efficient resource use and, in particular, to develop a system of pollution and user charges. The use of economic instruments has also been recommended through the report Immediate Measures for the Implementation of the NEAP ("NEAP Immediate Measures"), the draft National Water Strategy, the Agricultural Development Strategy ('Green Strategy', adopted in 1998), the Forestry and Pastures Development Strategy (adopted in 1999, and incorporated into the 'Green Strategy') and the draft Energy Strategy.

The NEAP Immediate Measures defines concrete proposals that do not require substantial financing, but which can significantly and rapidly contribute to the protection of the environment. One of the key areas identified in this report is the increased application of economic instruments. The NEAP Immediate Measures proposes several environmental taxes that could be introduced or strengthened.

The most urgent proposal is the introduction of the carbon tax, because it generates reasonable revenues quickly and its collection is highly efficient. The Ministry of Environment has already drafted a law for the introduction of a carbon tax, which was circulated in 2001 and early 2002 within other ministries. The tax would be levied on the carbon content of each fuel. According to basic assumptions, the carbon tax would generate 0.5 million dollars a year, with a tax rate of 0.08 US$ cents per litre of petrol and diesel. The impact on current energy pricing would be limited and in any case not higher than 1 per cent. Revenues from the carbon tax would be earmarked for environmental purposes if the law were adopted.

Tax institutions include the Tax Department of the Ministry of Finance and local institutions in communes, municipalities and districts. The Tax Department supervises local tax institutions.

Instruments for air pollution management

No system of air emission charges exists in Albania. The introduction of air emission charges and non-compliance fees was planned through the proposed draft law on environmental charges and the creation of a national environmental fund of 1995. However, this draft law has never been approved because of strong resistance from the Ministry of Finance to extrabudgetary funds.

If emissions occur without permission from the relevant governmental bodies, fines can be levied on the basis of the 2002 Law on Environmental Protection. The environmental inspectors impose the fines for administrative contraventions defined in article 83 of the Law. The inspectorates can impose fines and penalties for non-compliance with air quality standards, on a case-by-case basis.

Albania has not introduced an environmental tax on fossil fuels (based on air emissions), nor is there a tax differentiation for more polluting fuels. Excise duties on fossil fuels do exist, and these are described below.

Instruments related to transport

Several transport-related taxes have been introduced through the Tax Code (No. 8435, 28 December 1998): vehicle taxes, air-travel-related taxes and harbour taxes. None of these taxes was set for environmental purposes and their environmental impact has not been estimated.

The following vehicle taxes have been introduced: an excise duty and value added tax (VAT) on transport fuels; an import tax on second-hand cars; a tax on vehicle weight; a vehicle registration tax; and a tax on the circulation of foreign vehicles. Their purpose is to raise revenue for the State budget. They are collected by the Tax Department, the Custom Directorate and the Road Inspectorate.

According to the Tax Code, the excise duty on petrol differentiates between leaded petrol, unleaded petrol and diesel. The excise duty on leaded petrol is 20 per cent, on unleaded petrol 90 per cent and on diesel 80 per cent of the retail prices. Most vehicles run on diesel; some run on leaded petrol. Diesel is cheaper than either leaded or unleaded petrol. Furthermore, a VAT of 20 per cent must be paid on transport fuels. Table 2.1 gives an overview of the different excise duties on fuels.

Table 2.1: Excise duties on fuels

Tax base	Tax rate
Leaded petrol	20%
Unleaded petrol	90%
Petrol with octane 45-90	77%
Petrol with octane above 90	90%
Diesel	80%
LPG	50%
Kerosene	50%
Heavy fuel	20%
Light fuel	20%

Source: Tax Code, 1998.

The import tax on second-hand vehicles was introduced in 1998 through the Tax Code. The tax amounts to 40,000 leks for passenger cars and 50,000 leks for lorries.

The annual tax on vehicle weight varies between 5,000 and 23,000 leks. The annual vehicle registration tax ranges from 600 leks for motorbikes to 8,400 leks for buses and lorries. Owners of vehicles registered abroad must pay a road tax upon each entry into Albania, and tax rates vary with the type and size of the vehicle.

Instruments for water resources management

Instruments for water resources management include abstraction charges, user charges for water consumption, sewage charges and non-compliance fees. There are no charges on effluent discharges.

The Government sets drinking-water prices, which may vary regionally. Rates differ according to the user group. Households pay a fixed monthly charge as water consumption is seldom metered. A family in Tirana pays a monthly charge of 600 leks. Enterprises and public institutions pay 70-85 leks and 28-30 leks respectively, per cubic metre of water supplied. Charges for water consumption are collected by the water authorities. The revenue of these charges covers only a fraction of the operating costs of water companies. Drinking-water prices are partially subsidized, though efforts are being made to liberalize them. The non-household users are obliged to install water meters at their own expense according to the Governmental Decision for the Water Supply Management of Household and Non-household Users (No. 236, 1993). Though the number of meters installed has not been counted, practice shows that the programme has not yet been completed. Table 2.2

presents water tariffs for the different water users with the minimum and maximum rates applicable in the country.

The revenues collected by the local water companies represent only 30-40 per cent of the water distributed. A large quantity of the water supplied is lost, however, due to broken water mains and illegal connections. Poor revenue collection, in turn, makes much needed investments in the maintenance of the distribution system impossible. Unless measures are taken to improve the system's financial base, the infrastructure seems doomed to decline further. In principle, investments in water infrastructure are financed by the State Budget. The Government, together with foreign donors, is making efforts to improve the management of the water companies and is encouraging their privatization.

At present, there is no waste-water treatment in Albania. Waste-water charges or sewerage charges are established in six cities, and differ according to user group.

The Government is trying to promote the rational use of water resources through abstraction charges for surface and groundwater. The principles for water extraction charges are defined in the Law on Water Resources, but the actual rates still need to be set. The only payments for water extraction are the administration fees from applicants for permissions, authorizations and concessions. The fees are collected by the water authorities. In addition, the Law on Water Resources defines a number of violations and sanctions for non-compliance. The fines vary from 100,000 to 2,000,000 leks (see also Chapter 6).

<u>Instruments for waste management</u>

The only economic instrument in this area is the user charge for municipal waste services (Table 2.3). Unlike most East European countries, where solid waste charges form part of the system of pollution charges, Albania has not introduced a charge on solid waste. At this moment, neither charges nor non-compliance fees for hazardous and industrial waste have been established by law. In general, industrial solid waste is dumped in sites not far from the industrial enterprises producing them, and no measures are taken regarding its final disposal.

Citizens pay an annual user charge for the collection and disposal of municipal waste, the so-called cleaning tax. The rate of this charge depends on the type of user. The charge for households is merely symbolic: 300 leks/year (US$ 2/year). Only 40-50 per cent of families, however, actually pay up. Companies from which waste is collected by municipal services pay a small amount, according to the category of activity generating the waste (see table 2.4). The revenues generated by the Cleaning Tax are not sufficient to cover the true cost of waste management. The Ministry of Territorial Adjustment and Tourism provides funds to subsidize all municipalities for waste management and other public services. In addition, the rate is far from sufficient to provide proper incentives for waste reduction and internal recycling. Revenues in 1999 totalled approximately US$ 746,000. The Ministry of Finance is considering a proposal from the Ministry of Environment to increase the rate of the cleaning tax.

Table 2.2: Water tariffs

	Lek/m^3
Households	15-27
Public institutions	28-30
Enterprises	70-85

Source: Ministry of Environment, 2001.

Table 2.3: Waste-water charges

	Lek/m^3
Households	3.0-4.5
Public institutions	4.0-6.0
Enterprises	6.0-10.0

Source: Ministry of Environment, 2001.

Table 2.4: Cleaning tax rates

User type	Charge/unit/year
Household	300 leks
Enterprise	5,000-15,000 leks
Restaurant	15,000 leks
Hospital	20-500 leks/room
Industry	15,000-50,000 leks
Construction	60,000 leks

Source: Ministry of Environment, 2001.

Economic instruments for natural resources management

Land management

As in most other East European countries, in Albania ownership of land and the right to use land is taxed through the land tax. The land tax is based on the Law on Leasing State-owned Agricultural Land, Meadows, Pastures and Forests (No. 8318, 1 April 1998). Criteria for the annual rent of State-owned land are set by the Council of Ministers. The charge is laid down in the land-leasing contract, signed by the Ministry of Agriculture and Food.

Mining

Mining and raw material charges are set out in the Law on Mining. The charge base is related to the permits issued. According to this Law, enterprises have to pay an administrative fee for a permit application to start the exploration and exploitation of minerals. A royalty, which represents a percentage (2 per cent) of the market value of the total amount of mineral resources sold each month, is payable as well. The charge rates for the exploration and exploitation permit are set by the Ministry of Industry and Energy, according to criteria decided by the Council of Ministers. Revenues collected in 2000 were US$ 134,000 according to the Taxation Department, and have a purely revenue-raising purpose.

Biodiversity and nature protection

A charge on hunting and fishing is in force, as well as a charge on cutting forest timber. The hunting and fishing charge is incorporated in the Law on Taxation of 1998. The fishing tax tariffs vary from 5,000 to 90,000 leks and are managed by the Fishery Department. The Hunting Association has the authority to collect the hunting fee. Fishermen and hunters need to have a licence from their respective Fishery Department or Hunting Association.

In Albania there have been increasing problems with illegal timber harvesting. To better control illegal harvesting and improve forest management on publicly managed land, the Law on Forestry and the Forestry Police Service (No. 7223/1992) was passed. It defines the country's forest assets, which comprise State, communal and private forests. In addition to the Law on Forestry and the Forestry

Police Service, a number of other laws and regulations have been issued. The Law for the Management of Revenues Generated from State Forests and Pastures stipulates that the income from State forests and pastures that are generated by timber sales, grazing fees, medicinal plants, hunting and other activities are managed by the General Directorate of Forestry and Pasture. According to this Law, 70 per cent of the income from State forests and pastures is earmarked for the General Directorate itself, and the remaining 30 per cent goes to the Government. Revenues from forest activities that are managed by the General Directorate are used for forest improvement and the protection of fauna and forest and pasture biodiversity, scientific research, forestation and improving forest roads. Revenues in 2000 totalled US$ 1.126 million or 156 million leks.

Fines and non-compliance fees

Fines and penalties can be imposed if there is evidence that environmental legislation has been violated. Furthermore, natural and legal persons who cause damage to natural resources resulting in environmental pollution shall be compelled to pay compensation for the resulting damage. Complaints are to be filed with the civil courts.

Liability for environmental pollution is also envisaged by the Penal Code and the Civil Code. The Civil Code states that persons or entities that harm the environment by changing or damaging it, partially or totally, are obliged to compensate for the damage. A lawsuit can be initiated by a public institution, as defined in the Law, or by the citizens whose private property has been damaged. The Penal Code defines seven criminal acts against the environment; the punishments vary from fines to imprisonment of up to 15 years. However, suits can only be filed against the authorities in civil courts when the rights of a person or organization have been infringed upon by an administrative decision.

It should be mentioned that the actual application of these articles is a different matter. Article 205 of the Penal Code, for example, stipulates that illegal woodcutting is punishable by up to one year in prison. Such sentences are rarely executed due to the lack of cooperation between the legal bodies and the police. There is no information available on the number of violations brought to the court, the sentences imposed or the compensation paid.

2.5 Environmental financing and expenditures

State Budget

To strengthen public expenditure management, the Government, with the assistance of international donors, has introduced a Medium-Term Expenditure Framework (MTEF). The MTEF should ensure that sectoral policies and public expenditures have a clear poverty-reduction focus and are designed within a realistic macroeconomic resource framework. Priorities that were identified under the Growth and Poverty Reduction Strategy have provided the strategic direction for the allocation of budgetary resources under the MTEF. The MTEF includes sectoral expenditure strategies for health, education, transport and agriculture, as well as for labour and social protection. Although the environment is not included in the MTEF, several environment-related investments are covered under the public works sector. The expenditure strategy for public works comprises investments to improve the water-supply and sewerage network, and to upgrade public services for waste collection, disposal and treatment.

The first MTEF, which covered the 2001-2003 period, achieved considerable success in providing a stronger framework for the preparation of the 2001 State budget. The recently completed MTEF for 2002-2004 proposes resource ceilings that reflect the sector's priorities. These ceilings specify the budgetary resources available to line ministries. The State budget allocations for the environment are very limited, due to the country's difficult economic situation. The environment is not considered to be a national priority. The MTEF does not specify the share of the total State budget to be allocated to the environment. Table 2.5 shows the budget allocations and projected allocations to the different sectors from 1996 to 2003.

The projections of expenditure by sector show that continuing priority is given to public order and safety. Substantial increases in spending on health and education are planned for the coming years. The relatively high levels of investment in agriculture and the transport sector are expected to be maintained.

The Ministry of Environment received no more than 0.02 per cent of the total State budget in 1995 and 0.04 per cent in 2000 (see table 2.6). The allocated resources covered only salaries, social insurance, administration and maintenance. Additional resources come from revenues from fines and licensing fees, which create a secondary fund.

Table 2.5: Sectoral resource allocations, 1996-2003

million leks

	1996	1997	1998	1999	2000	2001 planned	2002 projected	2003 projected
Total	**87,596**	**100,732**	**141,629**	**165,781**	**170,622**	**157,600**	**180,062**	**201,622**
Public services	5,850	6,303	11,065	15,722	14,366	13,944	13,425	14,602
Defence	4,774	4,668	5,343	6,407	5,655	6,617	7,211	7,859
Public order and safety	5,269	8,000	9,136	11,522	12,733	13,954	14,776	16,061
Education	10,310	11,197	13,612	15,938	17,192	19,937	24,854	27,243
Health	6,079	6,269	7,986	12,077	12,334	18,122	20,329	22,996
Social security and welfare	26,703	28,405	34,112	34,278	38,521	42,511	48,207	53,012
Housing and communal amenities	3,753	3,696	5,933	7,326	8,559	11,514	12,976	14,266
Recreation, culture, religious affairs	1,847	1,623	2,031	2,260	2,395	2,490	2,725	2,982
Fuel and energy	95	542	2,068	1,169	4,823	4,711	6,795	6,870
Agriculture, forestry, fishing, hunting	3,884	3,983	5,501	6,399	4,788	6,701	7,497	8,161
Mineral resources	793	638	748	3,698	1,499	851	936	1,029
Transport and communication	4,418	4,727	6,959	11,630	16,090	14,123	17,607	22,814
Other economic services	1,351	1,902	1,236	1,885	522	525	574	627
Other expenditures	12,470	18,779	35,899	35,470	31,145	1,600	2,150	3,100

Source: Medium-Term Expenditure Framework 2002-2004, 2001 and Fiscal Statistics of the Government, 2000.

Table 2.6: State budget allocations to the Ministry of Environment

	1995	1996	1997	1998	1999	2000
Total State budget (in million leks)	77,134	87,596	100,732	141,629	165,781	170,622
Ministry of Environment (in million leks)	17	17	20	27	65	66
Ministry of Environment (as % of total State budget)	0.02	0.02	0.02	0.02	0.04	0.04

Source: Fiscal Statistics of the Government, Ministry of Finance, 2000.

Figure 2.1: Expenditures of the Ministry of Environment, 1998-2001 (million leks)

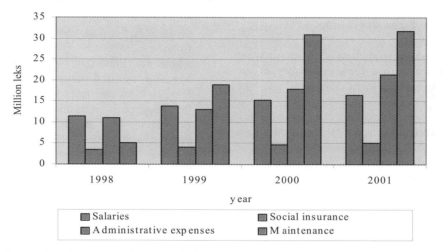

Source: Ministry of Environment, 2001.

The Regional Environmental Agencies are financed through the budget of the Ministry of Environment. The Regional Environmental Agencies do not have sufficient resources to do their work properly.

Extrabudgetary funds

In 1994, with the support of the Phare Programme, the Government began preparatory work to create an environmental fund. A draft law on environmental charges and the creation of a national environmental fund was prepared in 1995, following the Saint Petersburg Guidelines defined by the Organisation for Economic Co-operation and Development and the polluter-pays principle. This draft law foresaw the introduction of environmental taxes and charges and other economic instruments, as well as the establishment of an earmarked environmental fund. However, no consensus has ever been reached on this issue and the draft law has never been adopted. Both the Ministry of Finance and the International Monetary Fund (IMF) oppose it. One of their concerns is that the establishment of extrabudgetary funds would undermine the policy of fiscal integrity, which the IMF strongly advocates. The charges and taxes proposed under this draft law were effluent charges, product charges, taxes on natural resources, tariffs for obtaining permits, non-compliance and administrative fines.

The introduction of the carbon tax, proposed in the NEAP Immediate Measures report, could generate a significant amount of finance for the environment (see above). It is not clear how the revenues would be channelled to the environment, whether through the State budget or through an environmental fund set up for this purpose. Since in Albania the taxation system is unified, any environmental tax or charge would require amending the Law on Taxation.

Article 87 of the 2002 Law on Environmental Protection stipulates that income from permit tariffs and fines for non-compliance with the law should be used as financial support for the following activities:

- Elimination of pollution sources;
- Designing projects and taking rehabilitation measures in ecologically damaged zones;
- Undertaking scientific research, performance of studies and training of specialists;
- Providing staff and offices with the necessary means and supplies;
- Remunerating environmental specialists, experts and institutions which review the EIA; and
- Supporting the administrative expenses related to the supervision of EIA monitoring programmes or other programmes of this type.

The income generated from tariffs of services are used in accordance with a joint guidelines of the Minister of Finance and Minister of the Environment.

Total revenues varied from 2.5 to 4 million leks a year between 1998 and 2001, which is not more than 10 per cent of the total budget of the Ministry of Environment. Part of the money was used to finance different activities organized by non-governmental organizations, environmental monitoring and scientific research projects. The remainder was spent on maintenance of the Ministry of Environment's administrative buildings and on rewarding its staff.

Foreign financing

The multilateral aid agencies and international financial institutions have been the main source of external financing for environmental projects. The major donors are the World Bank, IMF, EU, the European Bank for Reconstruction and Development (EBRD) and the United States Agency for International Development (USAID). The total amount of foreign assistance to environmental projects is unknown. Details on various projects financed by international institutions are included in Chapter 3.

2.6   Conclusions and recommendations

Integrating environment-related economic instruments into economic development policies is difficult in Albania. A first attempt to introduce economic instruments for environmental protection coincided with the beginning of the political reforms and the transition to a market economy. The National Environmental Action Plan of 1994 recommended a set of measures to restructure economic incentives to encourage more efficient resource use. The economic and social situation since that time has been characterized by a growing budget deficit, high unemployment, tax evasion, corruption in the public administration and weak institutional capacity. These economic and social difficulties have diverted the Government's attention from the management of environmental issues.

Little finance is available for environmental policies. The State budget allocations for the environment are very limited, and in 2000 the Ministry of Environment received only 0.04 per cent. This amount was completely inadequate to finance even basic monitoring and inspection. An additional important source of income for the Ministry of Environment is revenue from permit fees, charges and fines for non-compliance. Part of this revenue is used to finance different activities organized by non-governmental organizations, environmental monitoring and scientific research projects. The remainder is spent on maintenance of the Ministry's administrative buildings and on rewarding its staff.

In a situation where resources are limited, it is of the utmost importance to allocate the available resources in a way that will achieve the greatest environmental improvement at the lowest possible cost. The selection and design of environmental policy instruments must therefore be based on the costs they impose versus the expected environmental improvements that they are expected to bring about.

A first step in increasing the effectiveness of policy instruments is to improve the legal and regulatory framework that is the basis for environmental management. The permit system in Albania needs to be improved to provide comprehensive solutions to polluting activities. The current permit procedures are neither transparent nor effective and need to be further developed. A first attempt could be made to set appropriate permit conditions with specific emission limit values for the pollutants likely to be emitted from the activity concerned. The inclusion of specific permit conditions could also lead to the introduction of an integrated permit taking into account the whole environmental performance of the activity, i.e. emissions to air, water and soil. This will also include local, site-specific factors such as the technical characteristics of the activity, its location and the local environmental conditions. For existing activities, the economic and technical viability of upgrading them also needs to be taken into account. The Integrated Pollution Prevention and Control Directive (96/61/EC, 24 December 1996) of the European Union could be used as guidance to develop a new integrated environmental permit.

The environmental quality standards referred to in the permit need to be upgraded to EU standards. The Ministry of Environment refers only to the 1974 Albanian quality standards in permits for existing (particularly State-owned) enterprises. New enterprises are required to apply EU quality standards as indicated in the permits, but the standards themselves are not specifically listed in the permit. To improve the system of environmental standards, it is important to focus on the major and priority pollutants that can actually be monitored at reasonable cost.

Recommendation 2.1:
(a) The Ministry of Environment should improve the current permit system by preparing clear procedures and guidelines, and when necessary adjusting the existing legislation. A first step should be to introduce appropriate permit conditions with threshold limit values for pollutants, in line with European Union legislation. A further step would be to introduce an integrated environmental permit regulating emissions to air, water and soil; (see also recommendation 9.1)

(b) The Ministry of Environment should update its environmental quality standards in line with European Union standards. As a first step, the system of environmental standards should concentrate on the major pollutants.

Enforcement of environmental legislation is in general very weak in Albania. The practical mechanisms for enforcement are incomplete and inadequate. The conditions stated in environmental permits are not respected and administrative fines for non-compliance are rarely paid. Inspections are carried out under the responsibility of the Ministry of Environment, but there is no separation between permit and inspection functions. The Ministry of Environment grants environmental permits and is at the same time involved in inspection and enforcement. The situation is exacerbated by the lack of basic resources and technical capacity within the regional inspectorates. In addition, cooperation with other regional bodies responsible for environmental matters (e.g. municipal, health, forestry, research institutes) in the enforcement of environmental legislation is not sufficient.

Recommendation 2.2:
Enforcement of environmental legislation needs to be improved by strengthening the Regional Environmental Agencies and establishing an independent inspectorate at national level to coordinate the regional inspectors and improve collaboration with other inspectorates. The Regional Environmental Agencies should be strengthened with training, equipment and operational means.

Economic instruments for environmental protection are not well developed in Albania. Its environmental policy is still dominated by command and control instruments. Few economic instruments are in place, with very low charge levels. While some of the economic instruments have environmental aspects, they do not give incentives to reduce pollution and to ensure sustainable resource use. It seems that the present environment-related instruments were not designed as incentives but rather to raise revenue for the State budget.

A draft law prepared in 1995 foresaw the introduction of a number of environmental taxes and charges. However, no consensus has been ever reached on this issue, and the draft law has never been adopted by Parliament. The proposed charges included effluent charges, product charges (carbon tax, pesticide and fertilizer user charges, and differentiated custom duties for imported used vehicles), natural resources user charges, and non-compliance fees and fines. Pollution charges can play a fundamental role in environmental policy and the implementation of the polluter-pays principle. The pollution charges were intended to raise revenue and encourage cost-effective abatement measures to reduce pollution.

The Ministry of Environment has drafted a law on carbon tax, whose revenues will be earmarked for environmental purposes. This tax could be a first attempt to develop a comprehensive system of economic instruments. The next step would be the introduction of pollution charges, such as water effluent charges, air pollution charges and natural resources charges, which need to go hand in hand with the permit system.

Recommendation 2.3:
The Ministry of Environment, together with the Ministry of Finance, should begin to develop a comprehensive system of economic instruments for environmental protection, in cooperation and negotiation with other ministries and stakeholders.

A first attempt could be made by adopting the draft law on carbon tax (earmarked for environmental purposes), and by adopting the proposals to introduce a packaging tax and to increase the cleaning tax.

Financial resources for environmental policies are extremely limited. One possible way to mobilize financial resources for environmental investments would be to create an "earmarked" environmental fund, which would collect the revenues generated by economic instruments as well as the contributions from foreign donors. The establishment of an environmental fund has been discussed and planned since 1995, and a draft law was prepared by the Ministry of Environment. However, the draft law has never been adopted because of strong resistance on the part of the Ministry of Finance (and IMF) to extrabudgetary funds.

A solution to this problem is to create a budgetary fund (environmental fund) within the State budget under the supervision of the Ministry of Finance. The fund's resources would then be subject to the regular State budget procedures. The financial resources could be held in a special account by the Ministry of Finance and subsequently be disbursed by the Ministry of Finance according to the fund's budget and identified environmental priority projects. To make the environmental investments more effective, priorities need to be set by the Ministry of Environment. These priorities could serve as a basis for selecting environmental projects to be financed. They should be in line with the new NEAP and updated regularly.

Recommendation 2.4:
The Government should take the necessary steps to establish and manage an environmental fund to channel financing for environmental purposes. This environmental fund could be established within the State budget under the supervision of the Ministry of Finance. To make the environmental investments more effective, priority projects need to be identified by the Ministry of Environment fully in line with the National Environmental Action Plan.

Chapter 3

INTERNATIONAL COOPERATION

3.1 Background

Geopolitical context

Since the political changes of 1991, Albania has strengthened its international links on environmental matters both globally and regionally. This effort is the result of Albania's interest in integration into Europe and the international community, so as to receive outside financial and technical assistance for solving its severe environmental problems, and benefit from the cooperation mechanisms of international environmental instruments.

During the past decade Albania has become a Party to several global and regional environmental conventions that now form an important part of its legal system. It strengthened its links with the United Nations system, established cooperation with international institutions, like the Organization for Security and Co-operation in Europe (OSCE), the North Atlantic Treaty Organisation (NATO), and the governments of neighbouring and other States. Albania has been a member of the United Nations since 14 December 1955 and participated in its principal environmental events – the Stockholm and Rio Conferences. On 8 September 2000 Albania joined the World Trade Organization (WTO) and it took part in the Ministerial Conference in Doha, Qatar (November 2001). For Albania, international cooperation with numerous organizations has already resulted in multimillion-dollar financial and technical assistance in such areas as:

- Health care and sanitation;
- Forest management;
- Seashore protection;
- Implementation of certain international conventions;
- Institutional strengthening and capacity-building;
- Agricultural development;
- Industrial and municipal waste; and
- Drinking-water supply.

Legal status and institutions

In accordance with the Constitution, international conventions enter into force when they are ratified by Parliament (Kuvendi I Shqiperise). According to articles 116 and 122 of the Constitution, international agreements ratified by Albania that are classified as laws become part of its national legislative system after publication in the Official Gazette of the Republic of Albania. Such agreements are enforced directly, except if they are not 'self-implementable' and their implementation requires a new law to be adopted. Once ratified (by law), international agreements take precedence over national laws. All the international instruments adopted by the international organizations of which Albania is a member take precedence. Should there be a contradiction between them and national laws, the former are to be complied with.

International environmental conventions are administered by the Ministry of Environment, which cooperates with line ministries when necessary. With only 40 professionals in its central office, the Ministry has insufficient capacity to ensure the proper implementation of international conventions. International cooperation is spread among different Directorates. Its Department for Environmental Policy and Project Implementation is responsible for general coordination, but the implementation of the conventions is carried out by the Ministry's technical directorates. Following a recent internal reorganization, a new Directorate on Legislation and Foreign Relations was established. Other State bodies play a major role in international cooperation. The Minister of State for European Integration coordinates the governmental activities related to the Stabilization and Association Agreement. The Ministry of Justice handles activities related to EU accession and its Department for the Approximation of Legislation (set up in July 1999 within the former Ministry of Institutional Reforms and transferred in July 2000 to the Ministry of Justice) is in charge of managing and coordinating the process of approximating Albania's legislation to the required status for EU association. To this end, it accomplishes activities needed for the Stabilization and Association Agreement too. The Ministry of Industry and Energy has administered around 100 investment projects with environmental components since 1992. The Ministry of Foreign Affairs and the Ministry of Economy, in cooperation with the Ministry of Environment, are responsible for the negotiation processes in the frame of different Agreements, Protocols of Cooperation and Programmes. The Ministry of Environment and the Ministry of Foreign Affairs are responsible for negotiation processes in general and for negotiating international environmental instruments in particular.

3.2   General principles and objectives for international environmental cooperation

In its international environmental cooperation Albania adheres to the principles of:

- Openness to cooperation with international institutions;
- Friendly relations with other nations;
- Supremacy of international rules; and
- Freedom of economic activities with due consideration for environmental concerns.

The main responsibility for international environmental cooperation is laid down in political documents and in several legal soft law and hard law documents, like the Law on Environmental Protection, the National Waste Management Plan approved in 1998, the National Biodiversity Strategy and Action Plan approved by the Council of Ministers in 1999, the Agricultural Development Strategy - the Green Strategy (forestry, fisheries, agriculture, aquaculture) – approved in 1998, and the National Environmental Action Plan approved in 1994.

According to these documents, Albania's policy objectives in international environmental cooperation are:

- Accession to the EU and the corresponding harmonization of environmental legislation;
- Integration into the global community through ratification of international environmental legal instruments;
- Strengthening of cooperation with East European countries to control potential pollution sources through coordinated investments;

- Development and implementation of the action plan for the Mediterranean Sea;
- Development of an implementation strategy for the Aarhus Convention;
- Improvement of implementation of international obligations;
- Promotion of foreign investment in the economy and environmentally sound technologies;
- Institutional strengthening; and
- Public awareness and civil society.

The 1994 National Environmental Action Plan (NEAP) was based on an internationally supported project (World Bank and the Government of Italy) and the Declaration of the Ministers of the Environment at the "Environment for Europe" Conference held in Lucerne, Switzerland, in 1993. In relation to international environmental cooperation, the NEAP makes the implementation of European environmental mechanisms a priority. The new NEAP, approved by the Government in January 2002, will strengthen environmental protection.

The National Biodiversity Strategy and Action Plan lists the international instruments that Albania views as priorities for its national environmental policy. Except for the Convention on International Trade in Endangered Species of Wild Flora and Fauna (CITES), Albania has ratified all the conventions listed in the Strategy (Bonn and Basel Conventions, Convention to Combat Desertification). Another priority in the international context is the conservation of transboundary lakes.

International cooperation is also addressed in the Strategy on Growth and Poverty Reduction, which the Government prepared with the World Bank. In accordance with the Strategy, environmental policy is viewed as a component of sustainable development. In the long term, the country will strive to achieve appropriate environmental standards in accordance with Albania's commitments to association with the EU. Provision is also made for the promotion of direct foreign investments in activities under the Strategy. In Albania, poverty is important in the environmental context: environmental degradation goes hand in hand with poverty, and poverty prevents many environmental problems from being solved.

3.3 Bilateral, subregional and regional cooperation

UNECE Conventions

The problem of air pollution, especially in the cities, ranks among the most serious environmental problems (see Chapter 5). There is no proper monitoring and no proper control over sources of emissions. Several draft laws, including a law of air protection and another on gaseous emission standards, are based on EU Directives. Albania has signed neither the *UNECE Convention on Long-range Transboundary Air Pollution* nor any of its protocols, although it did start preparatory work on assessing its possibilities of adhering to the Convention in 1998.

One third of the hydrographical basins of Albania's waters are located outside the country. Albania ratified the *UNECE Convention on the Protection and Use of Transboundary Watercourses and International Lakes* on 5 January 1994 and its *Protocol on Water and Health* on 8 March 2002. Several projects on international lakes – Ohrid, Prespa and Shkodra – that aim at establishing sound environmental management of the lakes and monitoring their quality provide important input for the implementation of the Water Convention (see Chapter 6, Box 6.1). So far, no bilateral agreements on transboundary river regimes or on their protection have been concluded with neighbouring countries. A project proposal, the Drini River Watershed and Erosion Masterplan, to be implemented by Albania and the former Yugoslav Republic of Macedonia, is now being prepared within the Regional Environmental Reconstruction Programme for South Eastern Europe (REReP).

On 4 October 1991 Albania ratified the Convention on the Environmental Impact Assessment in a Transboundary Context. To fulfil its international obligations, Albania has recently prepared a draft law on environmental impact assessment (EIA), which it is now considering. The law will further develop the general EIA provisions stipulated in the 2002 framework Law on Environmental Protection. At the same time, the new framework Law, in its Article 26, specifies the EIA process, and Article 27 establishes the foundation for EIA in a transboundary context, with specific reference to the UNECE Convention. The draft law on EIA stipulates that projects having transboundary environmental effects will be subject to a special EIA. Albania will be obliged to notify the potentially affected countries about such projects, to supply them with information on their environmental impacts and to invite representatives from interested States to participate in the EIA.

Albania ratified the *UNECE Convention on the Transboundary Effects of Industrial Accidents* on 5 January 1994. A policy for the prevention of, preparedness for and response to industrial accidents is being developed and relevant legislation is being drafted, including laws on the establishment of monitoring systems, on air protection and on gaseous emission standards. They aim to improve safety at hazardous installations, for instance by developing and installing alarm systems, training staff in safety measures at chemical installations, preparing information for the public, and developing contingency planning. The Ministries of Industry, Mineral and Energy Resources, Health, and Environment are involved in activities under the Convention and in administering it. For instance, there are small projects on environmental auditing for the Deep Oil Processing Refinery in Ballsh and Ferro-Chromium Plant in Elbasan. The Institute of Contemporary Studies has implemented a project on taking environmental liabilities into consideration during privatization. The Ministry of Environment has participated in coordinating technical assistance.

Albania ratified the *UNECE Convention on Access to Information, Public Participation in Decision-making and Access to Justice in Environmental Matters* on 27 June 2001. Under the Constitution the country must maintain "a healthy and ecologically suitable environment for present and future generations". Natural resources must be "rationally exploited" consistent with "the sustainable development" principle and there is "the right of everyone to be informed about the environmental situation and its protection". In 1998 the Minister of Health and the Environment approved the Guidelines on environmental information and public access to environmental information – a rather detailed procedural and substantive document. A draft law on public access to environmental information and the 2002 Law on Environmental Protection provide for basic rights that are formulated in quite broad terms. A strategy for the implementation of the Aarhus Convention is under preparation within REReP (see Chapter 4).

"Environment for Europe" and other agreements and programmes

Albania has been an active participant in the Pan-European "Environment for Europe" Ministerial Conferences since the second conference, held in Lucerne in April 1993.

Albania participates in a number of other regional initiatives to expand regional cooperation, including Corridor 8 (East-West Corridor, a highway across Albania from the Mediterranean to the West), the Southeast European Cooperative Initiative (SECI), the South-East European Cooperation Process (SEECP) and the Charter on Good-Neighbourly Relations, Stability, Security and Cooperation in South-Eastern Europe (signed on 12 February 2000). SECI is a regional initiative involving 11 countries, including Albania. It aims to encourage cooperation among the countries of the region and facilitate European integration. It is a forum at which representatives of the countries meet to discuss common regional economic and environmental problems. SEECP, another initiative for regional cooperation, was started in 1996 in Sofia. It now involves seven countries, including Albania. Its main aim is to promote and strengthen good neighbourly relations among the South-Eastern countries, and it covers various areas, including the environment. SEECP meetings take place once a year and are attended by the Ministry of Foreign Affairs, who have consultations and produce guidelines on cooperation. The Charter on Good-Neighbourly Relations, Stability, Security and Cooperation in South-Eastern Europe mainly focuses on political peace issues; it proclaims principles and outlines areas of cooperation, including environmental cooperation, which takes place through the systematic exchange of information, bilateral and multilateral agreements and concrete joint projects mainly in the border areas.

Cooperation with the EU

Cooperation with the EU on environmental matters takes place through EU accession policies and activities, including the harmonization of legislation, and also through projects benefiting from EU support. In September 2001 the Government of Albania and the EU agreed to begin negotiating a pre-accession agreement. The areas of cooperation encompass water quality, air pollution, the monitoring of pollution, the promotion of

energy efficiency and safety at industrial plants, the classification and safe handling of chemicals, urban planning, waste management, and the protection of forests, flora and fauna. In September 2001 a working meeting was held with the EU Commission in Tirana to discuss such issues as trade, customs and taxation, public procurement, competition, property rights, the free movement of capital and the reform of the public administration.

Most efforts are concentrated on the harmonization of Albania's legislation with that of the EU. These activities are supervised and coordinated by the Ministry of Justice. Its Department for the Approximation of Legislation is responsible for preparing a national harmonization strategy. In addition, it issues opinions and advice on draft laws, and makes comparative studies. Its mandate is to cooperate with countries already associated with the EU and with the other countries of the region that are eligible for stabilization and association agreements – agreements proposed by the EU in 1999 within the Stabilisation and Association process and to be signed by five countries in the region, including Albania. One of the process's objectives is to bring Albania closer to EU standards and principles, and to prepare the country for gradual integration into EU structures.

Since 1991 Albania has received substantial assistance for various sectors, including transport, agriculture, private sector development, local community development, public administration reform, water supply and sewage systems, and environment, from the EU under its PHARE programme. PHARE is one of the three pre-accession instruments financed by the European Union to assist the applicant countries of Central Europe in their preparation for joining the EU. Overall for the 1991-2000 period the EU allocated almost € 633 million to Albania. Environment (excluding water infrastructures) received less than 1 per cent (€ 5.4 million) - the smallest share of all sectors. However, some projects in agriculture and forestry, for instance, will also benefit the environment. The agricultural component of PHARE for the year 2001 was worth € 1,150,000 and aimed specifically at land improvement. This allocation between the environment and other project activities remains the same under the current PHARE programme. At the end of September 2001, the environment programme represented only € 1.9 million (less than 1 per cent). (see Figure 3.1)

Figure 3.1: Phare programmes breakdown (as % of total, excluding Special Programmes*), 2000

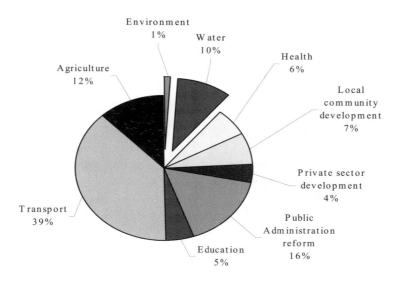

Source: EU. Phare, Cooperation Instruments Implementation Report, 2001.

Note: *Phare special programme include: Emergency Food Aid Triangular, Technical Assistance, Import Support, FEOGA, Balance of Payments Grant, Urgent Rehabilitation, Humanitarian Aid, Macro-financial Assistance, Support to Public Expenditure, Support Kosovo Refugees.

The EU has now started its Community Assistance for Reconstruction, Development and Stabilisation (CARDS) – a new, three-year programme of assistance to South Eastern Europe that will cover activities to strengthen Albanian environmental institutions, to raise their capacity to implement and enforce laws, to increase public access to credible environmental data, to implement EIA, to reduce health risks through improved water quality, better waste management and reduced air pollution, to enhance regional cooperation, and to improve urban planning. Assistance to Albania will support the priorities of the Stabilisation and Association process, including the environment. The Ministry of Economy will coordinate the different projects. Particular attention will be paid to the "hot spots" identified by the United Nations Environment Programme (UNEP). EU also plans to support environmental cross-border cooperation, for instance for natural parks and lakes.

Protection of the Mediterranean Sea

Protection of the Mediterranean Sea and its coastal zone in Albania is minimal. Urbanization, fisheries, resources extraction (sand, gravel) and tourism remain the principal pressures on the marine ecosystem. There is no specific national legislation concerning environmental protection of the coastal area (see Chapter 11).

In 2000 Albania ratified the *Convention for the Protection of the Mediterranean Sea against Pollution*, signalling its commitment to protecting the marine ecosystem. Programmes and joint activities implemented within the framework of the Convention by the activity centres help the country to improve its position. The Blue Plan Regional Activity Centre studies environmental conditions in the Mediterranean basin and on the basis of various parameters (human population, urbanization) models prospective scenarios. The Mediterranean Pollution Monitoring and Research Programme (MED POL) was initiated in 1975 as an environment assessment component of the Mediterranean Action Plan. Its task is to assist the Mediterranean countries in the implementation of pollution assessment programmes. The Regional Marine Pollution Emergency Response Centre for the Mediterranean (REMPEC) plays a coordinating role in the implementation of the emergency protocol, which provides for response action in emergencies. In cooperation with UNEP and the Mediterranean Action Plan, Albania started pollution monitoring in the Ionian and Adriatic Seas and in the main rivers that flow into the sea. Albania is also developing cooperation with the Mediterranean Technical Assistance Programme.

The Conservation of Wetland and Coastal Ecosystem in the Mediterranean Region is a United Nations Development Programme (UNDP) project to ensure the sustainable management of the biological diversity of coastal areas and wetlands through the development of adequate legal and regulatory frameworks, the creation of institutional organizations, capacity-building and awareness raising. The project is a national component of a Mediterranean regional initiative involving Albania, Egypt, Lebanon, Morocco, Tunisia and the Palestinian Authority. An inter-ministerial coordination mechanism for local and national projects has been established, and demonstration activities at the most significant sites shall also be funded. The amount allocated to Albania under the project is US$ 1.9 million, with US$ 1.75 million coming from UNDP/GEF and the remaining US$ 150,000 contributed by the Albanian Government. The project started in November 1999 and is scheduled to end in late 2004. The following outputs are expected: management plans for protected ecosystems and wetlands, policy documents to be adopted by decision makers, an inventory of and a monitoring system for threatened species and the hydrological conditions of the wetlands.

Although Albania ratified the Barcelona Convention, implementation is poor. Albania is one of few countries that do not have sewage-treatment plants, thus allowing untreated effluents to go directly into the sea. This poor implementation may be explained by economic problems and the Balkan conflict in recent years; however, further delays should not be permitted, and Albania should do more to protect the Mediterranean Sea from pollution.

Albania and the Stability Pact

On 10 June 1999, Albania signed the Stability Pact and in 2000 joined its Regional Environmental Reconstruction Programme for South Eastern Europe (REReP), which widened cooperation between Albania and other Balkan States.

The Stability Pact is an instrument to speed up transition and reform, and bring countries closer to

the EU. It is a new political agreement between donors and countries in the Balkans. Albania has initiated several projects under the Stability Pact and some have already found support from international partners under the "Quick Start" Priority Projects. Among them are:

- Strengthening National Environmental Protection Agencies and their Inspectorates in the South Eastern European Countries – € 477,580;
- Supporting capacity building for EU approximation in SEE – € 467,500;
- Supporting the development of strategies for implementation of the Aarhus Convention in SEE – € 908,295;
- Supporting ratification and implementation of multilateral environmental agreements – € 471,450.
- Promoting the networking and cooperation of environmental NGOs: the establishment of electronic computer networks on national and regional levels – € 750,000 for 2001-2003;
- Carrying out a feasibility study on the Change of the Hydraulic Regime of Lake Prespa and the Conservation of its biodiversity – € 600,000 (under consideration);
- Eliminating 800 tons of arsenic solution stocked near Semani River, which flows directly into the sea – € 1 million;
- Supporting environmental legal advocacy and advisory centres for SEE – € 500,000; and
- Developing a regional strategy for hazardous waste management – € 119,000.

Cooperation with the European Environmental Agency

Albania started its cooperation with the European Environmental Agency (EEA) with the assistance of EU PHARE in 1996. In 2000 it applied for membership of the EEA. It expects to benefit from the CARDS Regional Programme "Strengthening Capacities in Balkan Countries in Environmental Reporting and developing the EIONET Network", which would help it prepare for future membership of the European Environment Agency.

Bilateral cooperation

Albania has signed bilateral memorandums of understanding on cooperation with the former Yugoslav Republic of Macedonia and Montenegro that provide for the development of cooperation in various areas, including the environment. However, no environmental cooperation has yet taken place as a result of these memorandums.

Albania is also developing cooperation with Canada, Germany, Italy, Japan, Switzerland and the United Kingdom, which support mostly economic and social projects, such as security, infrastructure (roads, water management, sanitation and capacity-building) and health care.

The Swiss Department for Cooperation with Eastern Europe and the Commonwealth of Independent States supports the "Promotion of networks and exchange in the countries of South Eastern Europe" project under REReP and the Stability Pact. The project focuses on biodiversity protection and the recreational values of Lake Shkodra. It provides for transboundary water management, the protection of endangered species and their habitat, strengthening civil society institutions and the sustainable development of the region. The project implementation started in December 2000 with the establishment in Shkodër (Albania) of an office and five working groups to prepare: (1) a report on the Lake's potential and the threats to it; (2) a report on the water regime and quality; (3) a communication campaign; (4) an endangered species list and biodiversity database; (5) materials for use in schools to raise awareness. A similar office and working groups have been established in Montenegro. The groups from both sides stay in close contact, and have already had several joint meetings on the report on the possible risks to the Lake and on the communication campaign. The first phase of the project has ended and the following are already available: Bibliography on Lake Shkodra, Report on the Risks and Potential of Lake Shkodra, and List of Lake Shkodra species. The second phase is now being prepared, and a proposal has been made for a database on a compact disk with the above information.

Cooperation with the former Yugoslav Republic of Macedonia covers activities to protect the international lake Ohrid, shared by the two countries. The project amounting to US$ 2 million in Albania is funded by GEF. (see Chapter 6)

3.4 Global cooperation

Albania is a very recent participant in certain global environmental conventions (see Annex III), most of which it ratified in the past two years. Because of this short time, it has only just started implementation.

Implementation of Agenda 21

Albania participated in the Rio Conference and signed its conventions. Thereafter, certain actions mentioned below have been taken to implement these documents. However, implementation is still very slow due to economic hardship, the Kosovo conflict, and the low priority given by the Government to environmental protection. There are no sustainable development programmes or plans; however, as a principle it is proclaimed in the Constitution and the Law on Environmental Protection.

Assistance from UNDP is expected for some activities for Agenda 21. In particular, under its Second Country Cooperation Framework for Albania (2002-2005), UNDP is planning to help build and strengthen national and local human capacity for sustainable development. This will include training, raising local government and public awareness and helping to formulate Albania's Agenda 21. To meet this objective UNDP, in cooperation with the Ministry of Local Government and Decentralization and the region of Fier, will implement a set of activities. Agenda 21 facilitators will be trained and awareness of sustainable development issues in the Fier region will be raised with the intention of setting up a regional advisory commission on sustainable development there. The commission would coordinate the activities of the local government to introduce a sustainable development model in this particular region. A local Agenda 21 will also be developed in the Ballsh municipality and one or two demonstration projects will be implemented to promote and test models for sustainable development at community level. Finally, an evaluation report will be prepared to review best practices and provide input to the national Agenda 21 process.

Another input for Agenda 21 is the new NEAP and the preparation of local environmental action plans.

Global Air Pollution

In March 1999 Albania acceded to the *Convention for the Protection of the Ozone Layer and the Montreal Protocol on Substances that Deplete the Ozone Layer* by governmental decree. It is in the process of ratifying the three amendments to the Montreal Protocol. Implementation has not yet started, but Albania prepared its national programme for implementation and submitted it to the Multilateral Fund for the Implementation of the

Montreal Protocol. GEF decided to fund the institutional strengthening component and a memorandum of understanding to this end is being signed. However, no specific efforts have been made to reduce the production or consumption of ozone-depleting substances. There is no air monitoring system, no control over ozone-depleting substances and no decision has been taken to ban the production of ozone-depleting substances (see Chapter 5).

Albania is a Party to the *United Nations Framework Convention on Climate Change* since it ratified it on 1 January 1995 with the status of developing country. As a first step to implementing the Convention, the Government prepared its First National Communication to the Conference of the Parties with UNDP support. A contribution of US$ 263,744 from GEF aimed to help the Government to draw up an inventory of greenhouse gases for the base year 1994, to assess the potential impacts of climate change, to analyse potential measures to reduce greenhouse-gas emissions and to adapt to climate change, and to prepare a national action plan to address climate change and its adverse impacts. The First National Communication is to be formally submitted to the Conference of the Parties. It is also expected to raise general awareness and knowledge on climate-change-related issues in Albania, and to promote dialogue and an exchange of information among all stakeholders. Eight training and information workshops have already been held in Albania and abroad.

Albania is considered to be an insignificant contributor to the depletion of the ozone layer and climatic change. Accelerated growth in transport, especially in cities, is likely to change the situation though a lack of monitoring means, that this cannot be confirmed at the moment. Moreover, the use and export of ozone-depleting substances have not been estimated. Nevertheless, several new laws on air protection, on gaseous emission standards and on environmental impact assessment and government regulations that are now in the pipeline will help Albania meet its international obligations.

Biodiversity and nature conservation

On 5 January 1994 Albania ratified the *Convention on Biological Diversity*. In 1999 the Council of Ministers adopted the National Biodiversity Strategy and Action Plan, prepared with the support of the Global Environment Facility. Its main objectives are to enlarge protected areas to 14 per cent of the territory and develop scientific research.

Action plans for ecosystems, habitats and species are only now being developed and the Plan is not yet implemented. Albania has not submitted any national reports to the Convention's secretariat. To meet Albania's international obligations, the Minister of Agriculture, Food and Forests issued a special order on 20 May 1997 to protect rare and endangered species of flora.

On 29 March 1996 the *Convention on Wetlands of International Importance especially as Waterfowl Habitat* came into force for Albania. By its Decision No. 413 of 22 August 1994 the Council of Ministers declared the area of Divjaka-Karavasta a specially protected ecosystem and it is included in the Ramsar list. Under an EU-funded project (€ 0.7 million), measures have been taken to improve the state of the Karavasta lagoon. However, the project has not been implemented in full and € 0.4 million for the second stage has been withheld. Due to unacceptable bids EU could not approve the work. The project is to be terminated.

Albania signed the *Convention on the Conservation of European Wildlife and Natural Habitats* on 31 October 1995 and ratified it on 13 January 1998. In 1997 the Red Book on endangered and endemic species of Albanian flora and fauna was published. In implementation of the Convention the Institute of Fisheries Research in Durrës has studied endangered fish in collaboration with the EU.

Albania has ratified the *Convention on the Conservation of Migratory Species of Wild Animals*, together with three specific agreements (see Annex III).

According to its Biodiversity Strategy, Albania is moving towards accession to the *Convention on International Trade in Endangered Species of Wild Fauna and Flora (CITES)*. In particular, the Government is assessing its financial, human resource and material capacities to fulfil CITES obligations. The General Directorate of Forests and Pastures of the Ministry of Agriculture and Food controls the export and trade in game species.

Other global conventions

On 27 April 2000 Albania ratified the *United Nations Convention to Combat Desertification*. Up to now no specific decisions or actions have been taken to implement it; however, land degradation is very acute in the country.

Waste remains one of the most serious environmental problems. It also has an international dimension, as stocks of illegally imported toxic waste have been found. On 29 June 1999 Albania acceded to the *Convention on the Control of Transboundary Movements of Hazardous Wastes and Their Disposal*. According to the Decision of the Council of Ministers on Hazardous Wastes and Residues of 1994, the import of hazardous waste, bulk waste or waste refined for disposal is prohibited. The import of waste is accepted only with an import permit granted by the Ministry of Environment and valid for one year. The Decision prohibits the export of hazardous waste unless the exporter has all the proper documentation from the importing country.

3.5   International funding mechanisms

Given Albania's lack of financial resources, international organizations play a crucial role in resolving environmental problems. Environmental assistance is provided by some 15 international organizations and governments of various countries. Most internationally funded projects and activities concern social, institutional and economic issues; few are specifically environmental. However, by improving the social and economic situation, through poverty eradication, health care improvement, rural and urban development, or institutional strengthening, environmental issues are also addressed. Table 3.1 lists some environmental projects and their sponsors.

Cooperation with UNDP

UNDP plays an important role in providing support to programmes and projects relating to environmental protection in the country. UNDP is supporting three projects in Albania, including a GEF Small Grants Programme, enabling Albania to prepare its First National Communication in Response to its Commitments to the United Nations Framework Convention on Climate Change, and Mediterranean wetlands protection (for fuller descriptions, see above).

Since 1998 UNDP has been administering a GEF Small Grants Programme. The project is aimed at ensuring global environmental benefits in the areas of biodiversity conservation, climate change mitigation and the protection of international waters through community-based approaches. The approach is based on the belief that there are local solutions to global environmental problems. An amount of US$ 88,400 was allocated for the project in January 1998, mostly to help communities to obtain GEF small grants. Approximately 40 NGOs have been involved in about 35 local subprojects that address global environmental problems. It is intended to allocate annually some US$ 200,000 overall to the project. In future UNDP will support government efforts in disaster management, preparedness and reduction, and the cleaning-up of environmental hot spots – areas representing serious threats to the population due to the presence of highly dangerous substances produced by obsolete industries and left in the open (see Chapter 7).

Cooperation with NATO

Albania became a member of the North Atlantic Cooperation Council in 1992. It has also applied for full NATO membership. In 1994 Albania signed the Peace Partnership Agreement. In 1998 NATO opened the Peace Partnership office in the Ministry of Defence to coordinate and implement the individual peace programme. No environmental projects are currently implemented with NATO support.

Cooperation with OSCE

Albania joined OSCE in June 1991. OSCE has been acquiring an ever-increasing role in solving environmental problems, which are viewed as one of the risks to security in modern society. The main focus of the OSCE Economics and Environmental Office in Tirana is on raising public awareness helping Albania draw up a coherent environmental policy.

OSCE is not a donor organization; however, it assists Albania to find funding organizations for environmental projects. OSCE cooperates widely with NGOs. In 2001 it was involved in supporting a media project to launch a TV series on environmental issues, in promoting a "teach the teachers" project, and in awareness campaigns on the most burning environmental issues using available political means to put pressure on the Government to take environmentally favourable decisions.

Projects with the World Bank

Since 1991 the World Bank has supported a broad range of priorities, e.g. broad-based growth, strengthening governance, promoting rural development, improving health and education services. By July 2001 it had given Albania 43 credits totalling US$ 570 million. Of this amount, US$ 389 million have been disbursed for 22 projects that are now being implemented. In addition, the International Finance Corporation of the World Bank has approved US$ 66.4 million in financing.

At this point, the World Bank is supporting one environmental project for the conservation of Ohrid Lake, and another is expected to start soon on the rehabilitation of the environmental "hot spot" in Durres. At the same time, other current and future projects will have a positive environmental impact: for instance, Irrigation and Drainage II worth US$ 24 million; Forestry worth US$ 8

million; and Urban Land Management worth US$ 9.9 million. In addition, the World Bank intends to extend its activities to other areas, such as natural resources management, remedying "hot spots" identified by UNEP, setting up fishermen's associations and promoting tourism in the Karavasta lagoon.

The World Bank is currently preparing a new country assistance strategy for Albania that will be based on the Growth and Poverty Reduction Strategy being finalized by the Albanian Government with the support of the World Bank and other donors. In April 2001 a workshop was held in Tirana to discuss the strategy. According to the Albanian Government, the strategy will be the central focus of government policy and donor support. The strategy will formulate the country's policy in relation to foreign assistance. The availability of a governmental instrument will help the donor community to fund activities properly.

Table 3.1: Some environmental projects and their sponsors

Projects (from 1999 to May 2000)	Donor	Allocated funds in US $
Rehabilitation of the sewerage system and repairs to the roads to Shkxet/Durrës	DFID	18,330
Storm water management - Pusi ne Cati/Berat	DFID	64,220
Storm water management - Phase 2: 28 Nendori to the Osum River/Berat	DFID	18,520
Restricting access to Tirana National Park/Tirana	DFID	15,510
Clean-up of Krujë	DFID	68,000
Restoring fishing livelihoods Narta Lagoon/Vlorë	DFID	45,000
Tear Fund/Kukës	Tear Fund	559,703
Monitoring of coastal waters in the framework of MED POL	UNEP	40,000
Albania watershed assessment	USAID	1,400,000
Integrated pest management	USAID	600,000
Irrigation rehabilitation	World Bank	24,000,000
Forestry project	World Bank+Italy	21,600,000
Lake Ohrid conservation (GEF)	World Bank	4,280,000
Support programme for areas of Albania hosting refugees	World Bank	1,000,000
Municipal water supply in Elbasan	World Bank+Italy	50,000
Municipal water supply in Pogradec	World Bank+Germany	515,708
Clean-up of public beaches/Durrës	UNHCR	6,000
Reconstruction at seaside	UNHCR	46,626
Capacity 21 for Albania	UNDP	897,500
Environment Albania	Switzerland	1,546,426
Regulatory framework and institutional strengthening	PHARE	206,283
Disposal of pesticide waste	PHARE	1,547,125

Source: UNDP; World Bank; EU Phare; IMF and other donors, 2001.
Note: Exchange rates from IMF International Financial Statistics, April 2002.

3.6   Conclusions and recommendations

Albania is keen to strengthen its international links in environmental matters. Before 1990 the country had hardly any international environmental obligations (having ratified only the Convention concerning the Protection of the World Cultural and Natural Heritage), and in the following decade the total was some 20 regional and global instruments (see Annex III). Albania is now taking part in international environmental cooperation. However, regional destabilization, economic hardships, the low priority of environmental issues, the closed lifestyle and traditions of the recent past make it particularly challenging for the country to meet its international obligations fully.

Having demonstrated a strong commitment to environmental protection in the international context, the Government should pursue this policy, concentrating its efforts on fulfilling its international obligations. To this end, the Government should put environmental protection and international environmental cooperation high on its political agenda. International commitments require: the adoption of legislation; outlining the specific policies and obligations of each executive body involved in implementing international environmental conventions; and strengthening the role and capacity of the Ministry of Environment.

Recommendation 3.1:
The Government of Albania should put more emphasis on fulfilling its international obligations in practical terms. The role of the Ministry of Environment in these tasks should be strengthened. To begin with, the Ministry of Environment should prepare national implementation plans for each convention ratified, in cooperation with the other ministries and institutions involved.

Albania has signed up to many important global and regional conventions that widen opportunities for addressing environmental problems. However, Albania is still absent from the international cooperation processes to combat air pollution and its participation in international cooperation on biodiversity is limited.

Albania needs to sign up to more international environmental instruments if it is to benefit from wider international cooperation to solve its own acute environmental problems. For instance, Albania could get advice and financial assistance from other Parties and the international community. The secretariats of the conventions may also provide recommendations on implementation. Such instruments as CITES and the UNECE Convention on Long-range Transboundary Air Pollution should be a priority, as the environmental issues that they address have already become a serious national problem (health effects, degradation of natural resources) and could be a threat to the region.

Albania also has many endangered flora and fauna species and is preparing to accede to the Convention on International Trade in Endangered Species of Wild Fauna and Flora (Washington, 1973). With the liberalization of international trade, Albania increasingly risks becoming a transit route for the illegal trade in endangered species. Ratifying CITES would help to ensure better protection of endangered species inside the country and stronger customs control in cooperation with other Parties to CITES and its secretariat (see Chapter 8).

Although Albania does not export significant amounts of air pollution, its technologically outdated industry, its waste and its growing fleet of vehicles are definitely increasing the emission of pollutants into the air. Ratifying the UNECE Convention on Transboundary Air Pollution would open access to national and international experience in dealing with air pollution, and would help to install a proper monitoring system and to review the old air pollution standards.

Recommendation 3.2:
Albania needs to sign up to other international environmental instruments, in particular the Convention on Long-range Transboundary Air Pollution and its protocols and the Convention on International Trade in Endangered Species of Wild Fauna and Flora. (see also recommendation 5.3)

Albania's regional cooperation with other countries, with the EU, international partners and donors often concentrates on economic affairs. The emphasis is on trade, support to economic activities and privatization. Economic cooperation alone cannot address the problems of poor political and cultural communication that could hamper regional cooperation in the long term. Besides, if economic cooperation develops without due attention to environmental issues, it may contribute to further environmental degradation and will fail to ensure sustainable development.

Recommendation 3.3:
The Ministry of Environment should develop a strategic paper, including a list of environmental priorities and projects, for international cooperation. This paper should be disseminated to the Ministry of Foreign Affairs and to the Ministry of Economy.

International support from international partners and donors for Albania has been strong. Donors have funded more than 50 per cent of public investment made during the past five years. Multimillion-dollar aid has been provided to support economic recovery. However, environmental issues are not addressed adequately. In EU-supported projects, the environment's share is less than 1 per cent, and the World Bank is only supporting one project at the moment.

Recommendation 3.4:
The Government needs to adopt regulations and establish mechanisms for the administration of

funds that it receives from international donors, so as to ensure a transparent and well-controlled system for managing international financial assistance. Such regulations may be in the form of instructions for the ministries responsible for the projects on how to manage the projects, distribute the funds and report back.

Albania started its cooperation with the European Environmental Agency (EEA) with the assistance of EU PHARE in 1996. Closer association with the EEA is important for helping Albania strengthen its data systems and harmonize its methodologies for data collection and analysis with EU standards.

Recommendation 3.5:
The Ministry of Environment should intensify its efforts to strengthen its cooperation with the European Environmental Agency and fulfil all obligations accordingly.

Chapter 4

ENVIRONMENTAL MONITORING AND INFORMATION

4.1 Environmental monitoring

Organization of environmental monitoring

The monitoring programmes started in the late 1970s but were completely interrupted for some years after 1990. In 1995, the programmes were revived by decision of the Council of Ministers. The present monitoring system is partly managed by the Ministry of Environment, whose main objective is to provide information and initiate collaboration with national scientific institutions. There are no monitoring facilities within the structure of the Ministry of Environment, which includes the twelve Regional Environmental Agencies. In order to manage this task the Ministry contracts a number of institutions, including: (1) the Geological Survey; (2) the Institute of Hydrometeorology; (3) the Institute of Public Health; (4) the Institute of Nuclear Physics; (5) the Institute of Biological Research; (6) the Institute of Forests and Pastures, (7) the Research Institute on Fishing, (8) the Museum of Natural Science, and (9) the Soil Science Institute, and asks these institutions to provide data both on monitoring issues, such as groundwater, surface water, air, noise and urban waste, and on nature conservation, such as soil, arable lands, ecosystems, green areas and biodiversity (see Table 4.1). The Ministry of Environment defines the monitoring and nature conservation parameters on the basis of international requirements and available measurements in the country. Altogether it has eight annual contracts worth about US$ 40,000 with the monitoring institutions.

There is no national environmental monitoring programme that includes different monitoring subcomponents such as an environmental radioactivity surveillance programme. The responsibility for monitoring is spread across several institutions. For instance, air quality is monitored by the Institute of Public Health (in urban areas) and the Institute of Hydrometeorology (in urban and suburban areas). Additional monitoring is carried out by other ministries and institutes. The Ministry of Environment does not finance these activities, but it receives the information, for example, on air quality measurements on SO_2 performed by the Institute of Hydrometeorology. Some of the information, such as drinking-water quality data from the Institute of Public Health, is not required by the Ministry of Environment.

In March 2002, the Government approved a Decision on Environmental Monitoring to set up a National Environment Monitoring Programme. It lists the environmental indicators and designates the entities responsible for measuring these indicators. The Ministry of Environment will prepare this Programme and coordinate the work for its implementation. According to this Decision, all physical and legal persons subject to an environmental permit monitor their pollution at their own expense.

Equipment and methodologies

In general, monitoring activities lack a standard methodology and sufficient monitoring equipment. The institutions use methodologies approved by their scientific councils and consultative bodies, often a legacy from the Soviet period. However, in cases where Albania has signed up to international standards, monitoring methodologies have been revised. One notable example is the Lake Ohrid Monitoring Programme. Component B of the Lake Ohrid Conservation Project ensures comprehensive, indicative monitoring of the Lake's ecosystem and US$ 0.9 million has been allocated for the monitoring component of the Lake Ohrid Monitoring Programme. It covers the construction of a new building (US$ 0.3 million) in Pogradec and the purchase of monitoring equipment (US$ 0.6 million). Sophisticated equipment, such as atomic absorption spectrometers, gas chromatographs, spectrophotometers, inverted microscopes and stereomicroscopes, has been purchased, which by the end of the project will belong to the Ministry of Environment. It is estimated that the laboratory equipment will be used at only 10 per cent of its capacity to carry out the monitoring tasks under the

Table 4.1: Measurements requested by the Ministry of Environment from other institutions, as of 2001

Subject	Institution	Measurements	Frequency	Place	Norms and standards
Groundwater	Geological Survey	Na^+, K^+, Ca^{2+}, Mg^{2+}, $Fe^{2+,3+}$, NH_4^+, HCO_3^-, CO_3^{2-}, Cl^-, SO_4^{2-}, NO_3^-, NO_2^-, mineralization, hardness.	Twice a year	25 observation points in 6 water basins	Norms issued by the Ministry of Health in 1974.
		Cu, Pb, Zn, Cr	Twice a year	9 observation stations	
		Pesticides	Twice a year	6 observation stations	
		Microbiological	Twice a year	25 observation points	
Rivers	Institute of Hydrometeorology	Temperature, pH, alkalinity, dissolved oxygen, P total, NO_3^-, NO_2^-, NH_4^+, BOD, COD.	Twice a year	13 observation points (in 13 rivers)	Norms issued by the Ministry of Health in 1974.
	Institute of Public Health	P total, NO_3^-, NO_2^-, NH_4^+, BOD, COD, turbidity, alkalinity	Once a month	32 observation points in rivers near Tirana, Shkodër, Durrës, Elbasan, Sarandë, Vlorë	Norms issued by the Ministry of Health in 1974. WHO guidelines are taken into consideration
	Institute of Public Health	Microbiological analyses (total *Coli, Faecal Coli, Faecal Streptococcus*)	Twice during summer	Shengjin, Durrës, Vlorë and Sarandë	Norms issued by the Ministry of Health in 1974.
	Institute of Nuclear Physics	Cl^-, K^+, Ca^{2+}, Ti, Va, Mn^{2+}, $Fe^{2+,3+}$, Ni, Cu^{2+}, Zn^{2+}	Twice a year	13 observation points	Norms issued by the Ministry of Health in 1974.
		Beta activity	Twice a year	13 observation points	Norms issued by the Ministry of Health in 1998.
Lakes	Institute of Nuclear Physics	Cl^-, K^+, Ca^{2+}, Ti, Va, Mn^{2+}, $Fe^{2+,3+}$, Ni, Cu^{2+}, Zn^{2+}	Twice a year	6 observation stations	Norms issued by the Ministry of Health in 1974.
		Beta activity	Twice a year	6 observation stations	Norms issued by the Ministry of Health in 1974.
Sea	Institute of Public Health	Microbiological analyses (total *Coli, Faecal Coli, Faecal Streptococcus*)	Twice during summer	4 observation points	Norms issued by the Ministry of Health in 1974.
	Institute of Biological Research	Vegetation associations, rare and endangered species, alien species, anthropogenic stress on indicator plants	-	Coastal zone and sand strip / 7 stations	No standards
	Museum of Natural Sciences	Monitoring of Faunas (mollusks, insects, amphibians, reptiles, birds and mammals)	-	Lagoons /6 stations coastal	No standards
Air	Institute of Public Health	Suspended particulate matters (SPM) PM10, black smoke, SO_2, NO_2, O_3, Pb	Five days a month	Tirana-5 stations, Korca-2 stations, Durresi-1 station, Elbasan-1 station, Shkodra-1 station, Fier-1 station, Vlora-1station	Norms issued by the Ministry of Health in 1974. WHO guidelines are taken into consideration
	Institute of Nuclear Physics	Beta total	Four times a year	Tirana, Shkodra, Korca	Norms issued by the Ministry of Health in 1998.
		Pb, Cu, Hg, Cr	Four times a year	Tirana-1 station, Korca-1 station	Norms issued by the Ministry of Health in 1974.
Noise	Institute of Public Health	Noise	10-day intervals for each season, three times a day. 9-11 a.m., 6-8 p.m. and background at night.	9 points in Tirana, 2 in the centre and 7 points at the busiest crossroads	No standards
Urban waste	Institute of Public Health	Content of urban waste: paper, glass, metal, stones, wood, plastics	One week every three months	Landfills of Tirana, Shkodër, Durrës, Fier	No standards
Soil	Institute of Soil	In industrial sites; heavy metals (Zn, Cu, Co, Cr, Ni, Pb, Fe, Mn, Mg, Na, K, P)			No standards
		Soil Fertility in agricultural land (pH, Na, Cl, SO_4, P, K, Mg, Ca, N); erosion			EU Standards

Ohrid Programme. The other 90 per cent of the time the equipment will be idle and could potentially be used for monitoring other samples.

With the help of international initiatives, some laboratories are adequately equipped. The Institute of Hydrometeorology and the Faculty of Natural Sciences, for instance, received analytical equipment as a result of their involvement in the monitoring programme for the Mediterranean marine coastal waters. In general, however, old and outdated stationary and field monitoring equipment exacerbate monitoring difficulties. In some cases analyses are carried out by the laboratories of other institutes due to a lack of equipment. The air quality samples for the analysis of heavy metals (Pb, Cu, Hg, Cr) in urban areas that are taken by the Institute of Public Health, for example, are analysed by the Institute of Nuclear Physics. After determining a series of general parameters, the Institute of Hydrometeorology provides its water samples to the Institute of Nuclear Physics for the analysis of more specific parameters (Cl^-, K^+, Ca^{2+}, Ti, Va, Mn^{2+}, $Fe^{2+,3+}$, Ni, Cu^{2+}, Zn^{2+} and Beta radioactivity). The lack of equipment prevents such selected environmental quality analyses as carbon monoxide measurements in the air.

Procedures, intercalibration and accreditation

The monitoring standards are applied and selected according to those provided by the Directorate of Standardization of Albania. Harmonized procedures and intercalibration are essential to ensure the comparability of monitoring results from different monitoring networks. In Albania this is not possible. An intercalibration exercise is done sporadically within selected international monitoring programmes or projects. The EQUATE project at the Institute of Hydrometeorology ensures quality measurements for national and international water monitoring. It seems that there is no national system of laboratory accreditation. Few laboratories are accredited internationally.

Measuring the pollution level in air and water samples demands so-called background monitoring stations. Their purpose is to measure background concentration levels of air and water in places far from pollution sources. These background stations were established for air in Albania, but some of them are out of date or their location is inappropriate, as in Tirana, where buildings and traffic surround the air-quality background stations.

It seems that no background stations for water have been established.

Data validity

Because most monitoring analyses are done irregularly, the quality of the environment is represented only partially, if not erratically. Air monitoring samples for suspended particulate matter (SPM), PM10 (particulate matter including organic and inorganic substances less than 10 μm in diameter), black smoke, SO_2, NO_2, O_3, and Pb are taken five days per month in Tirana (5 stations), Korçe (2 stations), Durrës (1 station), Elbasan (1 station), Shkodër (1 station), Fier (1 station) and Vlorë (1 station) by the Institute of Public Health. There are no measurements of greenhouse gases such as CH_4 (methane) or CO (carbon monoxide). Monitoring of core indicators for water (P total, NO_3^-, NO_2^-, NH_4^+, BOD_5 and COD), heavy metals in surface waters, and pesticides, heavy metals and nitrates in groundwater is performed only twice a year.

Of the eight polluted sea areas, namely the coastal regions of Lezhë, Laç, Shengjin, Durrës, Kavajë, Lushnjë, Fier, Vlorë and Sarandë, identified in the UNEP assessment report, the Institute of Public Health monitored only four (Shengjin, Durrës, Vlorë and Sarandë), taking measurements twice during the summer of salinity, turbidity, suspended matter and microbiological pollutants: total *Coli*, *Faecal Coli*, *Faecal Streptococcus*. Within the Mediterranean Pollution Monitoring and Research Programme (MED POL), the Natural Sciences Laboratories monitor heavy metals (Hg, Pb, Cd, Zn, Cr, Cu), biological samples (*Mytilus Galloprov*), and some specific organic compounds twice a year in Durrës and Vlorë.

Most of the monitoring points are chosen at random and only a minimum number of parameters are measured. For certain parameters, such as carbon monoxide, precipitation kinetics, bacterial count in surface and bathing water, organic chemicals (e.g. detergents) in surface water, there is no monitoring at all.

4.2 Data reporting and analysis; reliability of data and use of environmental indicators

The information flow

There is no national environmental information system in Albania. Although efforts have been made by the Ministry of Environment to collect and systematize the information available in the country, the information from scientific research institutes is not systematically organized. Environmental information generated by sector goes directly to the specific ministry, i.e. health data to the Ministry of Health and soil data to the Ministry of Agriculture and Food. Within the Ministry of Environment, monitoring data are collected according to the above-mentioned contracts with scientific institutions, and through projects that are financed by the Ministry, such as the Lake Ohrid Monitoring Programme. The monitoring data are collected and kept by the Ministry in its data archives, mainly in hard copy and sometimes electronically in Word format. Since 2000 the State Statistical Institute has been requesting environmental data from various ministries. So far the Ministry of Environment has submitted state-of-the-environment reports and quarterly newsletters to the Statistical Institute. In January 2002 the Statistical Institute for the first time published an annual report that included environmental information.

The data and information flow within the Ministry of Environment is organized through monthly meetings with the 12 Regional Environmental Agencies. Environmental information systems, including the monitoring of environmental quantity and quality and the development of indicator sets, are still designed primarily on the basis of the capacity of existing technical equipment and data storage. Neither monitoring nor the information flow is focused on producing elements for decision-making in environmental management.

At present, the information flow by electronic means among the ministries and between the national and the local offices is underdeveloped. In Albania Internet access is provided mainly through dial-up connections with local servers at a speed of not more than 33600 bps. There are certain governmental and non-governmental organizations whose resources and capacities allow connection through a dedicated line. At the Ministry, all employees have a computer, which may be old, but they have no direct access to the Internet. However, its Regional Environmental Agencies are small. Some agencies have office space for only one person. In most cases these Agencies are equipped with only a typewriter and telephones. This low technical capacity prevents them from establishing a regular and instantaneous information flow to the Ministry.

The State-of-the-Environment Report

The 1993 Law on Environmental Protection required the publication of an annual state-of-the-environment (SoE) report. In the new (2002) Law on Environmental Protection, the Ministry is obligated to prepare, publish and distribute the SoE report every two years, in Albanian and English. The approved report is made accessible both as a publication and electronically. In addition, the Ministry publishes periodically its official bulletin and prepares other publications on environment.

To this end, specialists in the Ministry of Environment collect, systematize and analyse the information available in the country. Although the lack of reliable and sufficient environmental data affects the reliability of environmental reports, the first official SoE report was published in 1995, the second in 1999, and the 2000 report is being drafted. The latest report is based on a common indicator reporting methodology following the "Driving Force-Pressure-State-Impact-Response" framework, which is recommended by the European Environment Agency. The reports are available in computerized form.

As far as environmental monitoring, and data collection and processing are concerned, the Ministry of Environment has started cooperating with the European Environment Agency, which offers assistance to European countries through the PHARE programme. Albania took part in the preparation of the Dobris +3 Report and the preparation of a SoE report on the Internet. Although its data contribution is weak, Albania is part of the European Environment Information and Observation Network (EIONET).

The Environment Information Centre

The Environmental Information Centre project (COP-97 Phare) was established in 2001 and is managed by the Environmental Centre for Administration and Technology (ECAT) in Tirana. The project aims to disseminate environmental information for national and local decision-making processes and raise awareness on environmental problems. The Environmental Information Centre is located at the Ministry of Environment. One of its current tasks is the development of system that will provide access to environmental information for decision makers and the general public. More specifically, it involves setting up a database of primary and secondary indicators, unifying terminology, exchanging information with other institutions and programmes, promoting information on the Internet, and raising awareness. With a total budget of US$ 21,000 for two operational years, the Centre has been equipped with a server for setting up a local area network. There is one information technology specialist responsible for the operation of the Centre. The Centre has sufficient facilities for raising public awareness; it has a library, a TV set, photocopiers, and access to the Internet. However, the lack of a sufficient flow of information means that it is unable to effectively disseminate environmental information. To fulfil its goals and objectives the Centre needs to clarify and prioritize its activities, and at the same time seek political support, which is lacking at the moment.

The Environmental Information Centre has made an attempt to draw up a set of specific environmental indicators, but at the moment there are few data available. The data are archived in Microsoft Word and Excel format. As the Centre does not have a sufficient flow of information, i.e. it does not coordinate directly with primary information sources, data collection is not sustainable.

4.3 Awareness raising and access to environmental information

Legal framework

Up to the early 1990s there was very little access to or dissemination of environmental information in Albania. The concept of providing information, particularly environmental information, is relatively new. The Albanian Constitution of 1998 recognizes everyone's right "to be informed on the environmental situation and its protection" and "to participate in decision-making processes".

Another step forward was the approval of the Guidelines on environmental information and public access to environmental information, No. 7, dated 19 January 1998 by the Minister of Health and Environment. These Guidelines determine the type of information that the Ministry of Environment should possess and guarantees the right of every citizen to information on the environment, the activities that have or might have a negative impact on the environment and human health, as well as environmental protection measures, including administrative measures and programmes for environmental management and conservation policies and strategies designed for

this purpose. The Guidelines also determine how the requests must be presented and the deadlines for providing the information or refusing the request.

One of the priorities of the National Environmental Action Plan (NEAP) of 1994 is the "development of environmental knowledge and increased public participation in environmental issues". The participation of non-governmental organizations in environmental issues as foreseen in the NEAP of 1994 aims at increasing public awareness of environmental issues through the mass media, seminars and conferences, and also through policies that enable public participation in decision-making and the development of environmental standards.

Albania signed the UNECE Convention on Access to Information, Public Participation in Decision-making and Access to Justice in Environmental Matters, commonly known as the Aarhus Convention, on 25 June 1998 and ratified it on 27 June 2001. This was a significant accomplishment in public information and participation. Before ratification, the Convention was translated into Albanian in 1999, and then distributed to national institutions and NGOs for comments and then to the Ministry of Foreign Affairs for submission to the Council of Ministers and Parliament.

To fulfil the obligations of this Convention, a law on public access to environmental information was drafted. This project was undertaken with the legal assistance of the PHARE Programme. In collaboration with the Regional Environmental Center (REC), a meeting of the Parliamentary Commission on Health and Environment and the Parliamentary Commission on Legislation was held in July 2000 to facilitate the Convention's ratification by Parliament. According to the Stabilization and Association Agreement with the EU and the government programme for 2002-2006, the law has to be approved in 2002.

In addition, Albania adheres to several other international legal frameworks with provisions on access to environmental information, public participation and access to justice, such as the Universal Declaration of Human Rights, the United Nations Framework Convention on Climate Change (ratified on 3 October 1994) and the Convention on Biological Diversity (ratified on 5 January 1994).

Access to Information

Environmental information is mainly disseminated through electronic and print media. A considerable number of information leaflets, posters, and fact sheets on the environment have been produced and distributed. The regular publications include the Environmental Bulletin of the Ministry of Environment (100 printed copies, four editions per year), the State-of-the-Environment Reports in Albanian and English (1,000 printed copies), and the REC Daily Environmental News (disseminated electronically to approximately 300 addresses). The 2002 Law on Environmental Protection stipulates that the National Environmental Information System is open to the public.

Information about the Ministry of Environment is available through the Internet at http://www.nea.gov.al/, although the web site is not regularly updated. There are about five articles or news stories per day in the eight to ten independent daily newspapers. Limited environmental information is disseminated through TV and radio. In collaboration with ECAT-Tirana, for instance, environmental problems resulting from traffic pollution, logging, and illegal construction in green urban areas were presented on TV.

Efforts to raise environmental awareness have achieved positive results such as information about the demolition of illegal construction in central parks and squares in Tirana. However, environmental information in general does not reach its intended audience. Newspaper articles are very much focused on "news" and not analysis. There is a lack of investigative journalism that could give more in-depth analyses of environment-economic-related issues.

Although there is an attempt to popularize environmental information, the attention of the public is still focused on economic concerns. For instance, emigration and the search for a better socio-economic environment have been the priority for many. Efforts to raise environmental awareness outside the capital are very minimal. As a result Albanians are not generally well informed about the risks of pollution, the relationship between the environment and public health, and the benefits of a clean environment for the economy and society as a whole. This is also true among national and local politicians. There is a great need for improved environmental awareness at all levels of society. Additionally, measures should be taken to facilitate and promote the public's right to environmental information.

Even if the Ministry of Environment receives only about four to five official requests for environment-

related information a month, public interest in and concern for environmental issues have increased over the past few years. In the newly established Environmental Information Centre one or two individuals visit the Centre each day and search for environmental information.

If the public is interested in certain environmental issues, requests for information have to be made to the public authorities. There are procedures for responding to such requests. The procedure is defined by the Guidelines on environmental information and public access to environmental information (see above). In practice, however, some of the requests made to the former National Environmental Agency have been denied.

There is no accessible pollutant release and transfer register (PRTR) or similar system at the moment. However, theoretically the public has the right to access environmental information from individual facilities on, for example, released pollution, generated waste and waste water either from the authorities or directly from the facilities. On the other hand, practice shows that the inspectors of the Regional Environmental Agencies do not have the right to enter a factory if the owner does not agree. Requests to the public authorities for information on confidential activities, international affairs, national defence, public security, issues under investigation or already investigated, materials which if announced might further damage the environment, and unfinished draft materials, may be refused.

The way information is collected and maintained does not facilitate public access. However, a large part of all materials available in the Ministry of Environment's and in the Environmental Information Centre's libraries can be used and copied in limited numbers free of charge. If the requested information is copied in larger quantities, the actual cost for copying must be paid.

Environmental education

Environmental education in the country today is poorly funded and it is only offered to a limited number of young Albanians. It seems that schools are not actively promoting environmental education through environmental projects or similar activities. Methodological materials, textbooks and training are lacking for teachers and students. The Albanian Development Education Project (Soros Foundation) has proposed a new curriculum model for primary and secondary schools and higher education, but aspects of environmental education are not incorporated. To try out the curriculum, 16 schools were chosen as pilot schools. Otherwise, bilateral projects on environmental education, such as projects between Albanian and Greek universities, are being undertaken.

4.4 Public participation in decision-making, NGO activities

Democratic traditions are not yet strong in Albania. One way to promote the participation of people in democratic dialogue is by increasing the influence of civil society as represented by non-governmental organizations (NGOs). Since 1991, more than 75 different organizations and groups working in different aspects of environmental conservation and public education have been created in Albania. In practice, 20-25 per cent of these are active. In the beginning, most NGOs were established in Tirana, and their membership was limited to specialists in environmental sciences: biology, chemistry and geography. More recently NGOs have been established with broad-based memberships involving students and the general public. In 1994 and 1995, many NGOs were established outside Tirana, especially in districts with acute environmental problems, such as Shkodër, Korçe, Pogradec and Elbasan.

Some environmental associations, NGOs and foundations have been established as international initiatives. Among these are the Regional Environmental Centre in Tirana (REC-Tirana), *Obschestvo Remeslenovo i zemledelcheskovo Trouda* (ORT), the Society for Trades and Agricultural Labour, Democracy Network (supported by USAID), Environmental Centres for Administration and Technology (ECAT-Tirana) (established by the European Commission) and MilieuKontakt (established on the initiative of the Netherlands).

There are good examples of campaigns organized by NGOs in Albania, such as the clean-up of the beach in Durrës organized by REC and ECAT-Tirana in 1996. A scientific symposium, bicycle races and a poetry night were also organized during the Day of Lake Ohrid as part of the Lake Ohrid Conservation Project. At present, however, the environmental movement through NGOs is powerless. In fact, many NGOs are established to carry out consultancy services rather than to lobby. In such cases, they are reluctant to bite the hand that might feed them. Considering this pattern, there is a paucity of initiatives from NGOs,

although they could have a great moral influence on politicians by educating people.

Another weak point of the NGO community is the lack of cooperation among themselves. There is no umbrella association that could serve as a basis for developing major NGO movements. A strategy document with inputs from four NGOs is in preparation.

The Constitution stipulates that everyone has the right to take part in decision-making processes. As far as environmental issues are concerned at the moment, Albanian legislation does not contain provisions that satisfactorily describe public participation in the decision-making process although there are good practices, for example, on the protection of the Karavasta Lagoon, where public hearings took place. Environmental impact assessments (EIA) are rare, and if they do take place it is in general without public participation (see Chapter 1). There are no clear rules or criteria for identifying the "public concerned" or for participating in the decision-making processes.

Although there is no legal provision that mentions simply proposing legislation to governmental bodies, several laws have been proposed by different NGOs on both environmental and social issues. In 1995, a group of NGOs began to draft the first environmental law that dealt with biodiversity. In 1997, another NGO developed a proposal that was finalized with a draft law on the conservation of caves.

4.5 Access to Justice

No environmental cases have so far been brought to court in Albania, and there is no legal ground which describes the review procedures available to the public if requests for environmental information are refused or ignored. The present legal situation does not review procedures available to the public, such as decision-making as part of public participation, or violations of environmental law either by the public authorities or by polluters.

4.6 Conclusions and recommendations

There is no system for monitoring environmental conditions in Albania despite its importance for environmental management. The responsibility for monitoring is spread across several institutions, which makes it impossible to strengthen and streamline data collection. There is no national environmental monitoring programme that would define different monitoring sub-components. Monitoring in general is not goal-oriented; its needs are not defined. It is, therefore, difficult to meet legal commitments. Timely and accurate data are missing (including data on monitoring frequency, monitoring methods, equipment and its use). The recent Decision on Environmental Monitoring of March 2002 should be implemented rapidly, and Albania should continue to strengthen its cooperation with the European Environmental Agency. (see recommendation 3.5)

Recommendation 4.1:

(a) *A national centre for environmental monitoring, subordinate to the Ministry of Environment, should be set up as a management unit to fulfil the goals and objectives of monitoring activities and information flow for environmental management purposes. The centre should:*

- *Draw up a monitoring programme that prioritizes the measurements needed (goal-oriented approach) for environmental management nationally and internationally, following requirements of the European Environmental Agency; monitoring institutes should be involved in this process;*

- *Make the environmental monitoring network more reliable;*

- *Assess and interpret monitoring and other data;*

- *Draft reports on the state of the environment;*

- *Establish a pollutant release and transfer register with reference to the current negotiations on Pollutant Release and Transfer Registers under the Aarhus Convention.*

(b) *To set clear-cut objectives and ensure coherency in the information programme, the national centre for environmental monitoring should prepare a conceptual framework on the flow of environmental statistical data from collection to the target audiences, in cooperation with the national statistical institutes.*

(c) *The environmental monitoring centre should benefit from the equipment obtained under the Lake Ohrid Programme. To fulfil monitoring tasks, the budget of the Ministry of Environment for monitoring should be increased.*

There are several institutions and projects in Albania that deal with the collection of environmental information, provide access to such information and create awareness of the environment. One such project is the Environmental Information Centre established and managed by ECAT-Tirana. There is no national information system that could be considered as part of the environmental management system. There is no pollutant release and transfer register in Albania.

Recommendation 4.2:
The Ministry of Environment should strengthen the information and public relations unit within the Ministry, inter alia, to assume the functions currently undertaken by ECAT-Tirana. The tasks of the information unit should include: dissemination of information to decision makers and the public, and promotion of awareness about the environment.

There are no strong democratic traditions in Albania; therefore public participation in the decision-making processes is weak both nationally and locally. As a result of the Constitution and the Aarhus Convention, the public is given the opportunity to participate in decision-making on specific activities. However, there are no clear rules or criteria for identifying the "public concerned" or mode of participation.

Recommendation 4.3:
The Ministry should ensure that the relevant provisions of the Aarhus Convention are fully implemented, taking into account the Convention's implementation guidelines. The new Law on Environmental Impact Assessment should incorporate public participation mechanisms at both the national and local levels. Even though the country has knowledgeable experts, general training for governmental and municipal officials (inspectors, clerks) on public participation and awareness raising should be developed in the near future.

Albanians are not generally well informed about the risks of pollution, the relationship between the environment and public health, and the benefits of a clean environment to the economy and society as a whole. Every-day thinking has not been focused on living in a clean and safe environment, which is beneficial for citizens themselves and for economic development. The Ministry of Environment has not utilised television to inform the population, especially youths, and to broadcast programmes about Albania's environment.

Recommendation 4.4:
(a) A strategy on awareness raising on environmental issues should be developed by the Ministry of Environment and thoroughly implemented by the Environmental Information Centre aiming at all user categories and using all kinds of media. A training programme for journalists, particularly on environmental issues, should be instituted;

(b) The public's right to access information should be ensured by the Ministry of Environment by establishing binding procedures. In the meantime, governmental and local authorities responding to requests from the public should take immediate action;

(c) To increase awareness, media briefings, public events, information materials, linkages with other government entities, schools and universities, and other environmental initiatives should be organized by the Ministry of Environment and its subordinated entities. Where possible, communication should be established through broadcasts on TV and radio and debates in newspapers.

The rise of Albania's environmental NGO community is a promising development. However, at the moment, the NGO community is not actively lobbying for environmental issues. A weak point of the NGO community is the lack of cooperation among themselves. There is no umbrella association that can serve as a basis for developing major NGO movements. Environmental education is not seen as an essential element of public information. No action has been taken to involve young people.

Recommendation 4.5:
Through the "access to environmental information and public participation" mechanism, the Ministry of Environment could encourage a more independent and active NGO network, which could help to consolidate democracy. The NGOs should actively lobby for environmental issues. The environment-related NGO community should also strengthen environmental education by organizing campaigns, exhibitions and other educational activities.

PART II: MANAGEMENT OF POLLUTION AND OF NATURAL RESOURCES

Chapter 5

AIR MANAGEMENT

5.1 State of and pressures on air quality

Air emissions

Emissions of air pollutants in Albania have fallen since the late 1980s and early 1990s. During that time the relative contributions from the different sources has also changed. Emissions from industrial production have fallen due to reduced industrial activity over the past 10-15 years. In the early 1990s household emissions also dropped for the same reason and because of the change from fossil fuels to electricity use. This trend seems to have continued throughout the 1990s. During the same period emissions from traffic have increased following a rapid growth in car ownership and use. Another factor is the age of Albania's car fleet as it imports large quantities of used cars from Western Europe. The fact that 90 per cent of all passenger cars registered in Albania are equipped with diesel engines explains why emissions of sulphur dioxide (SO_2) and particulate matter (PM) per vehicle-kilometre are relatively high.

So far, Albania has not compiled a comprehensive emission inventory. Only emission data for some industrial sectors have been published. As a Party to the United Nations Framework Convention on Climate Change, Albania has to present a National Communication with information on emission inventories, projections and emission abatement measures. The country has recently presented its first National Communication (September 2002). The report was developed by an Albanian team, and the work was partly financed by a UNDP programme set up to help non-industrialized countries to meet their reporting commitments under the Convention.

The National Communication presents 1994 (base year) emission data for the three greenhouse gases - carbon dioxide (CO_2), methane (CH_4) and nitrous oxides (N_2O) – as well as a number of indirect greenhouse gases, like nitrogen oxides (NO_x), carbon monoxide (CO), non-methane volatile organic compounds (NMVOC) and sulphur dioxide (SO_2). Emissions of NO_x, CO, NMVOC and SO_2 may also cause local air pollution and so health problems and damage to vegetation, while emissions of SO_2 and NO_x may contribute to acidification. Emission data for 1994 are presented in Table 5.1. All data are calculated according to methodology recommended by the Intergovernmental Panel on Climate Change (IPCC) in 1996 (revised). Albania has not published complete emission inventories for years after 1994.

In 1994 Albania's total non-biogenic emissions of CO_2 stood at 3.1 million tons, excluding the effects of land-use change and forestry and emissions from biomass burned for energy. Ninety-four per cent of the 1994 CO_2 emissions resulted from fuel combustion, 6 per cent from industrial processes.

Emissions of greenhouse gases (measured as CO_2 equivalents) from fuel combustion for the years 1990-1994 are presented in Table 5.2. The table shows an emission reduction of 60 per cent during this period. The reduction is largest for the combustion of coal, which has dropped 90 per cent during this period, while emissions from the combustion of oil has dropped by less than 30 per cent. The main reason for the changes is a drastic reduction in the activities of highly energy-intensive industries like mining, metallurgy, chemical and petrochemical industries, while GDP growth has taken place in less energy-intensive sectors like agriculture, the food industry and the building material industry.

In 1990 oil and coal contributed roughly equal amounts of greenhouse gases, 48 per cent each. In 1994 oil was responsible for 87 per cent of the greenhouse gas emissions from fuel combustion. The main reason for the change in the distribution of greenhouse gas emissions and the large reduction in the combustion of coal is a dramatic reduction in coal production in Albania. Only 6 out of 20 coal mines are currently operating.

Table 5.1: Emissions of selected air pollutants, 1994

	CO$_2$	CH$_4$	N$_2$O	SO$_2$	NO$_x$	NH$_3$	NMVOC	CO	Particles	Lead	Cadmium	Mercury	PAH
	Million tons	1000 tons	1000 tons	1000 tons	1000 tons	1000 tons	1000 tons	1000 tons	1000 tons	tons	Kg	Kg	tons
Total	3.101	101.7	1.0	0.0	17.8	0.0	29.0	130.4	0.0	0.0	0.0	0.0	0.0
Energy	2.902	8.1	0.1	0.0	17.8	0.0	18.6	118.0	0.0	0.0	0.0	0.0	0.0
A. Fuel combustion	2.902	5.1	0.1	0.0	17.8	0.0	18.6	118.0	0.0	0.0	0.0	0.0	0.0
Energy and transformation industries	0.575	0.0	0.0										
Industry	0.990	0.1	0.0										
Transport	0.794	0.1	0.0										
Residential	0.156	4.1	0.1										
Commercial / institutional	0.184	0.0	0.0										
Agriculture/forestry/fishing	0.203	0.8	0.0										
Other	0.000	0.0	0.0										
B. Transient emissions	0.000	3.0	0.0	0.0	0.0	0.0	0.0	0.0	0.0	0.0	0.0	0.0	0.0
Oil and natural gas system	0.000	0.0	0.0										
Coal	0.000	3.0	0.0										
Industrial processes	0.199	0.0	0.0	0.0	0.0	0.0	0.3	0.1	0.0	0.0	0.0	0.0	0.0
Agriculture	0.000	79.7	0.7	0.0	0.0	0.0	0.9	1.1	0.0	0.0	0.0	0.0	0.0
Enteric fermation	0.000	75.6	0.0										
Manure management	0.000	4.1	0.1										
Field burning of agriculture residues	0.000	0.0	0.0										
Use of nitric fertilizers	0.000	0.0	0.6										
Waste	0.000	13.9	0.2	0.0	0.0	0.0	0.0	0.0	0.0	0.0	0.0	0.0	0.0
Landfills	0.000	13.9	0.0										
Waste-water treatment	0.000	0.0	0.2										
Waste incineration	0.000	0.0	0.0										
Other	0.000	0.0	0.0										
Solvent use	0.000	0.0	0.0	0.0	0.0	0.0	9.3	11.3	0.0	0.0	0.0	0.0	0.0

Source : National Communication to the United Nations Framework Convention on Climate Change, 2002.

Table 5.2: Anthropogenic greenhouse gas emissions from fuel combustion, 1990-1994

(1000 tonnes of CO_2 equivalents)

Source categories	1990	1991	1992	1993	1994
Total	7,134	5,023	2,670	2,875	2,869
Energy					
- oil	3,517	2,795	1,923	2,393	2,504
- coal	3,423	2,089	619	390	316
- natural gas	194	139	128	92	49

Source: National Report to the United Nations Framework Convention on Climate Change. Greenhouse gases inventory for Albania, 2001.

Figures 5.1 (a) and (b) present CO_2 emissions in Albania in 1994 per capita and per million United States dollars of GDP compared with other countries. Albania's CO_2 emissions per capita were lower than those of industrialized countries, because:

- Its energy consumption is low;
- Its electricity production is almost entirely based on hydropower;
- Household energy consumption is almost entirely based on electricity;
- Energy consumption has fallen in the industrial sector, due to reduced levels of production.

However, in terms of CO_2 emissions per unit of GDP, Albania was a substantial emitter in 1994. This situation is explained as follows:

- Albania's industrial technology is very old;
- Productivity is lower in Albania than in industrialized countries, and energy intensity is higher;
- A large share of the energy consumption in Albania takes place in the household and not in the production sectors.

The main sources of SO_2 emissions are transport and industrial production, while transport, other energy users and industrial processes are the main contributors of NO_x emissions. The main industrial source of emissions to air is the processing of chromium ores and concentrate.

Emissions of particles are caused by the combustion of fuels like coal, fuel oil and diesel. Most carbon monoxide is discharged by car traffic.

Acidification is not considered a problem in Albania at present. The Institute of Hydrometeorology has analysed acidity in rainfall at monitoring stations in Tirana, Elbasan and Korçe, and the analyses show few pH values below 5.6 (non-acid pH value). The lowest daily value was 4.17 in Tirana in October 1998. However, time series observations in Tirana show a decrease in annual pH values from 7.85 in 1995 to 6.4 in 2000. These observations indicate that acidity is increasing slightly in Tirana. A possible cause could be the rapid growth in traffic during recent years and the extensive use of diesel fuel.

Albania is not a party to the Convention on Long-range Transboundary Air Pollution or its eight protocols. Consequently, the country has not presented data on critical loads or emission data to the relevant bodies under the Convention, nor is it included in the modelling activities carried out under the Cooperative Programme for Monitoring and Evaluation of the Long-range Transmission of Air Pollutants in Europe (EMEP). However, EMEP has estimated that in 1996 imported air pollution contributed to more than 80 per cent of the sulphur deposition in Albania and more than 90 per cent of the deposition of oxidized nitrogen. Greece and Italy are the main contributors. Albania is likely to start contributing to the deposition of sulphur and nitrogen in its neighbouring countries as its economy develops. Although the National Environmental Agency prepared the necessary documentation for adherence to the Convention on Long-range Transboundary Air Pollution and its protocols in 1998, the country has not yet become a party to them (see Chapter 3).

In 1999, Albania acceded to the Vienna Convention on the Protection of the Ozone Layer and the Montreal Protocol on Substances that Deplete the Ozone Layer, but not to any of the four amendments to the Protocol. The two agreements set the "elimination" of ozone-depleting substances as their "final objective." The Parties are committed to gradually phasing out the production and use of ozone-depleting substances (ODS) within certain time limits. Albania temporarily comes under

Figure 5.1. a: Emission of CO$_2$ per capita (tons/capita), 1994

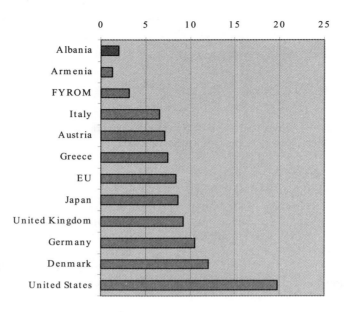

Source: National Report to the United Nations Framework
Convention on Climate Change. Greenhouse gases inventory for
Albania, 2001.

Figure 5.1. b: Emission of CO$_2$ per unit of GDP (tons/million US$), 1994

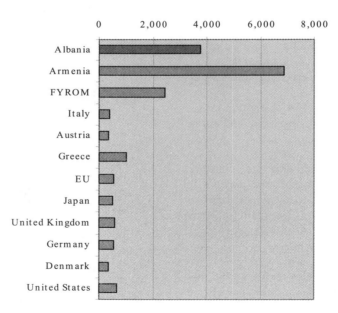

Source: National Report to the United Nations Framework for
the Climate Change Conference. Greenhouse gases inventory for
Albania, 2001.

article 5, paragraph 1, of the Montreal Protocol (a developing country with a low consumption per capita of certain substances) and is entitled to delay for ten years its compliance with certain control measures. Albania is committed to participating in relevant programmes regarding the country's strategy for managing substances covered by these two agreements and to complying with all other requirements. Albania has already prepared a National Plan for phasing out the ODS substances towards 2010. Albania does not produce or use halons or chlorofluorocarbons (CFCs) and it has reduced its use of hydrochlorofluorocarbons (HCFCs) as required. Thus, Albania complies with its basic commitments under the Vienna Convention and the Montreal Protocol.

The Ministry of Environment will soon start submitting air emission inventories according to CORINAIR methodology, which was developed within the framework of the European Environment Agency.

Ambient air quality

Air quality data are reported to the Ministry of Environment by the monitoring institutions, namely the Institute of Public Health and the Institute of Hydrometeorology. However, data are not published, analysed or reported on a regular basis (see Chapter 4).

The data show a striking decrease in SO_2 and soot levels since 1990. 1990 measurements showed that in Tirana and other major cities levels were more than twice the national air quality standards. According to monitoring data compiled by the Institute of Public Health and the Institute of Hydrometeorology, present concentrations of CO, O_3, NO_2 and SO_2 do not seem to breach Albanian standards or WHO limit values in any part of Albania. This is especially interesting given the fact that the city of Tirana has more than tripled in size, and the number of cars has grown perhaps even more. Still, it should be noted that measurements are limited both in terms of geographic scope and the methodology employed.

The NO_2 concentration in Tirana's city centre is much higher than in its suburbs. This situation is due to the level of exhaust gases from cars. The highest levels have been observed near the main traffic arteries like that around the City Hall.

Ambient air quality is a problem in some urban areas, like Tirana. The concentration of toxic particulates (PM_{10}) has been monitored regularly at three points in Tirana since 1997. 1997 and 1998 measurements show that the concentration of PM_{10} in some areas is higher than accepted values according to Albanian and WHO standards based on health criteria (see Table 5.6). Monthly average values of PM_{10} vary between 70 and 200 $\mu g/m^3$ exceeding the WHO 24-hour and annual mean limit values (respectively 60 and 90 $\mu g/m^3$). In Tirana WHO limit values for PM_{10} are exceeded throughout the winter.

Radon

Radon is a radioactive colourless, tasteless and odourless gas that may cause lung cancer. The possibility of high concentrations of radon in indoor air gives rise to concern among Albanian specialists and authorities. During the past years, attention has been given to monitoring radon concentration in indoor air at different locations in Albania, first and foremost in urban and suburban areas. Based on international literature the Geological Survey of Albania considers a radon level of up to 150 Bq/m^3 as a low cancer risk. A level between 150 Bq/m^3 and 400 Bq/m^3 is considered a medium risk, while levels exceeding 400 Bq/m^3 entail high risk. The European Commission recommends a maximum of 400 Bq/m^3 for old houses and 200 Bq/m^3 for new ones. Since 1999, measurements have been carried out in 200 indoor environments (about 15,000 observations) in Albania, mainly in Tirana. Radon concentration has been measured in places like governmental buildings, domestic buildings, schools and kindergartens. Eighty per cent of the objects investigated in Tirana showed values below 150 Bq/m^3, 14 per cent showed values between 150 and 400 Bq/m^3, while 6 per cent indicated radon concentrations above 400 Bq/m^3, of which some showed concentration above 1,000 Bq/m^3.

Sectoral pressure and underlying factors

Overall trends

The main sectors contributing to air emissions in Albania are transport and energy production. Other sources are industries and open-air burning of waste. In 1994, 38 per cent of the country's CO_2 emissions came from industry while transport was responsible for 25 per cent and energy production and transformation was responsible for 19 per cent. Five per cent of CO_2 emissions came from household energy use.

Transport

In urban areas traffic is of particular concern. The growth in car ownership and traffic has been explosive. In 1993, there were only 57,000 passenger cars registered in Albania, in 1999 the number stood at 99,000 (Table 5.3). In terms of cars per capita this figure is still lower than in other countries. While in 1998 the number of vehicles per 100 inhabitants in Albania was 4, in Turkey it was 8, in Hungary 27, in Greece 35 and in OECD countries 51 on average. Thus, the number of vehicles, and consequently road traffic, in Albania is likely to continue to grow as the economy develops.

At present 90 per cent of passenger cars registered in Albania are equipped with diesel engines. In general a diesel-fuelled car emits more SO_2 and particulate matters (PM) than a petrol-fuelled car. The reason why Albanians seem to prefer diesel cars is assumed to be the relative fuel prices. Petrol costs about 120 leks a litre, diesel only about 75. As most imported cars are second-hand cars, Albania's car fleet is relatively polluting. Also, most cars have relatively powerful engines, which consume more fuel. Moreover, the sulphur content in diesel fuel used in Albania is high. In 2000 the average was above the present standards that only allow 0.2 per cent. It is assumed that fewer than 1,000 cars are equipped with a catalytic converter. Due to the poor quality of the fuel it is likely that few of the catalytic converters still work. Unleaded fuel is being marketed. However, due to poor fuel quality control it is not known whether the lead content is sufficiently low so as not to ruin the cleaning function of the catalytic converters.

The emission of lead from cars is not a concern in Albania today since only about 10 per cent of passenger cars use petrol. However, the concentration of lead in the air could increase if traffic grows and leaded petrol continues to be used.

It is likely that the concentrations of pollutants other than PM_{10} will exceed recommended air quality standards in urban areas in the future if appropriate control measures are not taken to reduce car emissions and to control traffic.

Also, freight transport by road is slowly growing, after substantially shrinking during the early 1990s (Table 5.4). Due to its geographical location, Albania is expected to serve as a transit country for transport from Durrës harbour to other Balkan countries like the former Yugoslav Republic of Macedonia and Bulgaria to the east as well as for transport from Croatia and parts of Yugoslavia to Greece.

Public transport is poorly developed. Road transport is the dominant and growing transport sector. The national road network is slowly being developed. Furthermore, plans exist for substantial road network investments through the international transit corridors in Albania. The international financial organizations have proposed financial support to Albania in order to develop the international road network. However, existing plans for upgrading Albania's railway system do not seem able to attract similar financial support.

Energy

Albania is rich in energy resources like oil, gas, coal and hydro energy. The country's need for electricity has mainly been met by hydroelectric stations (90-95% during recent years in terms of kWh produced in Albania) and to some extent by thermoelectric stations. At present the only operating thermoelectric station is in Fier with a production capacity of 159 MW (currently only up to 40 MW is working). Total production capacity of the thermoelectric station amounts to 1,662 MW, while the hydroelectric stations produce 1,444 MW. The production of thermo-power in Albania is highly polluting. The thermoelectric station in Fier burns oil with a sulphur content of 6-8%. In 1997-1998 it emitted 1,650 tons of ash, 7,100 tons of SO_2 and 14,200 tons of CO_2 into the air. Albania is at present experiencing a serious electricity crisis. Electricity demand is much higher than domestic production. Different strategies to solve this crisis are being discussed, including demand management and ways to increase production.

The baseline scenario presented in Albania's first National Communication to the United Nations Framework Convention on Climate Change foresees the installation of new thermoelectric power plants with a total production capacity of 700 – 850 MW up to 2020. Together with the foreseen increase in energy consumption in sectors like transport, industry, services and households, total CO_2 emissions are expected to increase during the same period (see table 5.5 for emissions of 1994). Also, emissions of other pollutants from the production and consumption of energy are likely to

Table 5.3: The number of vehicles registered, 1990-1999

Road vehicle fleet on 31 December	1993	1994	1995	1996	1997	1998	1999
Passenger cars	56,728	67,960	58,682	67,278	76,822	90,766	99,220
Lorries	31,084	42,271	25,790	27,774	30,105	34,378	37,880
Road tractors	8,251	8,842	3,334	2,638	3,151	2,731	3,018
Buses and minibuses	..	2,806	6,651	7,612	8,747	9,227	..
Trailers	12,116	3,969	3,497	..	3,990	4,245	..

Source: UNECE Common database, 2002.

Table 5.4: Volume of passenger and freight transport, 1990-2000

	1990	1995	1997	1998	1999	2000
Passenger transport (million passenger-km)						
- Road transport	2,174	4,955	..	..	..	..
- Rail transport	779	201	95	116	121	125
- Marine transport	5	10	..	..	..	..
Freight transport (million ton-km)						
- Road transport	1,195	2,097	..	..	..	..
- Rail transport	584	52	23	25	26	28
- Marine transport	907	594	..	..	..	..

Source: ECMT 1990 and 1995; INSTAT The National Institute of Statistics 1997-2000.

Table 5.5: Emissions of CO_2 (non biogenic) in 1994

Million tons

	1994
Total	**3.101**
Energy production and consumption	2.902
Energy and transformation industries	0.575
Industry	0.990
Transport	0.794
Residential	0.156
Commercial/institutional	0.184
Agriculture/forestry/fishing	0.203
Non energy use	0.199

Source: National Report to the United Nations Framework Convention on Climate Change. Greenhouse gases inventory for Albania, 2001 and Greenhouse gases abatement analysis, 2001.

increase. Consequently, it is vital that the Ministry of Industry and Energy should develop and implement a comprehensive energy strategy that respects environmental needs. The National Communication outlines abatement measures like improving energy efficiency in different sectors of the economy, replacing coal with less polluting fuels like gas in thermoelectric power stations, the use of renewable energy sources and different energy demand management measures.

Industry

Cement plants, which are working at full capacity at the moment, are causing heavy pollution in some cities (Elbasan and Fushë-Krujë). They generate high amounts of particulate matter, of which 10 per cent are emitted into the air.

5.2 Policy objectives and management

Objectives and legislation

The 1993 Law on Environmental Protection with amendments adopted in 1998 sets the basis for developing, adopting and implementing new air pollution combating programmes. In 2002 a new Air Protection Law was adopted and a Decision of the Gaseous Emission Standards was approved. The new Law and Decision set requirements for self-monitoring, recording and periodic reporting, applying cleaner production and best available technology, complying with different emission standards, and taking remedial action against heavy pollution. Emission standards are established as either general limit values (ambient air quality standards) or special values for particular industries, equipment and plants (emission standards).

The existing set of air quality standards was established in 1974 in a regulation approved by the Ministry of Health (Table 5.6). Generally these standards were based on maximum allowable concentrations (MAC) as in the former Soviet Union. There have been no regulations on the emission standards for ozone and PM_{10}. For the latter, WHO air quality standards have been used. In the new Law on Environmental Protection, Article 50 states that the definition of norm values, as the admissible level for the use of the environment and its elements, is to be "based on EC Directives, objectives of the national environmental state policy and best available techniques."

In general, Albania has expressed its intention to align its environmental legislation, including that on air protection, with EU legislation. However, no time schedules have been set.

Monitoring of air quality

The legal obligation to monitor air quality derives from the Laws on Environmental Protection and on State Health Inspectorate. Nevertheless, it is important to emphasize that the rules and regulations for the enforcement of these two laws are incomplete: they do not lay down clear and precise definitions and do not spell out the duties and responsibilities of the different institutions. This has led to frequent misunderstandings and misinterpretations, which have affected progress. According to the Council of Minister's Decision No. 541 of 25 September 1995, the Ministry of Environment is responsible for the quality, extent and financing of ambient air quality monitoring, while the actual monitoring is carried out by the Institute of Public Health and the Institute of Hydrometeorology. The requirements from the two institutions are laid down in annual contracts. In 1998 the National Environment Agency developed a national air-monitoring programme and identified relevant environmental indicators. A joint project involving the two above-mentioned institutes started with the intention of upgrading the air monitoring network. The project was financed by the National Environment Agency in 1998 and 2000.

Together the two institutes monitor concentrations of sulphur dioxide (SO_2), suspended particulate matters less than ten microns in diameter (PM_{10}), soot, nitrogen oxides (NO_x), ground-level ozone (O_3) and carbon monoxide (CO). The Institute of

Hydrometeorology also monitors depositions of acid substances and particulate matter.

The Institute of Public Health operates the central air pollution control laboratory in Tirana. The laboratory started operating in its present form in 1997 and is equipped with modern instruments. The Institute of Public Health also operates air quality monitoring stations in Tirana, Korçe, Durrës, Elbasan, Shkodër, Fier and Vlorë. Concentrations of particulate matter (PM_{10}), black smoke, SO_2, NO_2, ground-level ozone (O_3) and lead (Pb) are monitored. The Institute's air quality monitoring network is in general based on active sampling, and wet chemical and gravimetric methods. Due to limited technical and financial resources, active monitoring takes place on an average of five days a month at each monitoring site. This makes a total of no more than 60 days a year at each location, which results in an annual data completeness of only 16 per cent. This is far below the minimum of 274 days a year (or 75 per cent) that WHO recommends. Passive monitoring is used only for monitoring O_3 and some parallel measurements of NO_2. Six passive samplers are operated in Tirana, at points with different traffic intensities.

The Institute of Public Health has also operated an automatic air quality monitoring station since 1996. The automatic station is located in Tirana and measures non-stop the dynamics of the following pollutants: O_3, SO_2, CO and NO_x. The automatic station provided a complete time series for the first time for the period 1997-1999. The automatic monitoring programme was suspended in 1999 due to a lack of spare parts and of an external calibration service. The air pollution laboratory at the Institute of Public Health is planning to resume automatic monitoring in 2002 at a new location in the city centre. It should be noted that the automatic station is situated in an area relatively far from the centre of Tirana. In the present situation of growing urban traffic the frequency of registrations is considered to be insufficient. While concentrations of PM_{10} in general are registered four or five times a month, at least 274 daily observations a year are required to obtain representative data.

The Institute of Hydrometeorology operates a national network composed of 25 meteorological stations (3 observations/day), 65 thermometric stations (1 observation/day) and 25 pluviometric stations. The Institute also monitors air quality at six of its meteorological stations. Five are located in urban and suburban areas in Tirana, Elbasan, Fier, Korçe and Shkodër, one in Petrela in a rural area. At four of these stations information ondeposited matter (gravimetry) and rainfall acidity (pH) is collected, while at the Tirana station concentrations of SO_2 and atmospheric turbidity (3 times/day) are also monitored. The Tirana station of the Institute of Hydrometeorology is located in a built-up urban area. The monitoring is not continuous due to poor maintenance of the equipment and an irregular power supply. The information collected is not shared with the Institute of Public Health. In addition, there is no

Table 5.6: National air quality standards

Pollutant	Maximum permissible concentration (in mg/m^3)		Pollutant	Maximum permissible concentration (in mg/m^3)	
	For a given moment (maximum)	For 24 hours (average)		For a given moment (maximum)	For 24 hours (average)
Nitric acid	0.40	0.40	Nitrogen dioxide	0.50	0.15
Sulphuric acid	0.30	0.15	Cyclohexane	1.40	1.40
Hydrochloric acid	0.20	0.20	Dichloroethane	3	1
Acetic acid, acetic anhydride	0.20	0.06	Ethylene	3	3
Acetone	0.35	0.35	Ethyl benzene	0.02	0.02
Acrolein	0.30	0.10	Phenol	0.2	0.1
Methylic alcohol	1.50	0.50	Hydrogen sulphur	0.05	0.015
Ethylic alcohol	5.00	5.00	Chlorine	0.100	0.015
Formic aldehyde	0.07	0.035	Chlorobenzene	0.1	0.1
Ammonia	0.40	0.20	Chlorophos	0.04	0.02
Phosphoric anhydride	0.15	0.05	Chloroprene	0.01	0.1
Sulphur dioxide	0.50	0.15	Fluor compounds, highly soluble fluorides in water (HF, SiF$_4$, NaF, Na$_2$SiF$_6$, etc.)	0.03	0.01
Aniline	0.05	0.03	Fluor compounds little soluble in water (AlF$_3$, CaF$_2$, Na$_3$AlF$_4$)	0.20	0.03
Arsenic (inorganic compounds, except AsH$_3$)	-	0.003	Fluor compounds mixed (soluble and unsoluble)	0.03	0.01
Naphthenic petrol (low content of S, calculated on basis of "C")	5.0	1.5	Chromium 6+ (calculated as CrO$_3$)	0.0015	0.0015
Petrol (high content of S, calculated on basis of "C")	0.05	0.05	Xylene	0.2	0.2
Benzene	3.0	0.8	Manganese and its compounds (calculated as MnO2)	0.03	0.01
Soot	0.2	0.1	Metaphos	0.008	-
Butiphos carbophos	0.015	0.01	Naphthalene	0.003	0.003
Lead and its compounds, except tetraethyl lead (calculated as Pb)	-	0.0015	Nitrobenzene	0.008	0.008
Carbon sulphate	0.050	0.015	Carbon monoxide	6	2
Lead sulphate	-	0.0017	Vanadium pentoxide	-	0.002
Carbon tetrachloride	0.0	2.0	Pentane	100	25
Toluene	0.6	0.6	Pyridine	0.08	0.08
Mercury	-	0.0003	Non-toxic dusts	1.0	0.5

Source: Ministry of Health, 1974.

intercalibration to compare the results of the two laboratories. However, both laboratories have taken part a few times in international intercalibration exercises organized by the WHO Collaborating Centre for Air Quality and Air Pollution Control at the German Federal Environmental Agency, and obtained results comparable to those of the other participants.

Integration into other sectors of activity

The transport sector

The Ministry of Transport and Telecommunications is responsible for developing vehicle emission standards and for ensuring that standards are met. Current standards only set limit values for smoke. Due to a lack of equipment, the control of vehicle emissions is poor in terms of both frequency and the number of pollutants controlled. Work to draw up new vehicle emission standards as well as control mechanisms has started.

The import of large numbers of highly polluting used cars is giving rise to concern among the authorities. Consequently, the 1998 Law on Taxation imposes an additional tax amounting to about 40,000 leks on the import of a used vehicle, compared to the tax on new cars. The rapid growth in traffic has increased concern about the urban pollution that it causes. Special attention is being paid to the traffic situation in Tirana. Public transport is of poor quality in Tirana as well as nationwide, and road traffic keeps growing.

A "Tirana Urban Transport Improvement Study" has been financed by the World Bank, the Albanian national authorities and the municipal authority of Tirana. As part of this study a five-year action programme for the 2001-2005 period has been set up. Investments totalling US$ 102.3 million have been proposed under this programme. Among the proposed actions are:

- A five-year road rehabilitation programme for the definite improvement of the road network and to start ordinary management;
- An inner ring project, an intermediate ring project and an external ring;
- Parking areas, new traffic signals and lights and new bus routes;
- A south and an east by-pass project;
- Urban road regulation;

- A preliminary study for a five-year public transport action programme;
- Cycle tracks.

Within the action programme, a technical report on parking management in Tirana as well as a technical report on legal and policy reforms was presented to the Ministry of Transport and Telecommunications in July 2001. The latter report recommends, among other actions, a new organization of public transport and administrative management of the city's road traffic. It recommends that limited-traffic areas, pedestrian precincts and dedicated bus lanes should be established and a tax and tariff system be introduced for the use of areas, services and utilities provided by the Municipality. These actions are expected to improve the environmental performance of transport in Tirana, including better control of air emissions, by better controlling traffic and encouraging less polluting transport modes – public transport and bicycling.

The energy sector

The Ministry of Industry and Energy is responsible for setting fuel standards and for verifying that fuels marketed in Albania meet them. Albania's current fuel standards were adopted in 1987. The diesel fuel standards limit the content of sulphur in diesel fuel (maximum 0.2% by weight), while petrol standards limit the content of lead (maximum 5 ppb) and sulphur (maximum 0.001%). There are no plans to revise the standards.

Although control procedures relating to fuel standards are laid down in regulations, the fuel being used does not comply with these existing regulations.

Other standards and implementing instruments

No economic instruments to reduce emissions to air, other than the additional tax levied on the import of used vehicles, have been used in Albania. Moreover, the relatively high excise tax on unleaded fuel (90% compared to 20% on leaded petrol) is likely to discourage the introduction of petrol-fuelled cars with catalytic converters.

Article 25 of the 2002 Law on Environmental Protection indicates that environmental taxes will be imposed on polluters, and that these will be regulated with a special law.

Albania's National Communication to the United Nations Framework Convention on Climate Change presents alternative measures to mitigate emissions of greenhouse gases in the country. However, it does not present any concrete policy instruments. As part of the report on Immediate Measures for the Implementation of the National Environmental Action Plan, a carbon tax levied on the carbon content of different fossil fuels has been proposed. The plan is to phase in the carbon tax gradually both in terms of tax rate and tax base. A major concern is the possibility of unwanted changes in energy demand, as the Albanian energy sector is under serious pressure. The carbon tax is due to be introduced in the near future through an amendment to the Law on Taxation (see Chapter 2).

In 1998 a research project to monitor the quality of the air in the main cities of Albania received a grant of 960,000 leks (i.e. about US$ 6,400) from the State budget.

5.3 Conclusions and recommendations

Cooperation to combat air pollution in Europe, North America and Central Asia takes place within the framework of the Convention on Long-range Transboundary Air Pollution. Besides establishing air pollution abatement policies, the Convention also brings together experts in air pollution monitoring, emission inventories, effects, and modelling. Their networks also serve the work of the European Union. Albania is now the only country in Europe that is not a Party to the Convention. At present it does not contribute substantially to air pollution in Europe. However, emissions are likely to increase as its economy develops. Moreover, participating in the international specialists' work within the framework of the Convention could help to train Albanian specialists. In the longer run Albania should consider taking on commitments regarding emissions of pollutants addressed by the different protocols to the Convention, like sulphur dioxide (SO_2), nitrogen dioxides (NO_x), volatile organic compounds (VOC), ammonia (NH_3), persistent organic pollutants (POPs) and heavy metals.

Recommendation 5.1:
Albania should accede to the Convention on Long-range Transboundary Air Pollution and its protocols. (see also Recommendation 3.2)

Albania does not publish comprehensive annual air emission inventories. However, the Ministry of Environment plans to start submitting air emission inventories according to CORINAIR methodology in 2002. The methodology of the Cooperative Programme for Monitoring and Evaluation of the Long-range Transmission of Air Pollutants in Europe (EMEP has been harmonized with that of CORINAIR.

Recommendation 5.2:
The Ministry of Environment should start submitting air emission inventories as soon as possible, following the methodology of CORINAIR and the Cooperative Programme for Monitoring and Evaluation of the Long-range Transmission of Air Pollutants in Europe (EMEP).

The monitoring of ambient air quality in Albania has just started. At present it is carried out by two different institutes, the Institute of Public Health and the Institute of Hydrometeorology. One primarily monitors urban air quality, while the other primarily monitors background levels in rural areas. To some extent, there is overlap between their networks. Measurements are quite limited in scope and the methods do not follow internationally accepted norms. Neither of the institutes has sufficient monitoring equipment to be able to monitor air quality and deposited matter according to such standards. In general manual methods are used. Monitoring frequency differs from the standards recommended by the World Health Organization.

Recommendation 5.3:
The Ministry of Environment and the Ministry of Health should cooperate in planning and establishing a unified network to monitor ambient air quality and deposited matter that will comply with ambient air quality European Union standards and the standards set by the Cooperative Programme for Monitoring and Evaluation of the Long-range Transmission of Air Pollutants in Europe (EMEP) under the Convention on Long-range Transboundary Air Pollution.

The possibility of high concentrations of radon in indoor air gives rise to concern among Albanian specialists and authorities. Measurements indicate that recommended levels of radon concentration are being exceeded at various locations.

Recommendation 5.4:
The Ministry of Health should study further the occurrence of high radon concentrations in indoor air. Mapping areas with a high concentration of radon in soil, water and air would greatly help land use and construction planning.

The concentration of particulate matter (PM), carbon monoxide (CO), sulphur dioxide (SO_2) and nitrogen oxides (NO_x) in air in Albania is expected to increase, especially in urban areas, as traffic grows. It is not known how the energy sector will develop. Though Albania does not at present have an industrial sector that contributes heavily to air pollution, it is important to develop adequate emission standards to mitigate the effects of new polluting activities. Albania's vehicle emission standards and fuel standards are old and insufficient. The control of car emissions and fuel quality is poor. The Ministry of Environment has drawn up proposals for air quality standards and emission standards for new and existing stationary sources, respectively. The Ministry of Transport and Telecommunications is about to draw up proposals for new vehicle emission standards.

Recommendation 5.5:
(a) *The Ministry of Environment, together with the Ministry of Health, should adopt and implement new air quality standards and emission standards for stationary sources. Air quality standards should be in line with World Health Organization's guidelines on ambient air;*

(b) *The Ministry of Transport and Telecommunications, in cooperation with the Ministry of Environment, should develop, adopt and implement new emission standards for new mobile sources according to relevant European Union standards. Adequate vehicle emission control schemes should be set up as soon as possible. Relevant European Union control schemes could serve as examples;*

(c) *The Ministry of Industry and Energy, in cooperation with the Ministry of Environment, should adopt and implement new fuel quality standards. Adequate fuel quality control schemes should be set up as soon as possible. It is vital to establish appropriate schemes to control the content of sulphur in diesel fuel and the content of lead in petrol.*

The average Albanian car is old due to the large number of used cars imported, in spite of an additional tax amounting to about 40,000 leks being levied on the import of a used vehicle. Most of the vehicles in use in Albania are equipped with diesel engines and the content of sulphur in the fuel used in Albania is high. Consequently, car traffic causes high concentrations of particulate matter in air, especially in certain urban areas. At present the excise tax on leaded fuel is 20%, while the tax on unleaded fuel is as much as 90 per cent, (see Chapter 2). Such a tax policy is likely to discourage the introduction of petrol-fuelled cars with catalytic converters. The tax policy should be modified. Differentiated fuel tax schemes have been implemented successfully in other European countries. This will, however, require the development of an adequate fuel quality control system.

Recommendation 5.6:
Immediate action should be taken and policy instruments should be examined to curb the import of the most polluting vehicles. One possibility could be to further differentiate the import tax on cars, e.g. according to the European Union standards they were required to meet when they were first registered. In order to reduce the sulphur content in diesel fuel, as well as in fuel oils, the introduction of a sulphur tax levied on the content of sulphur in fuel could be considered. Regarding petrol, the tax policy should be modified in order to stimulate the changeover to unleaded-petrol-fuelled cars.

As public transport is poorly developed in Albania, road transport dominates and continues to grow. Plans have been developed to improve public transport and traffic management in Tirana. Plans also exist for upgrading the Albanian railway system. However, most resources seem to be allocated to the development of the road network. The development of rail networks does not seem to be given priority in the corridors passing through Albania.

Recommendation 5.7:
(a) *To avoid uncontrolled growth in emissions and other environmental problems from the transport sector, the Government should give more priority to the development of urban public transport and better traffic management;*

(b) *The Government should consider allocating more resources to the development of rail transport through the most important international and national transport corridors, for passenger as well as for freight transport.*

Chapter 6

WATER MANAGEMENT

6.1 Albania's water resources

Overview

Albania is rich in water resources, including rivers, groundwater, lakes, lagoons and seas. Overall its resources exceed by far its consumption (Table 6.1), although locally water shortage and conflicts among users may occur in the dry season. The hydrographic basin of Albania covers 43,305 km², of which 28,748 km² lie within its boundaries (Figure 6.1). The rest (i.e. 33 per cent) is in Greece, the former Yugoslav Republic of Macedonia and Yugoslavia, so Albania shares upstream and downstream water resources with its neighbours. Since 1990, the monitoring of water is much less frequent, and in particular the quality of the water resources is not well known.

Rivers (quality and quantity)

The most important rivers are the Drini, the Mati, the Ishmi, the Erzeni, the Shkumbini, the Semani, the Vjosa and the Bistrica (Table 6.2). The overall river flow is 1,308 m³/sec. Rivers are mountainous with steep slopes and a flow ratio between the wettest and the driest month averaging 10. Their regime is torrential. In general, river flows are the highest in winter or early spring during the wet season. The rivers carry large quantities of solid matter: an estimated 1,650 kg/sec on average.

A water quality survey was conducted in 1997-1998. It showed that rivers were in general slightly alkaline (pH from 7.5 to 8.25), with a mineral content of 200-400 mg/l. Surface waters are largely contaminated. The two main contaminant factors are: (i) urban waste water directly discharged into surface water bodies; and (ii) pollution by industry, though the latter has lessened during the economic crisis. Many rivers (Ishem, Tirane, Erzeni, Shkumbini, Semani) show a deficit in dissolved oxygen, with high chemical oxygen demand (COD) and biological oxygen demand (BOD) values, which indicate pollution by organic matter, generally of domestic origin. The Gjanika and Semani Rivers, in which waste water from oil extraction and processing are discharged, are amongst the most polluted in the country. They contain high phenol concentrations (0.98 to 3.90 mg/l), high COD contents (60 to 190 mg/l) and high BOD values (20 to 63 mg/l) - far above the European Union standards for river water quality (i.e. phenols less than 0.05 mg/l, COD less than 30 mg/l and BOD less than 15 mg/l for category IV, i.e. bad quality) - and a high content of oil products. Other rivers, such as the Ishmi (industrial and domestic waste in particular from Tirana), the Kiri (industrial waste), the Great Fan, Little Fan and Mati (copper mining), are heavily polluted by pollution discharged from ore-dressing factories. The Shkumbini River downstream of Elbasan is also severely polluted even though metallurgical and mining activities have decreased since 1990. The rivers in the south (Vjosë, Bistrica, Pavlla and Pallasa) seem generally cleaner.

Lakes and lagoons

Lakes cover 4 per cent of Albania's territory. Ohrid, Prespa and Shkodra are the major lakes, but there are also many smaller ones (247 in total). An analysis of the transparency and the nutrient contents (nitrogen and phosphorus) of the lakes indicate that they are oligotrophic, except in specific areas where tributary rivers sharply increase the concentration of nitrogen and phosphorus (0.064 mg of phosphorus/l in the Cerava, up to 0.156 mg of phosphorus/l in the Pogradeci). In Lake Ohrid, the phosphorus content varies from 0.003 to 0.007 mg/l, in Prespa from 5 to 10 mg/l.

Also, 626 reservoirs, with a total capacity of 562 million cubic metres, were built along the main rivers (Drini, Mati and Devolli) for irrigation.

There are some large lagoons along the Seacoast, such as Karavasta, Narta and Butrint (see Chapter 8 and 11); all of them are wetlands of key importance for flora and fauna protection.

Table 6.1: Water balance, 1997

(million m³)

Surface water	Inflow	Outflow
Rainfall/evaporation	42,690	15,773
River flow	15,670	41,280
Groundwater	..	915

Water abstraction	Intakes	Discharges
Public supply and industry *	258	..
Waste-water discharges**	..	134
Irrigation **	675	..
Drainage **	..	..

Source: Draft National Water Strategy, 1997.

Note : *from groundwater; ** into surface waters

Groundwater

Groundwater is relatively abundant in Albania and well distributed over the country. It is exploited from wells mostly in valleys or plains or through springs in mountains. The water is of good quality (good physico-chemical and microbiological characteristics) at the source, but in some specific locations little is known about its quality since monitoring has been neglected for several years. Only the water table level has been monitored without interruption. Potential problems that have cropped up in recent years are the intrusion of saline water into the aquifers (such as in the coastal regions of Shkodër, Lezhë, Durrës, Lushnjë and Fier), the degradation of water quality in rivers underlying aquifers where the extraction is too intense or sanitary protection perimeters are lacking around water wells (e.g. Ishmi aquifer for the supply to Tirana), and the drying-up of springs during the dry season (Mati basin aquifer). Another risk is the upstream pollution by all kinds of wastes discharged in karstic zones, where the water penetrates quickly in the ground through fissures and then feeds the aquifers without being filtered by soil layers. The Shkodër aquifer is one such vulnerable area.

Groundwater resources are Albania's major source of drinking water. Seventy per cent of the main cities are supplied by wells. About 20 per cent of the groundwater is also used for irrigation and agriculture (in Shkodër and Vlorë areas). Today, it is estimated that about 30 per cent of the available resources of water are used; however, not much is known regarding their availability, the potential extraction capacity, the locations of water-uptakes, the real extracted amounts and the hotspots for pollution or for over-exploitation. Figure 6.2 shows the use of groundwater based on the most recent available data, i.e. these of 1996.

6.2 Water uses and pressures on the water resources

Overall situation

The current situation as far as the use of water resources in Albania is concerned is very difficult to assess because of insufficient monitoring and the fast changes in agriculture, mining and industrial activities since 1990, as well as major internal population movements (see Chapter Introduction). Roughly, irrigation and mining rely on surface waters, and households and industry on water from aquifers. Nearly all water used in industry is supplied by public drinking-water networks. There is no recent data on the quantity and provenance of water abstracted and its uses by the different sectors of activities.

Table 6.2: Major rivers

Rivers	Catchment area Total	Catchment area In Albania	Annual flowrate volume	Main tributaries and lakes	Transboundary with
	(km²)	(km²)	million m³		
Drini	..	19,582	11,100	Buna river with Lake Skhodra; Fierza reservoir:2.7 km³;	FYR of Macedonia and Yugoslavia
Mati	2,441	2,441	3,250	Fani river; Ulza reservoir: 0.24km³	-
Ishmi	..	..	..		-
Erzen	..	..	..		-
Shkumbin	2,445	2,445	1,900	Rapuni, Gostima and Zaranica rivers	-
Seman	5,649	5,649	2,700	Devoli and Osumi rivers; Banja reservo	-
Vjosë	..	4,365	5,550	Drino	Greece
Bistrica	..	..	..		-

Source : Draft National Water Strategy, 1997.

Figure 6.1: Albania hydrographic network and hydrographic basin boundaries

Source: Department of Public Information of the United Nations (UNDPI), Cartographic Section, New York, Post-Conflict "Environmental Assessment-Albania", United Nations Environment Programme (UNEP).

"The boundaries and names shown on this map do not imply official endorsement or acceptance by the United Nations"

Box 6.1:   Lake Ohrid Conservation Project

Lake Ohrid is a transboundary lake located in the east of Albania and the southwest of the former Yugoslav Republic of Macedonia. It covers 349 km², of which 118.9km² (34 per cent) belong to Albania. UNESCO classified it as a world natural heritage site in 1979. It is a natural, cultural and historical monument and the cradle of very ancient civilizations (Neolithic). The Lake is one of the oldest lakes in Europe. Because of its oligotrophic state, it is one of the largest biological reserves in Europe, sheltering unique flora and fauna that are extinct elsewhere. Due to its age, many of Lake Ohrid's aquatic species are endemic, including 10 of its 17 fish species. At present, more than 100,000 people live and work along its banks, and exert environmental pressure (domestic activities; tourism; textile, metal, electrical industries; and agriculture and fishing). In 1996, in an attempt to protect the lake from anthropogenic pressures, both countries adopted the Lake Ohrid Conservation Project financed by GEF and executed by the World Bank.

The three-year project started in 1998 at a total cost of US$ 4.4 million. The Albanian part is US$ 2 million, of which 93 per cent is covered by GEF and 7 per cent by the country. The main objectives of the Lake Ohrid Conservation Project are to:
*   Develop a basis for the joint management and protection of the Lake by the two border countries,
*   Create conditions for promoting environmentally friendly solutions for the management of natural resources and economic development of the watershed.

The first step consisted in developing a participatory watershed management approach. This step aimed at raising public awareness of the project and its results at an early stage, by actively involving the population, stimulating local initiatives through NGOs, and setting up a water management committee. Still under debate are the establishment of a joint monitoring programme and the sustainable management and control of fish stocks. Pilot projects in forestry, tourism, spatial planning, sewage, waste management, and the use of phosphorus-free detergents are developed in cooperation with NGOs. A recent opinion survey shows that 80 per cent of the local population is now aware of the project. Other concrete results are the building of the first Albanian waste-water treatment plants in Pogradec (30,000 inhabitants); the improvement of the sewage collector and the drinking-water-supply system; and the creation of a landfill for solid waste. Germany and the European Union Phare programme will finance these projects, beginning in June 2002. The success of the project has been ensured by the active involvement of all the local stakeholders; the water management committee is a good example for the establishment of river basin management committees in the rest of the country.

Figure 6.2: Use of groundwater (as % of total), 1996

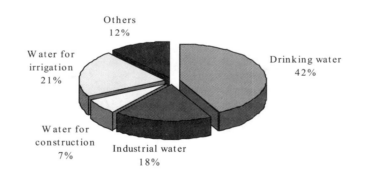

Source: Draft National Water Strategy, 1997.

Protection from floods

Protection of the urban centres and the agricultural lands from floods is a major undertaking in Albania as the rivers are subject to sudden spates in rainy periods (winter and spring). Flood protection works are wide-ranging: 300 km of channels in the mountains collect and drain the rainwater into reservoirs, lakes and sea; kilometers of

embankments along the rivers protect rural zones and urban areas and 864 km of dikes stand along the seacoast. These protection works have practically not been maintained over the past 15 years. The Ministry of Agriculture and Food, which is in charge of the maintenance of all flood works (except in the urban areas where the authorities responsible are the municipalities), has received an annual budget of about US$ 0.3 million per year in the past decade for these works' overall maintenance. This is far too little. The problem is further compounded by the fact that pebbles and gravel from the riverbeds have been illegally exploited for road building, resulting in drastic modification and displacement of the water streams. Today, new buildings are mushrooming in all fertile plains and in urban areas. They are made of gravel illegally and carelessly extracted from riverbeds and of sand from beaches. This practice causes a deep modification in the river courses and their estuaries, leading to an acceleration of the water flow, making existing flood protection works inefficient, causing the erosion of agricultural lands, threatening urban areas with possible floods and causing adverse modifications of the seashores and coastal zones.

Domestic uses

Urban water supply and waste-water systems are plagued by problems. Albania has been operating underdeveloped and obsolete infrastructures built before 1990. Over the past decade, the migration of about 13 per cent of the population from rural to urban zones and the concentration of 44 per cent of the urban population in the Tirana-Durrës-Fier-Elbasan area has put significant pressure on the water infrastructure. A particular feature is the spectacular growth of the population in major urban centres between 1990 and 1999, especially in Tirana, Durrës, Fier and Lushnjë. (In the coastal zone and in Tirana, the population density has increased from 82 inhabitants/km^2 in 1960 to 179/km^2 in 2000.) This is accompanied by a boom in building construction, illegal siting of new construction due to the absence of urban planning, and illegal connections to both water-supply pipes and sewage pipes. The situation is not better in rural areas, where land use planning is non-existent. People put up their farms and houses in the middle of the countryside, far from any public infrastructure and then illegally dig their own wells for drinking water.

Water supply

About 80 per cent of drinking water is abstracted from underground and 20 per cent from surface waters. The drinking-water-supply network covers the whole country. Most of the population (85 per cent) is supplied through a public system at home in urban areas and essentially from standpipes and public taps in rural areas. Ten per cent also have access to groundwater through private wells, 4.9 per cent of families use treated surface waters, and 0.1 per cent use untreated surface water. The water is distributed in general without preliminary treatment with the exception of that from three drinking-water plants (two in Tirana and one in Durrës) that have recently been renovated as a result of international funding (Box 6.2). The average quantities supplied are very low, i.e. about 20-50 litres/person/day at the tap and 120 litres/person/day at the origin, i.e. at the supply enterprise. The latter figures reflect the importance of the amounts lost in the distribution system.

Overall the supply is not yet satisfactory and the quality of the drinking-water at the taps is mediocre. Water demand has increased not only because of population growth and urban density but also because of the mismanagement of water resources and obsolete infrastructure in poor repair. (On average, pipes, now 30 years old and made of cast iron, are corroded.) Losses for the water enterprises run at about 50-70 per cent. Insufficient storage capacity and frequent cuts in electricity interrupt water supply, in some places for several hours a day. This intermittent water service and the lack of chemicals and disinfectant reagents for treatment increase the risks of contamination in the supply pipes by external biological, chemical or microbial agents. In the ground, infiltrations of waste water from parallel sewer lines contaminate the old supply pipe network.

In rural zones, the construction of public water pipes began in the 1960s but accelerated only after 1986 as a consequence of Decision No. 428 on supplying cities and villages with drinking water. Drinking water in rural areas is supplied by public taps for groups of houses. The network was never completed, however, and, even where it exists, it has been poorly maintained and was damaged in approximately 400 villages during the 1991-1992 civil unrest. Villagers often dig their own wells without any monitoring of the water quality or reference to rules of sanitation. In some valleys, the wells are dug on the banks of heavy polluted rivers (e.g. along the Seman valley) and fed almost directly with unfiltered water, unsuitable for human consumption (see Chapter 12). There is therefore a strong need to complete and rehabilitate the water-supply network.

Box 6.2:   Water supply and waste-water management in the Tirana and Durrës region

The population of the capital, Tirana, has mushroomed over the past ten years (150,000 people in 1991, 523,000 in 2001), as has the population of the valley from Tirana to the sea, Durrës included. In the surrounding countryside, new farms are emerging everywhere right in the middle of fertile plots, without building permits, and are scattered far from any road, electricity and water infrastructure.

For the past two to three years, Tirana has experienced one of the highest development rates in cities worldwide. Seventy per cent of the new buildings breach municipal planning and building regulations. Tirana has no water-supply and sewerage master plan. The existing water-supply infrastructure is in a critical condition, and the water is provided for only four to six hours per day. Drinking water is distributed by two water enterprises that have recently benefited from funds from the European Union/PHARE and Italy for the rehabilitation of their facilities (reservoirs and treatment plants). PHARE has also funded the rehabilitation of part of the supply pipe network in the Kombinat, Paskutan and Koder Kamez areas; however other zones are still in dire need of renovation (Ali Demi, Tirana e Re).

Tirana has 530 km of mixed sewage system (collecting rain and sewage altogether) functioning by gravity. Illegal buildings and illegal connections have damaged the sewerage system designed for a capacity of 200,000 people in 1962. In the new suburbs there is no sewerage infrastructure; new buildings are equipped with septic tanks, which are emptied by pumping trucks, and sludge is discharged into the sewerage system. In 1997, the Government of Japan funded a study on the rehabilitation of the sewage collection system and designed a waste-water treatment facility. In 2001, the reconstruction of secondary collectors started. Overall the cost of total immediate and long-term rehabilitation has been estimated at € 55 million.

The prices of water in Tirana differ according to the user (see section on economic instruments). They do not cover the full cost of operation and maintenance. Ninety-three per cent of the price charged to consumers is for drinking water and 7 per cent for sewage collection. The collection rate, at 91 per cent in September 2001, has much improved over the past two years for people and legally registered enterprises.

The situation in Durrës is not better. As the country's second city with 183,000 inhabitants in 2001, its population doubles every summer since it is the most important domestic sea resort in Albania. Durrës has also been the destination both of refugees during the Kosovo conflict and of internal migrants. The water problems in Durrës are similar to those of Tirana, exacerbated further by the uncontrolled building of homes and hotels along the seashore, which are discharging their waste water directly into the sea. The pollution of the sea is at its highest in the summer when people are most likely to be exposed. Hepatitis, dysentery, gastroenteritis, and other diseases transmitted by water are frequent. There is no waste-water treatment at all at the moment.

Waste-water discharges and treatment

The situation regarding sewage is critical. Because of the economic crisis, the waste-water collection and treatment infrastructure has not been maintained and has not developed quickly enough to cope with the increasing flow of discharged pollution. No new waste-water infrastructure has been built to keep pace with the increasing population in Tirana and along the coast of Durrës (see Box 6.2). In urban areas, only 40 per cent of the population has access to sewerage connections. The poorer neighbourhoods are without any access at all. At best, buildings and houses are equipped with septic tanks. There are no sewage treatment facilities for domestic waste water in Albania.

Waste water has been discharged in an uncontrolled manner, and might have polluted groundwater, but this has not yet been investigated.

Agricultural uses

Agriculture is the main economic activity in Albania and remains the most important water consumer. The climate makes irrigation a necessity.

Crop water deficits between June and August range between 400 and 500 mm. Out of its 2.9 million hectares, Albania has 0.7 million hectares of arable land. In 1990, 60 per cent of this arable land was irrigated and produced 80 per cent of the agricultural value. More than half the irrigated area is located in the coastal plains. The development of irrigation was accompanied by flood protection works for 0.13 million ha and drainage systems for 0.3 million ha. Since the fall of the previous regime and of the State farms, the irrigation network has been badly maintained or even destroyed. There are no recent measurements or reporting of the quantities of water abstracted (see Chapter 10).

Over the past decade, fertilizer and pesticide consumption have seriously declined, thus lessening the risk of polluting water bodies, in particular aquifers, a threat that existed in the past. Nevertheless, since 1994, the use of fertilizers and pesticides has been picking up steadily with the take-off of agricultural activities (Chapter 10). This growing demand is leading to an increased interest in rehabilitating fertilizer factories, potentially heavy polluters.

Industry uses and pressures

Hydro energy

Albania has a large potential for hydropower production resulting from the combination of large water quantities and steep riverbanks. Ninety-eight per cent of the electricity generated in the country is from hydropower; 93 per cent of this production is from dams on the Drini. Other hydropower plants have been built along the Mati. In the rest of the country (centre and south) hydropower plants are driven by river-flow without dams. The dams originally built only for hydropower generation also play a role in river-flow regulation. Other multipurpose dams were envisaged. For instance, the Chinese Government has just approved a loan for the construction of the Bushati hydropower plant in 2002, a construction which, though approved by the World Bank, is contested by environmental NGOs. The project has a transboundary character and would badly affect Lake Shkodra in Montenegro, a wetland classified as a Ramsar site.

Mining and ore processing

Before 1991, mining was an important activity in Albania. It has significantly decreased since then (see Chapter 9), as have its pollution discharges (Table 6.3). The mining industry is a strategic sector that has been open to privatization since 1999.

Copper ore is still extracted (930,000 tons in 1990, 260,000 in 1995, 34,000 in 1999) in the Drini basin, the Mati basin and the Semani basin, and some enrichment factories still operate but at reduced capacity. Most of the pollution (iron, copper and other elements) originates from the enrichment process through the discharge of waste water and from the leachate of inert materials deposited around the plants. Today, only one metallurgic copper plant is still working in Rubik on the Mati River. The waste water is very acidic and contains sulphur, sulphates, arsenic, iron and phosphate, and has a high COD.

Chromium ore is another important mineral resource for Albania. In 1992, one million tons of chromium ore were extracted, but, eight years later, extraction was reduced to one tenth (80,000 tons in 1999). Chromium ore mines are located in the Drini and Mati basins. Enrichment factories are still operational at reduced capacity. Chromium metallurgic complexes are still working in Elbasan

Table 6.3: Industrial liquid discharges into water bodies, 1996-1998

in thousand m³

	1996	1997	1998
Total	10,814	5,340	12,450
Mining/ total	7,158	2,434	..
of which:			
Chromium extraction	..	..	..
Chromium enrichment	3,250	1,913	..
Chromium melting	547	377	..
Copper extraction	..	..	..
Copper enrichment	1,909	144	..
Copper melting	1,452	..	..
Oil /total	3,156	2,513	..
of which:			
Extraction	546	359	..
Refining	2,610	2,154	..
Thermo power plants	500	393	..

Source: State of the Environment Report, 1997-1998.

and Burrel and produce ferrochromium compounds. They generate waste water that is highly toxic (heavy metals) and that is not treated before being discharged. The Fani River is polluted with hexavalent chromium (the most toxic form of chromium), due mostly to heaps of sludge of high chromium and copper contents that have been dumped along the riverbanks and are leaching into the river. There have been no regular measurements of pollution since 1995.

Lake Ohrid is polluted with iron and chromium leaching from a mining plant.

Industry

Industry is also discharging untreated polluted water. Before the 1990s, a few big industrial State-owned facilities were equipped with waste-water treatment plants. Over the past decade, most of these industrial facilities have closed down because of the economic crisis and the few that remain operational have not maintained their waste-water treatment plants. According to the environmental legislation, every new enterprise has to obtain an environmental permit (or licence) (see Chapters 1 and 2) as a prerequisite for a building authorization and a guarantee that the necessary environmental equipment will also be incorporated into the project. But when production starts up no operating permit is required and there is no obligation to monitor and report pollution that is then discharged.

In the past, Albania had much heavy polluting industry, including an important chemical industry producing nitrogen and phosphate fertilizers, pesticides, soda, pigments, paints and solvents; oil refining; metallurgical plants for iron and copper melting; cement production; and a wood and paper industry. With the exception of oil refining and cement production, most of them have ceased operating, without any prospect of resuming production. The heavily polluting fertilizer factories in Fier are no longer in operation due to the lack of a natural gas supply. Other active industries include tanneries, construction materials and food processing. The majority of these industries use very old technology and do not treat their effluents.

The oil sector is the major industrial water polluter. In the Visoke-Patos-Marinez-Ballsh zone, polluted water is directly discharged into the Gjanica and the Semani, causing heavy pollution by organic aromatic compounds (see the specific environmental survey financed by PHARE in 1997). The Ballsh refinery, the most important in Albania, discharges a significant amount of pollution (in particular phenols) into the Gjanica River, as the refinery's waste-water treatment plants are inadequately managed. In the same region, the water from irrigation and drainage canals has a toluene and benzene content several times higher than the standards. Almost 10,000 tons of pollution (in particular oil and grease) per year were discharged this way in 1999 and 2000, and 100 highly polluted spots have been identified.

Statistical surveys of industry show that the food and beverage industry, the textile industry and the leather industry (respectively 26, 8 and 9 per cent of 1999 manufacturing output) are rapidly expanding their activities. Most of these private small and medium-size industries are developing in the suburbs of the big towns. Leather industries are found in Tirana, Durrës, Korçe, Gjirokaster and Berat; the textile industry in Tirana, Korçe, Berat; sugar and spirit factories in Maliq and beer factories all over the country, the biggest of them in Tirana. These branches traditionally generate heavy water pollution. How much polluted effluent they discharge is not known, nor are the characteristics of the pollutants it contains.

Tourism

Tourism is still in its infancy, but domestic tourism is developing steadily. It is developing along the coast essentially in the south of the country (see Chapter 11) and also in the vicinity of the large lakes in the east of the country (Ohrid, Prespa). Along the coast the population doubles during the high season (Durrës, Vlorë, Sarandë). Illegal buildings along the coast have mushroomed, while

municipalities have been unable to regulate their development and provide adequate water infrastructure. The new buildings are equipped with private reservoirs for storing the intermittently supplied drinking water, a practice that is not safe since the residual chlorine content disappears in time and certainly does not ensure that the stored water will be kept uncontaminated for long. Domestic waste water is discharged into septic tanks, where it is sometimes partially treated before going directly to the sea along the coast. In summer, the efficiency of this type of treatment is highly questionable as this technology is not adapted to the sudden chock-loads occurring from the high population increase (see Box 6.2).

6.3 Policies, strategies and framework management

Policies and strategies for water use and protection

Albania has no national water strategy and no master plan for water management. A national water strategy was drafted in February 1997 under the European Union's PHARE Programme. Although drawn up under the close supervision of all the members of the National Water Council, in its final stage the strategy met with opposition from a few Ministries and local authorities and has therefore never been adopted.

The draft national water strategy promotes water resource conservation and the sustainable use of water resources in harmony with the environment and other natural resources. It defines the national objectives of water uses and water resources management, as well as the appropriate institutional structures for implementing the strategy. It also indicates the legal, regulatory and technical framework to be developed, as well as the coordination among the different partners. It indicates how to fulfil the requirements of each different use in agreement with national and regional development and individual sectoral policies. It identifies specific programmes and priority projects for the short, medium and long terms.

Legislation

National

The Law on Water Resources (No. 8093/1996) is the main legislation on water resource management. It established the National Water

Council (NWC) and its Technical Secretariat as well as other water institutions in place today. The Law provides for the protection, development and sustainable use of water resources, and it organizes water resource management and administration by river basin according to its use and purpose. It introduces permits, concessions and authorizations for using water and for discharging waste water. Although the Law is concerned with controlling and preserving the quality of water resources, it does not define very strict conditions for the discharge of pollution, nor does it introduce pollution charges to encourage polluters to reduce their pollution loads. The Law also calls for the drawing-up of a water strategy.

The Law on Water Supply and Sanitation Sector Regulation (No. 8102) was also issued in 1996. This Law is concerned with securing a safe and reliable drinking-water supply and domestic waste-water treatment, and promoting private investments in the sector. The Law makes licences compulsory for all entities wanting to distribute drinking water and collect and treat waste water. The Law also establishes the national Water Supply and Sanitation Regulatory Commission, which grants licences and approves the water charges or prices and the terms and conditions of services provided by the licensees. The Commission is under the Ministry of Territorial Adjustment and Tourism.

The Law on the Construction, Administration, Maintenance and Operation of Water and Drainage Systems, (No. 7846/1994), concerns the irrigation and drainage systems. Its implementation is under the responsibility of the Ministry of Agriculture and Food. The 1999 Law for Irrigation and Drainage (No. 8518), which updates the Law of 1994, essentially provides for the decentralized management of irrigation and drainage infrastructure, and paves the way for their privatization or for concessions and management by water users' associations.

A draft Law on Water Protection, proposed in the new NEAP, has been prepared and is under review of the line Ministries. It focuses exclusively on reinforcing existing legislation to protect and preserve water quality. The ultimate goal is to protect human health. The draft law clarifies and reinforces the tasks of the National Water Council and gives the Ministry of Environment more responsibilities for protection. The draft law forbids "the discharge of any substances that might pollute water resources, either directly or indirectly". Regulations on the discharge of waste water and

emission limit values for polluting substances should be laid down. Under the draft law, the Ministry of Environment would be entrusted with setting up water protection areas, issuing regulations regarding the siting and functioning of treatment facilities, regulating the use of fertilizers and pesticides, and monitoring the implementation of the law on water protection, including water monitoring. The municipalities would be responsible for the planning, management, connection to and discharge from public sewerage in their jurisdiction. In addition, the draft law calls for national standards for drinking water and for strictly and strongly enforcing these standards. Sanitary protection perimeters must be set for protecting the water resources used for drinking.

Starting in January 2002, the Law on the Organization and Functioning of Local Government (No. 8652/2000) gives full administrative, service, investment and regulatory powers for water supply, sewerage and drainage system and flood protection canals to local governments (municipalities and communes). This increase in responsibilities also requires that municipalities should improve their capacity for water management and urban planning. International organizations and the European Union are helping Albania to face this challenge (see Chapter 1).

The critical issue in Albania is not the availability of appropriate legislation but the lack of implementation and enforcement. Called for in the Law on Water Resources, the draft water strategy of 1997 was never adopted. Neither the Law on Water Resources nor the draft law on water protection indicates how the permitting system should be enforced and by what authority. For the time being, Regional Environmental Agencies and the Health Inspectorate of the Ministry of Health are responsible for inspection, but they lack the means and real authority to undertake this work.

International

Albania has been a Party to the Barcelona Convention for the Protection of the Mediterranean Sea against Pollution and to four of its protocols since 1990. Albania also ratified the UNECE Convention on the Protection and Use of Transboundary Watercourses and International Lakes in 1994, and signed its London Protocol on Water and Health in 1999. Further developing bilateral agreements on transboundary rivers is the task of the National Water Council, but no significant action has yet been taken. The most important achievement regarding international water cooperation is the agreement with the former Yugoslav Republic of Macedonia on the common management of Lake Ohrid (see Chapter 3 and Box 6.1).

Institutions

According to the 1996 Law on Water Resources, the management of water resources is entrusted to the National Water Council (NWC, i.e. the former Water Authority) and its Technical Secretariat (implementing body) at central level and to water basin authorities at local level. As many strong sectors were benefiting from the free use of water, the NWC was set up at a very high level to ensure that it had enough clout. The National Water Council is headed by the Prime Minister, co-chaired by the Ministry of Territorial Adjustment and Tourism and the Ministry of Transport and Telecommunications, and is made up of representatives from the Ministry of Agriculture and Food, the Ministry of Industry and Energy, the Ministry of Transport and Telecommunications, the Ministry of Foreign Affairs, the Ministry of Health, the Ministry of Environment and the Ministry of Local Government and Decentralization. Since Decision 240 of 1998, its Technical Secretariat, made up of one person only at the beginning, should include five staff (director, economist, hydrologist, hydrotechnician and lawyer). At the moment, there are only three persons.

While the structure and tasks of the National Water Council are well defined and the Council has adequate coordination with other ministries, little progress has been made to implement the provisions of the 1996 Law on Water Resources. In 1998, the NWC delineated the boundaries of six river basins: the Drini-Buna, the Mati, the Ishmi-Erzeni, the Shrumbini, the Semani and the Vjosa basins. Two years later, a decision called for the establishment of a water basin council and implementing agency for each of the six basins. However, this decision has never been implemented. In early 2001, another NWC decision (No. 63) defined the responsibilities of the previous water basin councils and water agencies regarding the granting of abstraction permits according to the type of applicant and the quantity requested (Table 6.4). De facto, the decision cannot be implemented, since the water agencies do not yet exist. Therefore, ministries have complete discretion over whether or not to issue permits, and, in general, water is withdrawn illegally. Water extraction charges exist and are calculated according to the type of use. However, users are not registered, the quantities extracted are neither measured nor reported, and the abstraction taxes are not paid.

In short, despite its best efforts, the National Water Council has only partially succeeded in enforcing the Law. It has failed to introduce a water strategy. It has not drawn up an inventory of water resources. It was not able to issue any authorizations for the use and discharge of water under its direct responsibility. Moreover, there is neither an implementing mechanism nor a budget for the decisions that have been taken.

Since 1998 the National Environmental Agency, now the Ministry of Environment, has been responsible for protecting water. The Ministry of Environment is responsible for water quality monitoring and emissions monitoring. It is also competent for setting water quality standards and water emission limits in coordination with other ministries, chiefly the National Water Council. Through environmental permits, the Ministry of Environment has the task of regulating emissions (domestic and industrial) into water. The Ministry of Environment and its Regional Environmental Agencies issue the environmental permits, and collect and process data on the state of the environment, including on water bodies, at district and regional levels.

The Ministry of Health, through the Institute of Hygiene and Epidemiology and the State Health Inspectorate, is responsible for monitoring the quality of drinking water. Local public health directorates carry out control and monitoring at local level. They control the toxic substance content and the bacteriological contamination of water, manage drinking-water and water-supply systems, and control the sewerage system. They regularly share information and coordinate with the Ministry of Environment at national and local levels. At local level the State Health Inspectorates verify that the quality standards for drinking water are respected. They are also entrusted with the monitoring of bathing waters; however, their overly tight budget prevents them from doing their monitoring jobs properly (see Chapter 12).

The Ministry of Territorial Adjustment and Tourism plans and manages the water-supply and water-treatment infrastructures, and provides for specialized technical support. Water supply is organized by district, each having at least one water-supply enterprise (52 in all, of which 38 are

State-owned entities and 14 given in concession to private firms). These enterprises often lack technical expertise, spare parts and maintenance capacity. Traditionally, the infrastructure investments have been financed by the State through the Ministry ofTerritorial Adjustment and Tourism, a situation that will change with the decentralization of authority (see the new Law on Local Government). The Ministry is also responsible for monitoring, data collection, and the compilation and storage of information from these enterprises. Sewerage management and waste-water treatment are organized in a similar way. The Water Supply and Sanitation Regulatory Commission, i.e. the leading decision-making body for regulating the water supply and sanitation sector, was established in 1999. It has the authority to issue licences to commercial water enterprises providing water for public consumption and to control their functioning, and to approve water supply and sewerage tariffs (prices and charges) submitted by the water enterprises and the municipalities. By law, the Commission should submit a yearly report on the state of the water industry.

The Ministry of Agriculture and Food, through its Regional Directorate for Irrigation and Drainage, was traditionally responsible for administering, maintaining and using the irrigation and drainage system. At present, this management is progressively being shifted to water users' associations. There is as yet no coordination with the National Water Council and the Ministry of Agriculture and Food, and, despite the Law, the National Water Council does not issue licences for the abstraction of irrigation water.

The local governments (municipalities) are responsible for the proper operation and maintenance of water facilities in their jurisdiction. As of January 2002, the responsibility of the local governments will be extended. Together with the basin councils, the municipalities will be responsible for sewerage planning and the construction of sewerage works within their jurisdiction in consultation with the Water Supply and Sanitation Regulatory Commission. Tariff-setting and regulatory authority for water supply and waste-water services will be exclusively under their responsibility from January 2002. All these tasks will be difficult to assume if the corresponding, currently weak, municipal water-management capacities are not strengthened. At the moment, only Tirana has an infrastructure department with a subsection for the water-supply and sewerage network.

Monitoring

A Decree of the Council of Ministers on Monitoring of 1995 stipulates who should monitor what in order to share and clarify the tasks of the different institutes and avoid gaps and duplications. This reallocation of resources was carried out because of economic difficulties and shrinking budgets, and does not reflect an in-depth rethinking and restructuring of the monitoring system itself. In 2001, the Ministry of Environment, which is responsible for monitoring the environment, subcontracted the monitoring of water for a total amount of 1.76 million leks (i.e. about US$ 12,000).

Table 6.4: Designation of competent authorities for water abstraction permits

Type of use	Units	Quantities		Competent authorities			Ratification	Implementing authority	
				Basin		Council	by	Water	Technical
		>	<	Councils	NWC	Ministers	Parliament	agency	Secrt NWC
Drinking-water supply	l/sec	0	100	X				X	
	l/sec	100	2000		X				X
	l/sec	2000				X	X		X
Industry through public supply	l/sec	0	5	X				X	
	l/sec	5	300		X				X
Irrigation and hydropower generation	Mln m3/y	< = 1		X				X	
	Mln m3/y	1	5	X					X
	Mln m3/y	5	10	X					X
	Mln m3/y	> 10				X	X		X

Source: National Water Council. Decision No. 63, January 2001.

Groundwater: For about half a century, the Albanian Geological Survey has monitored the groundwater and, in particular, aquifers, for water quantity, quality and movement. The Survey also carries out hydrological studies of groundwater and so has a precise idea of the current state of the resources. By law (Law on the Albanian Geological Survey, 1998), the Survey must protect the aquifers, but information on abstraction licences and the quantity of water withdrawn from aquifers is not reported to it. The Albanian Geological Survey does stress that the current use of groundwater is unsustainable because it is too intensive in certain aquifers and in certain locations.

Surface waters: The monitoring of rivers is subcontracted by the Ministry of Environment to the Institute of Hydrometeorology. According to the 1998 State of the Environment report, 80 per cent of the surface water would meet the European Union's first-quality category for surface waters, but the report also indicates that the monitoring stations have been deliberately located in places far from pollution sources. In fact, monitoring of surface water quality has dramatically decreased since 1990. Most of the initial 150 stations no longer function because they do not have sufficient staff, sampling and analysis equipment, or cars. Currently, two series of results are transmitted to the Ministry of Environment per year. The quality of each of the 13 most important rivers is described from one instantaneous grab sample taken at one precise sampling location through the measurement of global parameters (such as temperature, pH, O_2, COD, BOD, reduced and oxidized nitrogen, P and alkalinity) and sometimes bacteriological determination. This methodology cannot give a reliable picture of the situation. This problem was already pointed out in the 1997 draft national water strategy.

Drinking water: Drinking water and coastal water are monitored by the Ministry of Health (the Institute of Public Health and the Directorates for Primary Health Service in districts), subcontracted by the Ministry of Environment. About 15 parameters are monitored, including the standard global physico-chemical parameters and bacterial counts. Pesticides are sporadically monitored; hydrocarbons not at all. Here again, the frequency and representative nature of the sampling are insufficient. In particular, the local laboratories of the Institute of Public Health cannot carry out the monitoring satisfactorily; for instance, the monitoring of the bathing zones on the coast during

the high tourist season is done only sporadically, if at all (see Chapter 12).

Standards

Albania has no water quality standards for its water resources, be they surface waters, groundwaters or coastal waters and regardless of their use. There are no water emission standards either. Only drinking water standards have existed since 1997; they are similar to the WHO standards. The new Law on Environmental Protection calls for standards to be consistent with EC Directives, objectives of the national environmental state policy and best available techniques.

Economic instruments

Charges for water abstraction and discharges: According to the 1996 Law on Water Resources, the Council of Ministers was to define the charges payable for the use of water. The fees and payments for using water were to be collected by the water authorities: the National Water Council at national level and the basin agencies at local level. While the different categories of users and of permits have been defined (Decision No. 63/2001 of NWC), no charge levels have been set, so no charges are levied. Because of this lack of revenue, it has not been possible to set up the water-basin structures that are required for proper and efficient water resource management.

Neither law mentions *pollution charges*, although the 1996 Law on Water Resources provides for the collection of charges on discharged waters by the water authorities (National Water Council and basin agencies). In addition, the 2002 Law on Environmental Protection does call for environmental taxes to be imposed on physical and legal persons who discharge into the water. The details of the amount of taxes and the rules of tax collection are to be regulated by a special law.

The 1996 Law on Water Resources also provides for financial incentives such as loans and tax exemptions to those wanting to reduce their use of water or their waste-water discharges. None of these instruments has been created, however.

Violations are defined in the Law on Water Resources. The fines can reach a maximum of 2 million leks (about US$ 14,000 in 2001), depending of the kind of violation.

Water pricing: The price of water managed by public supply enterprises (so-called water enterprises) is set by the Water Supply and Sanitation Regulatory Commission of the Ministry of Territorial Adjustment and Tourism on proposals from the water enterprises and the municipalities. The cost of drinking water depends on the location, the treatment and the distribution network. It also depends on the client. The scale has recently been simplified from six (including hospitals, schools, private companies, etc.) to three tariff categories (households, industry and institutions). Drinking water is still partly subsidized. The Regulatory Commission adjusts the final price, taking into account social and regional considerations (see Table 2.3 in Chapter 2). Institutions and industry pay more to compensate for the lower price that households pay. In addition, in six cities, including Tirana, the price also incorporates sewage management (see Table 2.4 in Chapter 2). Some of the income of the water enterprises goes to the municipalities for maintaining the pipe network, and 0.5 per cent to the Regulatory Commission.

Currently only 14 of the 52 water enterprises, most of them partly or fully private, are under the control of the Water Supply and Sanitation Regulatory Commission. The other 38 are still State enterprises under the direct authority of the Ministry of Territorial Adjustment and Tourism; there is no obligation for them to join the Regulatory Commission. For water enterprises working with the Water Supply and Sanitation Regulatory Commission, water prices can be adjusted every year, and are based on the balance sheet of the water enterprises. In general, the price of water should cover operating and maintenance costs, not investments. However, even to cover only operation and maintenance, subsidies from the general budget are necessary. In principle investments are financed by the State budget, a burden difficult to assume at present. The State encourages the privatization of waterworks. In Elbasan, a German private company, the Berliner Wasser Co., has a 30-year concession to manage the water enterprise. It plans to invest DM 42 million and proposes to cover the full cost of operation, maintenance and investments. Water prices will rise to 40 leks/m^3 for households, 120 for institutions and 140 for industry, with more regular increases planned. Some 5000 families will not be able to afford these prices and will be subsidized by the municipality.

Expenditures and projects

From 1996 to 1999, expenditure on the water supply and sewerage remained stable. A big increase was expected in 2000, largely reflecting higher external financing of investments (Table 6.5). Expenditure on water infrastructures has long represented more than half overall public works expenditure. Nevertheless, funding for the operation and maintenance of water works is insufficient.

Water infrastructures are investment-intensive and are a real problem for countries facing a long economic crisis. This is the case in Albania. But, in spite of a shaky political decade, Albania has often received financing from abroad. The World Bank has conducted two projects for the rehabilitation of the irrigation system. The water supply infrastructure is currently benefiting from a number of projects financed by bilateral donors and international organizations. Recently, the European Union through PHARE has concentrated its efforts on sanitation projects, as these were attracting less interest from the international community. The main donors are the European Union (€ 40 million), the EU member States (Austria € 4 million, Germany € 84 million, Italy € 49 million and Norway 30 million kroner per year), the World Bank (€ 26 million) and Japan's International Cooperation Agency (€ 1.6 million). Foreign contributions to Albania's water supply and sanitation projects total some € 205 million.

However, donors find it difficult to identify the most useful projects for Albania. Until recently, information on its actual needs was not readily available. As a first attempt to improve the situation, a "water group" has been set up, on the initiative of the World Bank, to advise donors. The water group holds regular meetings with donor countries. In addition, in May 2001, the Ministry of Territorial Adjustment and Tourism issued its Strategic Framework for the Water Supply and Sanitation Sector in preparation for the national strategy that will be issued in 2002. The strategy will identify the country's infrastructure priorities, as well as set standards for the design and construction of facilities. The European Union has used the Ministry of Territorial Adjustment and Tourism's Strategic Framework to develop its own PHARE/Strategic Approach to the Development of the Water Sector (September 2001).

Table 6.5: Investments and expenditures in the water sector, 1992-2001

	1996	1997	1998	1999	planned 2000	2001
Overall public works expenditures (million euro)	33.9	28.1	30.8	32.7	51.5	..
% of water infrastructure expenditures	52.0	52.4	59.5	50.6	68.7	..
Water supply and sewerage expenditures (million euro)	17.7	14.7	18.4	16.5	35.4	..
Investments by the Albanian Government (million euro)	11.1	2.4	6.0	7.3	5.3	5.8

Source: Strategic Framework for water supply and waste-water sanitation, Ministry of Public Works and Transport, 2001.

6.4   Conclusions and recommendations

Albania is endowed with sufficient surface water and groundwater resources for its various needs, which is a real asset for a Mediterranean country with a dry climate. Moreover, the aquifers as well as the surface hydrographic network, including the artificial reservoirs, are evenly distributed throughout the country. Another advantage is that the groundwater is in most cases still of a good drinkable quality. It is still mostly used only for human consumption. It is vital to manage these resources in a sustainable way for future generations, a task that Albania is completely underestimating at present.

Water is a key resource for most economic and social activities. In Albania, surface waters are traditionally used for both non-consumption (as hydroelectricity, tourism) and consumption (irrigation, industry) and receive all the pollution generated and discharged by anthropogenic activities. The threat from industrial pollution has eased since the early 1990s, except in a few hotspots. Nowadays most of the pressure comes from domestic pollution in urban areas that are developing at full speed totally uncontrolled by any urban planning. Ultimately, the polluted rivers contaminate the coastal areas, which have lost their appeal and are no longer suitable for recreation and fishing. If this situation continues, the further development of economic activities and human welfare could be badly affected in the long run.

Therefore, in managing its water resources, the challenge for Albania is twofold:
- Keep the groundwater resources suitable for drinking, protect them from any contamination from the surface and further ensure their sustainable management for future generations;

- Improve the management of effluents in order to better protect surface waters and the seashore, so that fishing, agriculture and tourism can continue there in the long run.

Related short-term actions should be strategically targeted and implemented without delay. Longer-term developments should be in line with the policies of the European Union.

Short-term objectives

Albania should properly manage its precious water resources starting with the aquifers that show signs of contamination (below Tirana and its suburbs) or of salinization (along the seashores). The current situation is due to uncontrolled management: neither the quantities withdrawn, nor the location and methods of withdrawal are known or controlled. The 1996 Law on Water Resources was a first attempt to introduce sound and long-term management, and integrates the main principles of the EU Water Directive. The Law contains excellent provisions but has never been implemented. It should be enforced urgently and its provisions put into practice.

Recommendation 6.1:
(a) *The Government of Albania, through the National Water Council and with the support of all its members, should urgently enforce the 1996 Law on Water Resources and the related regulations. The Technical Secretariat of the National Water Council should set in motion the following expeditiously:*
- *Management by river basin should be put into practice as provided by the Law; river basin authorities should be set up and should manage their water resources;*

- *Water abstraction permits for groundwater and surface water should be properly registered; this should apply to all entities defined by the Law, i.e. hydropower plants, irrigation enterprises and drinking-water enterprises (be they private or State-owned);*
- *Proper implementation of sanitary protection perimeters is required around the water uptakes intended for drinking water;*
- *Enforcement of the water abstraction charges; the enterprises abstracting water should report on the quantity they abstract; the related data should be registered, compiled and used as a management tool, in particular at the basin level;*
- *The money collected from the water abstraction charges should help pay for the functioning of the river basin authorities and their projects.*

(b) The coordination role of Technical Secretariat of National Water Council should be strengthened and it should implement its tasks and obligations deriving from the 1996 Law on Water Resources.

The intense extraction of gravel from riverbeds is endangering agricultural land as well as urban areas. According to the 1996 Law on Water Resources, gravel and sand are in State ownership (art. 3) and their extraction from rivers is subject to a permit from the National Water Council (art. 20), an obligation never enforced. Measures should be taken to stop this practice and propose alternative building materials.

Recommendation 6.2:
The National Water Council, with the help of its river basin agencies, of the regional environmental agencies and of the construction police and State police, as appropriate, should combat the illegal uptaking of gravel and sand. Places where this practice can take place under control without endangering the environment should be defined under EIA procedures.

Improving the drinking-water supply in order to protect the population from diseases is high on the Albanian agenda. This is illustrated by the high number of ongoing projects for water supply and water treatment and the associated high investments. The Government is also pursuing an active policy to introduce market instruments into water management (concessions, semi-private companies, municipal companies, etc.) and transfer their ownership to local governments in order to ensure their efficient operation and maintenance. The Strategic Framework for the Development and Management of the Water Supply and Sanitation Sector in Albania is a useful attempt by the Ministry of Territorial Adjustment and Tourism to indicate priorities and guide donor countries.

The discharge of untreated water in rivers and coastal zones is also increasingly threatening human health and limiting numerous human activities. Treating these waters is another immense and costly task, too costly given the country's current economic potential. In the long run, all towns and villages with more than 2000 inhabitants (see European Union regulations) should be equipped with public sewerage and treatment facilities. But, in the short term, a targeted approach is to be followed: hotspots should be identified, prioritized and eliminated in the most cost-effective way. There are two kinds of hotspots: (i) discharges of domestic waste water in rapidly developing urban areas and in coastal zones; and (ii) discharges of polluted water from industrial sites.

Waste-water discharges from urban areas typically have a high concentration of organic matter and faecal bacteria, although their toxicity is low. The impact is especially detrimental in coastal zones, where there is tourism and fishing. The European Union, under PHARE, is paying particular attention to waste-water treatment in the coastal cities in southern Albania and intends to finance projects for extensive waste-water lagooning (oxidation lagoons). This unsophisticated technology is well adapted to the Mediterranean climate; it requires minimum maintenance and little energy for its operation. However, the main challenge will be to collect all discharges into one sewerage network connected to the facility, a task that is today impossible as urban planning is inexistent and buildings mushroom haphazardly outside urban zones. Organized urban planning in cities and land-use planning in the countryside have a strong impact on the development of all infrastructures and reduce their costs. If Albania wants to solve the problem, it has to take immediate steps, as the uncontrolled development of buildings will make their connections to water supply, waste-water, electricity, telecom utilities and roads very costly for society as a whole.

Recommendation 6.3:
The Ministry of Local Government and Decentralization should encourage all relevant administrative authorities, and chiefly the municipal authorities of the biggest cities, to develop urban plans and especially master plans for water supply and sewerage networks. Municipalities should strengthen their competences regarding water infrastructure planning and management, taking advantage of the numerous possibilities for assistance offered by the international community.

A similar targeted approach is necessary for industrial hotspots. Facilities that release significant amounts of toxicity should be identified and mapped. Particular attention should be paid to the medium-size but highly polluting industries, such as the leather industry, slaughterhouses, the dairy and food-processing industry and industrial animal-breeding installations. At present, the oil industry is a major concern. Its waste-water discharges pollute groundwater, rivers, reservoirs and the sea. For such big polluters, whether private or State-owned, an environmental permit should be compulsory.

At present, no real environmental operating permit exists in Albania. The so-called "environmental licence" does not regulate day-to-day pollution, although it does ensure that, at its nominal production capacity, an industry respects the water quality objective of the receiving water body. Due to their importance, environmental permits in the worst industrial hotspots should be issued at ministerial level, while all other less important permits should be the responsibility of the regional environment agencies. Moreover, incentives should be developed to encourage industry to improve its environmental performance. For instance, emissions charges or tax exemptions should be introduced and their amount re-invested for improving industry's environmental performance. To negotiate these permits, there should be a few well-trained and experienced inspectors at the Ministry, capable of working out measures with the enterprises and pressing them to comply within a defined but realistic timeframe. In extreme cases, production sites should be closed down.

Recommendation 6.4:
The Ministry of Environment should identify and draw up a list of industrial hotspots that have a significant adverse impact on the environment, and rank them. Environmental objectives, and in particular water emissions objectives, for these plants or for particular industrial sectors (firstly

the oil industry, private and State-owned), should be set or negotiated and introduced into the environmental permits. Environmental permits for these facilities should be compulsory and handled at the Ministry, and environmental, economic and other incentives worked out in parallel. (see also recommendations 2.1, 7.3(b), and 9.1)

Long-term policy objectives

Joining the European Union is Albania's ultimate objective. Therefore, the long-term objective in water management is approximation to the EU Water Directive 2000/60/EC that establishes a framework for Community action in the field of water policy. Already Albania is moving in the right direction with the upcoming introduction of river basin district management. However, protecting the water itself is not enough. An integrated approach will have to be envisaged in the future. First, the ecosystems surrounding the water need to be protected as well as the water itself. And second, further integration of water protection and sustainable water management into other policy areas such as agriculture, urban development, transport, tourism, fisheries and regional development is necessary. Albania will have to decide for which activities or uses the different water bodies will be responsible and will have to shape their protection and management rules and standards accordingly. This should be reflected in a national water strategy and a national water resources plan, encompassing the management and the protection of water resources (both requested under article 6 item 3 of the Law on Water Resources), and further refined at the river basin level (river basin management plans).

Recommendation 6.5:
The Ministry of Environment, in cooperation with the National Water Council and other entities (ministries and institutions) involved in water management, should draw up water quality standards and set water emission limits, taking as reference the corresponding standards of the European Union.

Recommendation 6.6:
Under the joint auspices of the National Water Council, the Ministry of Environment and the Ministry of Territory Adjustment and Tourism, should revise, adopt and implement the draft national water strategy of 1997 without further delay. It should define a clear policy towards a sustainable use, management and protection of Albania's water bodies. The strategy's revision

should involve all the ministries that are members of the National Water Council and institutes that carry out water management tasks. (see also recommendation 1.1)

Albania cannot afford comprehensive water monitoring at present. However, data requirements on water resources, their quantity and quality, as well as the impact of discharges, should be selected and prioritized according to national strategic goals (that should be defined in the water strategy). Under the leadership of the Ministry of Environment and of the National Water Council, all the institutions involved in water monitoring should work to establish a cost-effective and demand-driven water monitoring system to provide the

necessary information for effective decision-making in water resource management and protection. Recommendation 4.1 in Chapter 4 calls for the creation of a separate institutional unit for environmental monitoring. Water monitoring should increasingly follow the EU Water Directive (2000/60/EC) and in particular its annex V.

The poor supply of drinking water, which is sporadic and of mediocre quality, does not encourage people to respect their water resources and use them in a sustainable way. In parallel with the investments that aim at improving the distribution and quality of water, campaigns should be launched to raise public awareness. (see recommendation 4.4)

Chapter 7

WASTE MANAGEMENT

7.1   Introduction

The management of municipal and industrial waste is essential to sustainable development, but it cannot be considered in isolation from the overall political and economic conditions of the transition period. Waste management requires resources for infrastructure, operations, maintenance, research and development, and these resources have been lacking in Albania.

Industrial and municipal waste management is one of the top priorities of environmental management in Albania, for the following reasons:

- There is no legal framework for waste management;
- Abandoned contaminated industrial sites have serious adverse effects on the population and the environment;
- There is no sound management of municipal waste in the major urban centres;
- There is a lack of research and development in the methods of waste treatment and utilization;
- The demolition of illegal buildings in the big cities is generating much construction debris;
- Old cars are abandoned, and there is no system for utilizing scrap cars for spare parts.

7.2   Industrial waste

General situation in industry

In 1990 industry contributed more than 37 per cent of GDP; this share fell to about 12 per cent in 1999. Industry was based on the mining and processing of polymetallic ores and coal. The main industrial sectors were smelting, metallurgy, oil refining and chemical production. The volume of the main industrial products was sharply lower in 2000 than in 1989. At present few industrial facilities, such as those used for the extraction of crude oil and natural gas, lignite production, chromium ores, coke and refinery are still in operation. As a result, less industrial waste is being generated. Most metallurgy technologies were imported from China

in the 1960s and 1970s. These technologies do not have units for the utilization or treatment of industrial waste (solid, liquid and gaseous). All effluents from industrial facilities are discharged into the environment without any treatment.

Albania is fairly rich in mineral resources. According to the Geological Survey, 2001, the present potential reserves of mineral resources are (in million tons) chromium ores: 5; copper ores: 45-50; nickel ores: 500; coal: 350. Past and current industrial activities are based on the use of natural resources as primary raw materials.

Between 1992 and 2000 the industrial output of many major products decreased by 50-70 per cent; some are no longer manufactured at all. These products include all metallurgical concentrates, nickel, chemical products and lignite concentrates. The main reasons for this are the changing social and economic conditions, and the obsolete technologies and equipment used. The chemical industry as a whole has practically shut down. At present few big industrial plants are operating, but a significant amount of industrial solid waste is still stored at these sites. Many of these sites are contaminated by toxic chemicals and heavy metals; they are sources of soil, air and groundwater contamination.

Industrial waste generation

At present industrial production consists of mining and the enrichment of copper and chromium ores, coal (lignite) mining, oil exploration and oil processing, and construction materials (see Table 7.1), so most industrial waste is generated by these industries. For the industrial facilities that were closed down, the main environmental problem is accumulated waste from previous operations.

In 2000 the highest quantities of industrial hazardous waste were generated in the chromium and copper industry. The quantities of accumulated waste from mining and ore enrichment are given in table 7.2.

Table 7.1: The volumes of the main industrial products, 1996-2001

Product		Unit	1996	1997	1998	2000	2001 QI
1. EXTRACTING INDUSTRY							
Crude oil		tons	4,882,214	359,666	364,627	314,304	77,755
Natural gas		thousand m³	22,698	18,271	16,551	11,490	2,357
Lignite		tons	100,946	39,826	48,706	20,666	507
2. NON ENERGETIC RAW MATERIALS							
Chromium ore		tons	263,358	157,203	150,285	57,042	10,324
Chromium ore (42%)		"	113,361	84,423	81,994	156,399	..
3. MANUFACTURING INDUSTRY							
Benzene		tons	36,658	15,405	21,316	23,551	3,620
Gas-oil		"	94,616	57,035	90,670	72,193	7,462
Kerosene		"	25,385	10,959	1,870	2,420	..
Lubricating oils		"	50	35	42	24	..
Solar oil and distillate		"	75,599	43,867	65,102	65,836	7,913
Black oil (Mazout)		"	114,458	90,961	62,006	74,133	30,687
Petroleum bitumen		"	19,597	16,900	15,782	31,888	4,229
Petroleum coke		"	63,473	33,678	57,842	45,533	4,771
Carbonic ferrouschrome		tons	31,189	31,445	30,252	8,744	..
Copper wires and cables		"	121	..	..	111	51
Rolled wrought steel		"	21,367	20,533	19,527	64,736	26,604
ELECTRIC POWER PRODUCTION							
Electric power		Million kWh	5,926	5,184	5,068	4,737	1,025

Source: Ministry of Environment, 2001.

Table 7.2: Volume of solid industrial waste accumulated by 2000

(million m³)

Mining industry		
Coal mining		3.0
Iron nickel extraction		4.2
Copper extraction		12.0
Chromium extraction		18.8
Enrichment industry		
Copper ore enrichment		11.8
Chromium ore enrichment		2.5

Source: Ministry of Public Economy and Privatization, 2000.

About 18.8 million m³ of solid waste from the mining of chromium ores and about 2.5 million m³ from their enrichment have been stored. (see Table 7.2) This waste contains hexavalent chromium, which is highly toxic and a threat to people and the environment. Waste from the copper industry, including mine tailings, contain 0.2 per cent copper, 10 per cent sulphur, as well as zinc, other heavy metals and inert material (exact composition is not available). It is also considered hazardous waste.

Nearly all copper-ore mining and enrichment has been discontinued, but surface water and groundwater are still contaminated by copper and other heavy metals from industrial waste storage sites.

Industrial contaminated sites and hazardous waste

The United Nations Environment Programme, in its "Post-Conflict Environmental Assessment" of Albania, identified the main industrial sites contaminated by toxic chemicals as those at Vlorë, Durrës, Elbasan, Rubik, Patos, Ballsh, Fier and Laç (see Figure 7.1). They are described below.

The chlor-alkali and polyvinyl chloride (PVC) plant, at four kilometres from Vlorë, is a former chemical plant that produced chlorine, caustic soda, vinyl chloride monomer and polyvinyl chloride. It was closed in 1992 and considerably damaged in 1997. Chlor-alkali electrolysis was used and contaminated about 50,000-60,000 m² of soil with mercury to a depth 1.0-1.5 metres; the concentration of mercury is 1000 times the EU standard. Mercury-containing sludge is now stored between the site and the Bay. The site is also contaminated by chlorinated hydrocarbons, and it is located in a residential area. Farm animals graze around the sites, and vegetables are grown nearby. The groundwater is contaminated by mercury. The water is drunk by animals and used to irrigate vegetables, and it drains into the sea. Exposure to mercury may result in damage to the human brain, lungs and kidneys. It is especially dangerous for children. No measures have been taken to protect the local population or the environment.

The chemical plant in Durrës produced sodium trichromate, lindane and thiram pesticides. It is situated in a residential area, and was closed in 1990. A very large quantity of chromium-containing waste is stored on the site. The site and the adjacent land are contaminated by pesticides. Groundwater is also contaminated by pesticides and chromium. The concentration of chlorobenzene in groundwater is 4.4 mg/litre, which is 4,000 times the EU standard. A dumpsite for waste containing chromium and lindane is situated near the former plant. About 370 tons of toxic chemicals are stored in an open facility 1.5 km from the former plant. People continue to live in this area and to graze animals there. In addition, the site is situated on low-lying land with flood risks. In the event of a flood, the surrounding land, including some residential areas, would be contaminated by chromium and pesticides.

The metallurgical complex in Elbasan produced steel, coke, pig iron, and nickel. The plant was closed in 1990, although there is still a scrap smelter working with obsolete equipment and technologies. Tailings (about 1.5-2.0 millions tons) from the metallurgical operation contaminate soil and groundwater with heavy metals (chromium, nickel and manganese). Water in the Shkumbini River is also contaminated by heavy metals and phenol. As it has no gas purification system, the smelter causes air pollution, spewing out 20,160 tons of particles, 924 tons of CO and SO_2 into the air. There are no data on the quality of river water and groundwater because there is no monitoring.

The copper plant in Rubik was closed in 1998. It produced refined copper for wiring. For 60 years the plant generated about 30,000 tons of mineral residues a year. Groundwater, which is used for drinking, is contaminated by copper.

The Marize oilfield in Patos, with 200 km^2 and 2000 wells, was the largest oilfield supplying the Ballsh refinery. Capacity has now been reduced to 400 tons/day of crude oil, instead of 2,000 tons at full capacity. Environmental problems include groundwater and soil contamination by oil due to obsolete equipment (4-8 tons of oil lost per day) and sulphurous and hydrocarbon emissions into the air. The local population is exposed to the pollution and suffers serious health problems.

The Ballsh oil refinery processes 300,000 tons of oil a year. Insufficient treatment of its waste water has resulted in the contamination of the Gjanices River and groundwater. The high content of sulphur in the oil has resulted in the emission of sulphur dioxide and hydrogen sulphide. Other air pollutants, such as hydrocarbons and carbon dioxide, are also emitted. No system for the purification of stack gases has been introduced. There are no facilities for waste-water treatment, and there is no system for monitoring the quality of surface water and groundwater.

The chemical fertilizer plant in Fier plant functioned from 1967 to 1992. During this period it used oil with a high sulphur content. Arsenic solutions were used for purifying sulphur compounds, and 850 m^3 of these arsenic solutions, at a concentration of 25 g/litre, are deposited in four old steel columns. The soil samples taken by a UNEP team indicate that the level of arsenic pollution is 0.83-17.23 g/kg. Although the topsoil pollution is limited, arsenic percolated the groundwater, which drains into the Gjanica River. The local residents use the water from the Gjanica River for various domestic purposes, including drinking, because there are no other sources of water in this region. So far nothing has been done to treat the stored arsenic solution.

The superphosphate plant at Lac used calcium phosphate in its technological process. Nearly 300,000 tons of iron-rich residues are deposited on this site. At present nothing is being done to protect water from contamination. Samples of surface water show that it contains high levels of copper and arsenic. As a result, the upper secondary aquifer of underground water is probably being contaminated.

The environmental impact of these sites has never been assessed. Neither industry nor the Government is doing anything to clean up contaminated sites and protect the population. Protection could include relocating people and farm animals away from contaminated sites, because

Figure 7.1: Major contaminated sites in Albania

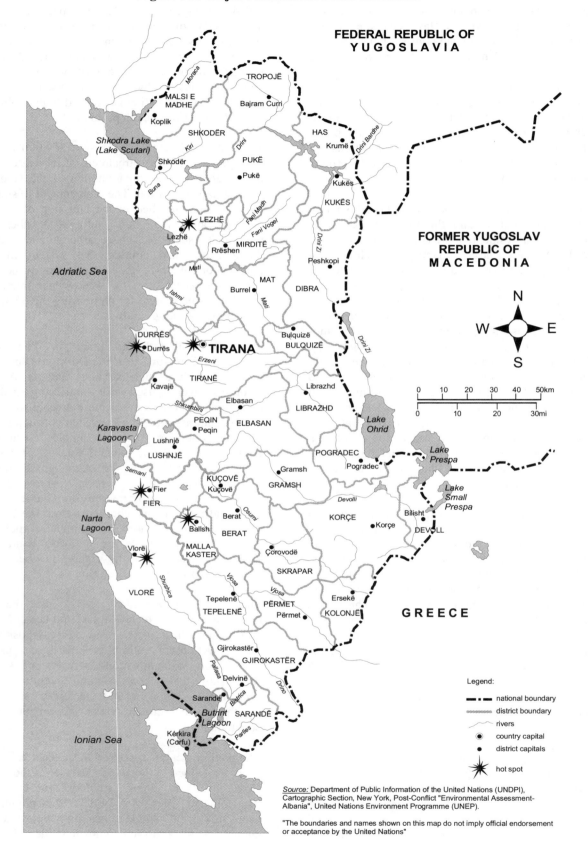

Source: Department of Public Information of the United Nations (UNDPI), Cartographic Section, New York, Post-Conflict "Environmental Assessment-Albania", United Nations Environment Programme (UNEP).

"The boundaries and names shown on this map do not imply official endorsement or acceptance by the United Nations"

homes could also be contaminated by these hazardous substances; decontaminating sites and preventing further contamination at other industrial facilities that are still in operation; monitoring groundwater and surface water at these sites, especially for sources of drinking water; carrying out environmental impact assessment studies with a special focus on health effects; introducing waste-water treatment for the industrial facilities still in operation; and preventing oil losses during oil exploration, transport and refinery by introducing more effective equipment.

Liability for past industrial contamination is a big issue in the cleaning-up of contaminated sites and their privatization. There is no specific legislation on the liability and responsibility for past industrial pollution and it is not clear who should pay. During the privatization negotiations a prospective buyer could discuss with the Ministry of the Environment and the Ministry of Industry and Energy who should pay. The Ministries may agree that the Government should shoulder part of the cost. Responsibility could also be shared between the Government and the future owner(s). For example, the environmental remediation project for the Patos-Mrinza oilfield includes both a license agreement and a petroleum agreement that assign responsibility to the Government and Albpetrol for significant environmental pollution that occurred before the collective partner group started operations. A separate project on the subject is envisaged.

In 2000 the Ministry of Industry and Energy drew up an inventory of hazardous substances at 36 enterprises, 40 trade organizations and 22 public service enterprises. Accumulated quantities of hazardous substances by category based on their properties are presented in Table 7.3. The data cover chemical enterprises.

Table 7.4 gives data on accumulated quantities of hazardous substances at other enterprises, including chemical companies.

By 2000 the quantity of hazardous substances accumulated at industrial facilities totalled 3,105 tons, of which 2,115 tons are stored as obsolete chemicals and 990 tons could be used as raw materials. No measures are being taken to destroy these obsolete hazardous chemicals. Most hazardous substances were generated in the chemical industry (1531 tons); other sources were the oil industry (706 tons) and light industry

Table 7.3: Accumulated quantities of hazardous substances by category, 2000

Chemical properties	Quantity (tons)
Total	1,531
Very toxic	40
Toxic	575
Extremely flammable	110
Oxidized	330
Harmful for health	300
Irritating	12
Others	164

Source: The Ministry of Public Economy and Privatization, 2000.

(501 tons) (see Table 7.4). There are no practical measures to prevent industrial waste generation at source, or to recycle or reuse it. All industrial waste is stored in uncontrolled landfills.

In addition, according to the former Ministry ofIndustry and Energy, about 1000 tons of obsolete pesticides have accumulated in agriculture (farms and storage). They are stored in environmentally unsatisfactory conditions and represent a real threat to the population and the environment. There are no facilities for their destruction or disposal.

Hazardous municipal waste, such as batteries and used oil, is not separated, and it is deposited at uncontrolled landfills. Hazardous industrial waste is stored at abandoned industrial sites or together with municipal waste. Unfortunately, there are no statistics on how much hazardous waste is accumulated or generated at present.

7.3 Municipal waste generation and disposal

Waste generation

In the past few years migration from rural to urban areas has considerably increased, and this has resulted in the generation of more municipal waste. The annual average increase in municipal waste generation during the past five years was between 8 and 10 per cent in the big cities. In 1998 the reported quantity of municipal waste disposed of was 520,000 tons. These figures are estimates, because there is no equipment to weigh the municipal waste delivered to landfills. In addition, only about 50-70 per cent of urban waste is taken to landfills; the rest is simply dumped illegally. There is a very urgent need for an information system for municipal waste collection, transport and disposal to obtain the full picture and plan accordingly.

Table 7.4: Quantities of chemicals accumulated by different industries by 2000 (tons)

Sector	Total	Usable	Obsolete	% of Total
Total	**3,105**	**990**	**2,115**	**100**
Chemical industry	1,531	351	1,181	49
Oil industry	706	306	400	23
Light industry	501	263	238	14
Metallurgical industry	218	70	148	7
Mining industry	83	0	83	3
Mechanical industry	66	0	66	2

Source : The Ministry of Public Economy and Privatization, 2000.

Figure 7.2: Municipal waste generation in selected countries, mid-1990s

kg/capita

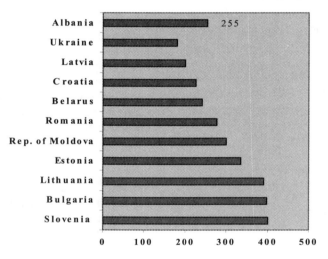

Sources : UNECE, Environmental Performance Review, various issues 1995-2001.

According to 1999-2000 data from the Ministry of Environment, municipal waste generation stood at 0.7 kg/inhabitant/day or 255 kg/inhabitant/year in the four main cities. A comparison of municipal waste generated per capita in selected countries in transition is given in Figure 7.2. The figure shows that the situation in Albania is similar to that in other countries in the early stages of transition.

In most cities waste is collected and transported by a municipal or privatized waste management service company. Rural areas are not yet covered by municipal waste management services. The main components of municipal waste in the biggest cities are inert material, plastics and vegetable scraps.

Waste disposal

The disposal of municipal waste requires a solution. All municipal waste, including waste that is collected and transported, is deposited at landfills that are uncontrolled and in many cases illegal. There is no inventory of such sites. The Sharra site is used for the disposal of municipal waste from Tirana. There is no control over the quantity and composition of its waste. A visit of the site revealed that all kind of waste can be found there, including municipal, industrial and medical waste.

Waste is also burned in open areas. Smoke containing toxic substances (dioxins, furans) is a source of serious air contamination, at a site situated 2 km from a residential area. Some people scavenge reusable materials from the waste, and some even live on the waste tips.

The Sharra site is situated on the slope of the Erzeni River valley. There is neither a drainage system nor a waterproof layer to prevent leaching and percolation into the groundwater. There are currently no investigations into the quality of surface water and groundwater, and there is no monitoring of the groundwater quality in the vicinity of the site. Groundwater, which is used as drinking water and for irrigation, could be contaminated by heavy metals and toxic organic substances. The same is true for the Erzeni River. However, there are no data on the composition of groundwater and river water.

The same unsatisfactory environmental conditions prevail at other landfills. For example, landfills in Durrës are situated near the city in a wetland. There is no waste management, no control and no monitoring.

There is a proposal to build environmentally sound landfills in six cities (approved by the Government in May 1999), but international funding has so far been available only for a feasibility study for the project at the Sharra landfill. This project aims to improve the overall management of both municipal and medical waste in the Tirana region. A new landfill was planned in Lezhë, but the site chosen was too low, and it was flooded once construction began.

There are no facilities for sorting, processing or recycling municipal waste. Some sorting of glass bottles (only bottles, not pieces of glass), paper and cardboard, scrap steel, aluminium cans and small quantities of scrap copper takes place. Scrap steel is sent to the Elbasan metallurgical plant. Glass bottles are collected, sterilized and reused by alcoholic or non-alcoholic drinks companies. Paper and cardboard are sorted only in small quantities at a paper-recycling plant in Tirana, where they used to be sent before the facility became subject to privatization. Aluminium cans are usually exported for reprocessing to neighbouring countries (mostly Greece), and a very small share goes to a small private Albanian aluminium smelter. There is no information available about the people or companies that sort and reuse such waste.

Few landfill sites for municipal waste disposal meet international landfill construction standards and health norms. There are no national norms and standards. Existing landfills (actually simple dumpsites) do not have any insulating plastic lining to protect groundwater against the leaching of hazardous substances. They are major sources of surface and groundwater contamination, especially industrial waste landfills that release heavy metals and organic chemicals. Other adverse effects of waste landfills are the contamination of surface and groundwater when nutrients and toxic substances seep into the soil. There are no bulldozers to cover waste with earth and no workers involved in waste disposal at the sites. None of the landfills has a drainage system. There are no special wells around landfills for monitoring.

Industrial waste is deposited either separately or together with municipal waste. When municipal waste is deposited together with industrial waste at uncontrolled landfills, the environmental impact includes the evaporation of toxic organic substances, soil contamination and the creation of unhygienic epidemiological conditions in the vicinity. This affects human health and results in the deterioration of the biodiversity of the ecosystems near waste disposal sites.

Villages are not covered by any municipal waste management service, and they have no landfills that meet environmental requirements. Waste is dumped on any available site in the villages or nearby. There are no enterprises to collect, transport and dispose of municipal waste in rural areas. There are no facilities for municipal waste incineration on an industrial scale.

Unfortunately, there is a lack of public information (e.g. brochures or other material) on municipal waste disposal, in particular with regard to sorting and recycling. There are no training courses on waste management for the public, no special TV programmes, or educational programmes on waste management in schools and universities in order to educate the population about how to collect and sort municipal waste. The information to the public should include how to prevent or minimize the generation of waste in each household (good housekeeping practices). Illegal dumping of municipal waste also could be prevented through public-awareness campaigns.

Hospital waste

At present there are 51 hospitals in Albania producing about 7.3 tons of medical and other hospital waste per day in seven cities. This amounts to 2,600 tons per year.

(Tirana, Durrës, Pogradec and Korçe) have privatized the collection and transportation of municipal waste.

The Law on the Organization and Functioning of Local Government stipulates that local government (villages and municipalities) can take its own decisions and fulfil its functions, including environmental protection as a whole and waste management (collection, transport, treatment and disposal), at the local level.

There are several institutions responsible for medical waste management, including hospitals, the Medical Commission, the Health Inspectorate, and the Technical-Consultant Commission (see also Chapter 12).

Economic instruments

Financial resources for implementing policies and projects to improve the overall waste management system throughout the country are not sufficient and not secure. This situation is not expected to improve in the near future. It is important to develop new economic instruments, such as taxes on gas, liquid and solid industrial discharges, to raise revenue for waste management. Such instruments could also help to prevent waste generation at source (see also Chapter 2).

Cleaner production

Albania has not yet introduced a cleaner production programme, and nor are there any international projects for cleaner production. It is important for Albania to start now, during the transition period, to establish and implement such a programme and to replace old and inefficient technologies. Its main goal would be to reduce waste generation at source and make technological processes more efficient.

The new NEAP does envisage the establishment of a centre for clean technologies to:

- Develop a legal framework for the development and introduction of cleaner production;
- Strengthen the inter-ministerial structure for the implementation of sectoral environmental and cleaner production policies and the development of environmentally sound technologies;
- Strengthen the national and local system for crisis management in the event of industrial accidents.

In addition, the centre could conduct environmental audits, provide training and disseminate information on cleaner production, provide technical expertise and draft policy documents on the introduction of cleaner technologies and modern technologies at new plants, and promote cleaner production processes to modernize existing enterprises (where possible). The centre could also promote the introduction of ISO 14000 standards for new enterprises.

The establishment of a cleaner production centre in Albania is an urgent and important task for the Government and the international community. The centre could be established within the framework of activities organized by the United Nations Industrial Development Organization (UNIDO) and UNEP for the creation of cleaner production centres in countries in transition, taking into account the positive experience of other such countries, for example Croatia.

7.6 Conclusions and recommendations

The management of industrial and municipal waste is one of Albania's environmental protection priorities. Urgent measures are needed to improve the overall situation, including a legal framework for waste management, the clean-up of abandoned contaminated industrial sites having serious adverse effects on the population and the environment; a system for the environmentally sound management of municipal waste in big cities and the introduction of waste management in rural areas; research and development in waste treatment and utilization methods; the allocation of financial resources to waste management at national and local levels; the disposal of construction debris resulting from the demolition of illegal constructions in big cities; and the utilization of car scrap.

There is no framework law on waste management in Albania, although both the 1993 and the 2002 Laws on Environmental Protection contain some provisions on waste management. The main legislation on waste management includes Decision No. 26 of the Council of Ministers on Hazardous Waste and Residues, the Law on Public Waste Disposal and the Law on Public Waste Disposal Taxation. This legislation is not enough to cover all aspects of waste management, because it does not provide for concrete measures for improvement. The main disadvantage of this legislation is that it does not include a policy on waste prevention, especially in industrial installations and service enterprises. In addition, there are no waste regulations to implement existing legislation.

Recommendation 7.1:
The Ministry of Environment in cooperation with the Ministry of Industry and Energy should speed up the development and implementation of a law and regulations on hazardous waste and chemicals management. This law should be consistent with European Union legislation.

At present municipal waste is disposed of at landfills that do not meet any environmental or health norms and standards. There are no facilities for the separation, sorting, treatment or recycling of municipal waste.

Existing landfills do not have any insulating lining or drainage system to protect groundwater from the leaching of hazardous substances. In addition, waste burned in the open, and toxic smoke containing methane and other toxic substances (dioxins, furans) constitute a source of serious air pollution. At present the surface and groundwater quality is not monitored in the vicinity of these sites. The environmental impact of existing landfills has never been assessed. There is no municipal waste management in rural areas. There is no system in place to educate the public and raise its awareness of municipal waste management.

Recommendation 7.2:
The Government, in close cooperation with the Ministry of Environment, the Ministry of Local Government and Decentralization and the municipalities, should take the necessary steps to find financial and human resources to:

- *Assess the environmental impact of existing municipal landfills and take measures to reduce that impact;*
- *Monitor groundwater and surface water in the vicinity of landfills;*
- *Introduce municipal waste management systems in rural areas; and*
- *Launch public information campaigns on municipal waste management, focusing on waste prevention, through the educational system and the mass media. In this context the Ministry of Environment should prepare special guidelines on the prevention, reduction and handling of municipal waste for municipalities and the public.*

Most big industrial plants are closed and abandoned. A significant amount of industrial solid waste is stored at these sites. All sites are contaminated by hazardous chemicals, oil and heavy metals. They are sources of soil, air and groundwater contamination. People living near these sites are exposed to toxic substances and contaminated water.

Recommendation 7.3:
(a) The Council of Ministers, the Ministry of Environment, the Ministry of Industry and Energy and the municipalities should focus on providing financial and human resources to mitigate the risks caused by abandoned dangerous industrial sites, in particular, they should:

- *Relocate people and farm animals away from contaminated sites, because homes are also contaminated by those hazardous substances which are at the sites;*
- *Decontaminate sites and prevent any further contamination;*
- *Introduce a groundwater and surface water monitoring system around the sites, especially for drinking water, and ensure that contaminated groundwater is not used for drinking or irrigation;*
- *Assess the environmental impact, and especially the human health impact, of all contaminated sites;*
- *Local authorities should, as the first urgent step, put up fences and special warning signs around contaminated sites in their jurisdiction, indicating that they are contaminated, and forbid access to them.*

(b) The Ministry of Environment and the Ministry of Industry and Energy should apply appropriate legislation to improve waste-water treatment for all industrial facilities in operation in order to prevent further contamination of the environment and, in particular, oil losses during oil exploration, transport and refinery. (see also recommendation 6.4)

The Ministry of Industry and Energy estimates that about 1,000 tons of obsolete pesticides have been accumulated by the agricultural sector. They are stored in environmentally unsatisfactory conditions and represent a real threat to the population and the environment. At present there are no facilities for their destruction and disposal. This problem is common in many countries in transition. Thermal or chemical methods could be used for this purpose. It is an urgent matter that should be considered as a priority for bilateral and multilateral cooperation.

Recommendation 7.4:
The Ministry of Environment and the Ministry of Agriculture and Food should collect and find ways to contain, store, and destroy obsolete pesticides and other toxic chemicals in order to reduce risk. Cooperation with neighbouring countries and the international community could help solve this problem.

Cleaner production has not yet been introduced in Albania. Its technologies are old and obsolete. They do not include any treatment of gaseous, liquid or solid waste. It is very important for Albania to start the development and implementation of cleaner production as a tool for reducing the generation of industrial waste at source. So far no action has been taken at government level to promote more environmentally friendly technologies. A centre could be established within the framework of UNIDO/UNEP activities for the creation of cleaner production centres in countries in transition, taking into account the positive experience of other countries in transition.

Recommendation 7.5:
The Ministry of Environment, in close cooperation with the private sector and line ministries, should promote the establishment of a cleaner production centre, which would: conduct environmental audits, provide training and disseminate information on cleaner production; and promote the introduction of ISO 14000 standards.

Albania has embarked on a programme to tear down illegal construction. The resulting debris is contaminated by metal, asbestos, paint and other decorations. All construction debris is landfilled together with municipal waste.

Recommendation 7.6:
The municipalities should undertake the necessary measures to collect and store separately the construction debris at the existing dump sites, so that it can be treated and possibly reused.

Albania generates about 7.3 tons of medical waste per day. At present there are no facilities for hospital waste treatment. There is one second-hand incinerator at the University Hospital Centre in Tirana. This incinerator is only used for the waste from one hospital. Because of a lack of financial and human resources, other hospitals do not collect and transport their waste for incineration. In general, medical waste is landfilled together with municipal waste at uncontrolled sites. This potentially hazardous waste includes infectious, anatomical or pathological waste, sharp objects, chemical, pharmaceutical and radioactive waste, as well as pressurized containers.

Recommendation 7.7
The Ministry of Health, in conformity with the Ministry of Environment, should improve the management of health care waste by standardizing record-keeping, monitoring and good waste-management practices. The Ministry of Health should also identify and encourage local independent suppliers of waste containers and equipment to provide appropriate equipment for health care waste. (see also recommendation 12.6)

Chapter 8

BIODIVERSITY CONSERVATION AND FOREST PROTECTION

8.1   Present state of nature

Introduction

Albania's natural environment is suffering from the adverse impacts of unsustainable agricultural and forestry practices, as well as from industrial pollution and uncontrolled building. Since the 1950s, the forest area has decreased from 45 per cent to 36 per cent of the territory, with consequent soil erosion. Wetlands too have been drained and reclaimed, changing most of the habitats permanently.

Nature conservation policy has developed since the democratic changes of 1990, but it has faced the difficulties that are typical of countries in transition, although more severely so in Albania due to its long isolation and the economic crisis of 1997. Since then, much effort has been put into institutional and legal development. Nature protection legislation is still changing, and should be harmonized with international standards. The National Report on the Convention on Biological Diversity - and the Biodiversity Strategy and Action Plan were issued, and Albania has become a Party to six international conventions on biodiversity conservation (Biodiversity, Ramsar, Desertification, Bern, Bonn and Barcelona Conventions – see Chapter 3). It is preparing to accede to two other instruments (CITES and the Pan-European Biological and Landscape Diversity Strategy). International organizations and various donors have supported this process.

Geography and habitats

Albania is a Mediterranean country on the Balkan Peninsula. Its coastline is 476 km long, with a Mediterranean climate that penetrates the hinterland along the river valleys. Precipitation ranges between 650 mm in the southern part of the pre-mountain zone, and 4000 mm in the alpine zone. Mountainous terrain prevails in the country,

the highest mountain being Korabi (2751 m above sea level). Most mountains are sedimentary and volcanic formations; though some are metamorphic. Alluvial plains, glaciers, marshes and lakes originated in the Quaternary age. The surface hydrographic network is complex. It consists of a dozen significant rivers and 274 either natural or artificial lakes. All these elements shape Albania's habitats.

The main habitat types and subtypes are:

- Coastal communities, which comprise marine communities, marine wetlands, coastal sands, and dunes and seaside rocky coast (see Box 8.1);
- Non-maritime waters, which comprise coastal wetland water (including brackish water) and freshwater bodies (see Box 8.1).

The coastal wetlands and lakes are important sites for the wintering of migratory species (particularly waterfowl). As coastal communities and non-maritime waters are important biological assets, they have been proposed for introduction into the future enlarged protected area network (Box 8.1).

- Bushes form several habitat subtypes, such as temperate heath grove, garrigue, maquis, alpine and sub-alpine habitats;
- Forests are spread over five phyto-climatic zones: (1) the Mediterranean shrub zone with broad-leaved and conifer species, as well as the (2) oak, (3) beech, (4) fir and (5) alpine zones. They cover about 36 per cent of the country (1,030,230 ha) (Box 8.2). Broad-leaved species dominate the forest fund (Table 8.1);
- Pastures occupy mainly meadows, alpine and sub-alpine zones over about 400,000 ha. Sixty per cent of that area is classified as "winter pastures" covering lowland areas up to 1,500 m altitude; the remainder is "summer pasture" at higher altitudes (up to 2,500 m and higher), including alpine vegetation.

Table 8.1: Structure of forest fund

TYPES	Area (ha)	% of total	Volume (thousand m³)	% of total
TOTAL	**1,044,640**	**100.0**	**82,820**	**100.0**
CONIFEROUS, Total	176,070	16.8	18,690	22.6
Black pine	109,840	10.5	11,183	13.5
Fir	16,730	1.5	3,936	4.8
Cluster pine	34,980	3.3	1,023	1.2
Other	15,020	1.5	2,548	3.1
DECIDUOUS, Total	600,680	57.5	56,894	68.7
Beech	194,850	18.6	38,175	46.1
Oak	330,760	31.7	14,455	17.5
Poplar	1,370	0.1	87	0.1
BUSHES, Total	267,890	25.7	7,236	8.7
Strawberry tree	59,440	5.7	2,180	2.6
Hornbeam	92,170	8.8	3,026	3.6
Other	116,280	11.2	2,030	2.5

Source: General Directorate of Forest and Pastures. State of the Environment report, 1997-1998.

Mountainous ecosystems occupy most of the hinterland. The biodiversity in the western part of the country, bordering with Yugoslavia, is also highly significant; therefore this land has been proposed in the enlargement of protected areas (see Box 8.2).

Apart from the terrestrial ecosystems (alpine pastures and meadows, continental and glacial lakes, oak and conifer forests), marines ecosystems and habitats (medium and infralittoral level), coastal ecosystems (sand dunes, delta rivers, alluvial and wet forests, lagoons and coastal lakes) are also endangered. The coastal wetlands and lakes are wintering places for migratory bird species.

Four of them (Karavasta, Narta, Shkodra and Ohrid) have international importance as they shelter more than 20,000 waterfowl species each. However, only Karavasta is classified as a Ramsar site.

Flora and fauna

There are about 3,200 vascular plant species and 756 vertebrate species in Albania. These data are mostly based on case studies and historical information, since there is no inventory or monitoring of species and ecosystems. The numbers of species by taxonomic group are presented in Table 8.2.

Box 8.1:   Proposal for introducing the "Shkumbini river outlet - Divjaka - Karavasta - Semani river outlet" national park into the network of protected areas

Proposed area: 8000 ha
Administration: Lushnjë and Kavajë districts
Current status: National park (1250 ha, Divjaka forest); strict nature reserve (5000 ha, Karavasta lagoon); managed nature reserve (815 ha, Kular)
Proposed status: Under the network of protected areas, the entire area is proposed as a national park

It is undoubtedly the area that deserves the highest protection status, as it contains the river delta, a lagoon, sand dunes, psammophyte, halophyte, hydrophyte and hygrophyte vegetation, pine forests with *Juniperus monocarpa*, three endemic plant species of *Orchis* sp. and *Aster* sp., and *Lutra lutra*. Over 45,000 wintering water birds of about 70 species can be found, giving the area regional and global importance. It provides breeding sites for the globally threatened *Pelecanus crispus*. The area was the first in Albania to be recognized as a Ramsar site. Additionally, it contains an archaeological and historic heritage, thus providing the basis for Eco-tourism development. A management concept for the area has been developed under an EU PHARE project.

Source: *Nature, Landscape and Biodiversity Conservation in Albania, REC, 1997.*

> **Box 8.2:** **Proposal for including the "Livadhi i Harushes - Tethi – Valbona and Gashi river" protected area into the network of protected areas**
>
> Proposed area: 35,000 ha
> Administration: Malsi e Madhe, Shkodër and Tropojë districts
> Current status: Parts of this area have been proclaimed forest national parks (Tethi forest national park 2300 ha; Valbone forest national park 8000 ha, and strict nature reserve Gashi 3000 ha).
> Proposed status: All three areas (now protected as national parks) of some 35,000 ha located in the northern Alps of Albania (including the protected sites of Tethi, Valbone and Gashi) are proposed to be included into the network of protected areas.
>
> It is a transboundary area with Yugoslavia (Serbia and Montenegro). Karst forms, with various high and sharp peaks, ranging from 2000 to 2600 m above sea level. Pine, fir, beech, chestnut forests, extended sub-alpine and alpine meadows and pastures cover the area. Big game, such as bear, wolf, lynx, chamois and wild boar inhabit it. The Valbona and Shala rivers provide a habitat for the globally endangered otter. This beautiful landscape could also become a tourist destination.
>
> Source: *Nature, Landscape and Biodiversity Conservation in Albania, REC, 1997.*

Table 8.2: Number of species by taxonomic group

Taxonomic group	Albania	World
Bacteria	Unknown	>4,000
Viruses	Unknown	>5,000
Protozoa	Unknown	>40,000
Algae	600	>40,000
Fungi	800	>70,000
Ferns	45	>12,000
Bryophytes	500	>14,000
Lichens	400	>17,000
Flowering plants	3,200	250,000
Molluscs	520 (700)	80,000
Insects	4,000 (14,000)	1,000,000
Crustaceans	115	8,000
Echinodermata	46	5,600
Marine fish	249	23,000-30,000
Freshwater fish	64	8,500
Amphibians	15 (16)	4,000
Reptiles	36 (38)	6,500
Birds	323 (335)	9,881
Mammals	70 (84)	4,327

Source: Biodiversity Strategy and Action Plan, 1999.

Note: The number in parentheses indicates the expected number of species.

Endangered and endemic species

About 91 fauna species are assessed as globally threatened, of which 21 are mammal, 18 bird, 4 reptile, 2 amphibian, 28 fish, and 18 invertebrate species. Deer (*Cervus elaphus*) is extinct, while bear (*Ursus arctos*), wolf (*Canis lupus*), lynx (*Lynx lynx*), jackal (*Canis aureus*), chamois (*Rupicapra rupicapra*), roe deer (*Capreolus capeoulus*), and wild boar (*Sus scrofa*) are particularly endangered by poaching. Five bird species are categorized as vulnerable, such as the curly pelican and the king quail. Some species of other terrestrial taxonomic groups (amphibians, reptiles, insects), as well as marine ones (fish species, molluscs, coral), are also endangered.

There are 27 plant species with 150 subspecies that are endemic to Albania, and another 160 plant species that are endemic to Albania, the former Yugoslav Republic of Macedonia, Greece and Yugoslavia. Endemic fauna species are generally less well known, although they are well studied in some particular areas, such as Lake Ohrid, where about 40 molluscs and 2 endemic fish species have been studied in detail.

The flora is mainly endangered by the reduction in habitat areas (particularly wetlands and forests due to agriculture), and by direct damage to or removal of particular species. Illegal logging, mostly for fuel, poses a serious threat to some forest species. The collecting of spice and medicinal plants – laurel leaves, mountain tea, common sage, wild marjoram, rockweed – is widespread.

The Red Books on endangered, rare and endemic plant and animal species were completed and published in the period 1995 - 1997. The number of animal species included in the Red Book for Fauna is around 573, including 273 species of vertebrates or 36 per cent of the country's total. The Red Book for Flora lists 320 species of flowering plants, 45 of mushrooms and 25 of marine plants. Both Red Books should be updated and based on a biodiversity inventory and monitoring, as defined in the Biodiversity Strategy and Action Plan.

Table 8.3: Structure of land use

Land use	1950		1990		1995		1997	
	Thousand ha	%	Thousand ha	%	Thousand ha	%	Thousand ha	%
Total	2,875	100	2,875	100	2,875	100	2,875	100
Agriculture	391	14	704	24	702	24	700	24
Forest	1,282	45	1,045	36	1,052	36	1,026	36
Pasture	816	28	417	15	428	16	445	15
Other	386	13	709	25	693	24	704	25

Source: Ministry of Agriculture and Forestry (Department of Statistics), 2002.

8.2   Pressures on nature

Land use changes

According to the State-of-the-Environment Report, almost 30 per cent of the forestland and about half the pastureland were turned into cultivated land between 1960 and 1980. As a result of the socialist central planning system that based its economic development on intensive agriculture, the area of agricultural land was almost doubled in this period, thus reducing the area of natural ecosystems (table 8.3).

Urbanization and uncontrolled land use occurred mainly in the past decade. General poverty has caused a significant migration of the population from rural areas into urban centres. It has resulted in an increase of illegal buildings throughout the country, but particularly in the coastal zone. Illegal houses have been built not only on land areas but also on forest (table 8.4), pasture and agricultural lands, changing their characteristics irreversibly.

This problem is a result of the lack of proper physical plans, and insufficient control of the application of land and building legislation. In 2001, the Government took some serious steps to control illegal building (i.e. it started to demolish illegal buildings in public city areas). The development of physical plans is a national priority, which should be based on an integrated approach to nature conservation and sustainable land use.

Agriculture

Since the 1960s, agriculture has had the strongest adverse impact on biodiversity in Albania. According to the Biodiversity Strategy and Action Plan, the drainage and reclamation of swamps (250,000 ha), deforestation for new agricultural land (290,000 ha), terracing and the establishment

Table 8.4: Buildings in forest land, 1997

Contraventions	Number of Cases	Surface, ha
Total	745	531
With approval	191	224
Without approval	554	307
Prosecuted	358	..
Penal	225	..
Administratively	133	..

Source: State of the Environment Report, 1997-1998.

of fruit tree plantations, and the cultivation of pastures were all widespread. They were 'justified' by the economic requirements of both extensive and intensive agricultural developments, but have resulted either in the loss or the degradation of ecologically important ecosystems, particularly forests, pastures and wetlands.

Overgrazing has posed a significant threat to ecosystems, since the pasture area decreased from 816,000 ha in 1950 to 445,000 ha in 1997 and can no longer maintain the national flock of about 3 million sheep and goats, which therefore have overgrazed pasture and forest areas, thus damaging forest regeneration (see Chapter 10).

Forestry

Forestry as a sector that uses forest resources is faced with both deforestation and the management problems of its own institutions and agencies undergoing transition. Deforestation is one of the major environmental problems, particularly in peri-urban and rural forests (easily accessible forest areas). Rural poverty, especially during the economic collapse in 1997, caused severe forest damage by illegal logging. It was reported that in 1999 the General Directorate for Forests and

Pastures sold only about 30 per cent of all timber and 40 per cent of all firewood; the rest was cut illegally. In 1997 alone, 5,494 fines for illegal logging were registered for an estimated damage of 232 million leks. Overall, the forest has declined from 45 per cent to 36 per cent in the past half-century.

The companies that harvest forests are mainly private. The General Directorate does not set any conditions on cutting technology and methodology to contractors; thus harvesting is not performed according to good forestry practices. Current forest management is based on outdated plans. It was reported that private companies were drawing up new forest management plans (10 of the 36 were completed by the time of the EPR mission). Scientific forestry institutions were not involved in the preparatory process.

Minor produce from forests is very important for the country's economy. According to the Environmental Centre for Administration and Technology, Albania is one of the most important suppliers and traders of medicinal plants in Europe. In 1995, 7,962,763 kg of medicinal plants were exported. In 1997 the amount decreased to 6,220,852 kg, but still earned Albania 1.8 billion leks. Since 1995, the uncontrolled collection of these plants has increased, while cultivation has decreased, thus leading to over-exploitation and biodiversity degradation.

To improve the forestry sector, the General Directorate issued the Strategy for the Development of the Forestry and Pasture Sector in Albania – Action Plan, in 2001. There are six main forest policy goals:

- To maintain the integrity of the forests and pastures;
- To promote sustainable natural resource management;
- To promote the transition to a market-driven economy;
- To transfer management responsibility for selected State forests and pastures to the local government;
- To improve State management of production forests and the summer pasture resource base; and
- To develop recreation and tourism opportunities in forests and protected areas.

To resolve the forestry and environmental problems, the Forestry Project was established with the support of the World Bank, the Food and Agriculture Organization of the United Nations (FAO) and other international organizations, to provide financial, technical and scientific assistance to the Albanian Government. Rehabilitation of degraded forests is reported to be slow. The support provided by the Forestry Project is insufficient compared to the environmental protection requirements.

A World Bank and FAO review of the forestry sector indicates a steady increase in the General Directorate's annual budget (US$ 4.4 million projected for 2001), amounting to about 0.4 per cent of Albania's public expenditure. More than half the forest budget is spent on personnel costs. Only about 16 per cent are invested in forests and pastures. The review also indicates that forestry expenditures will continue to exceed fiscal income from forest activities.

Forest fires

Forest fires occur mainly in spring and summer, as in the rest of the Mediterranean region. In 1997, the most affected districts were Vlorë, Përmet, Berat, Gramsh, Tirana, Skrapar and Devoll. The burnt forest area amounted to about 2900 ha and burnt pasture to 7000 ha. The General Directorate is responsible for forest fire management. It is reported that other State institutions, as well as district and local authorities, are insufficiently involved in fire prevention and control, or are not involved at all. To improve the situation, the FAO Technical Assistance to the Forestry Project has supported the development of a national forest fire management strategy and action plan.

Hunting

In 1997-1998, hunting decreased considerably as foreign hunters cancelled their visits to Albania following the 1997 crisis. The increase in hunted game species in 1998 points to increased poaching (Table 8.5).

Uncontrolled hunting is a major factor of disturbance for biodiversity, especially during the winter, when migratory winter birds are at risk. Illegal hunting methods are used, even poison. Carnivorous mammals and birds of prey are chiefly affected. The result is a reduction in the population of some species.

Table 8.5: Number of hunted animals, 1997-1998

Name*	1997	1998
Bear	521	536
Beaver	841	1,823
Wild cat	354	202
Lynx	23	25
Otter	442	446
Chamois	441	583
Roe deer	772	521
Badger	1,937	1,608
Wolf	2,656	2,565
Fox	34,262	43,105
Marten	854	892
Wild boar	1,154	954
Hare	..	82,341
Pheasant	..	..
Heath cock	..	187
Mountain grouse	..	85,490
Field grouse	..	13,236
Pelican	..	..

Source: State of the Environment Report, 1997-1998.

* Species declared as game, according to the Law on Hunting and Wildlife Protection.

Fishing

Fishing did not pose a serious threat to biodiversity in the past. In recent years, however, growing populations in coastal settlements and poverty have resulted in increased fishing along the coast and in Lakes Ohrid, Prespa and Shkodra.

Coastal fishing is carried out mainly by small boats, nets and hooks. The species most endangered by fishing belong to the *Sparidae*, *Soleidae* and *Mullidae* families. The breeding sites of *Posidonia oceanica* are also degraded. Foreign vessels fishing offshore damage the habitats of fish and crustaceans, and cause severe damage to benthic forms off the Ionic coast. This mostly affects the rocky areas of the coast.

Besides traditional techniques, the use of explosives and poisons in lakes is reported. The main fishing species are carp, trout, sturgeon and eel. Much of the fishing is illegal, a particular threat to these lakes' endemic species. Since there is no proper monitoring, it is impossible to assess the damage to fish stocks.

8.3   The framework for biodiversity protection

Institutions

The government body responsible for biodiversity management is the Ministry of Environment. Within the Ministry, the Directorate for Natural Resources Management and Biodiversity formulates biodiversity policy and proposes related legislation. There are four persons in the Directorate (including the Director). Their tasks cover:

- Flora and fauna conservation and implementation of the Convention on Biological Diversity;
- Conservation and management of wetlands;
- Forestry and protected areas; and
- Agriculture and soil protection.

The Regional Environmental Agencies were established in 1994. They are responsible for cooperation in the application of legislation for the protection of the environment, the collection of information related to the environment, imposing fines according to the law, control over the management of protected areas within their jurisdictions, the organization of environmental impact assessments (EIA), and environmental inspection. Generally, one or two persons per county are engaged in nature conservation.

Other institutions are also responsible for environmental protection. In the Ministry of Agriculture and Food, the General Directorate for Forests and Pastures is responsible for the management of protected areas. It consists of the following units:

- Local government forest pastures and extension service;
- Forest police;
- Forests and pastures (forest management and cadastre, silviculture and forest resources, marketing, pastures);
- Protected areas; and
- Finance.

Another four sectors (personnel and foreign relations, services, auditing, legal office) report directly to the Director-General. Three of the

Directorate's specialists are directly engaged in protected areas management. The General Directorate employs altogether 43 permanent experts (including the three for the protected areas).

The Institute of Biological Research (under the Academy of Science) is involved in national (monitoring, conservation measures, climate change, and other) and international biodiversity projects (Ecological Survey of high forests – World Bank; Vegetation Map of Albania – German support; Implications of climate changes on the Albanian coastal ecosystems – UNEP; Study Centre for conservation and preservation of Mediterranean species – EU; Inventory of wetlands – UNEP).

The Museum of Natural Sciences is subordinate to Tirana University (under the Ministry of Education and Science). It has three departments dealing with biodiversity: Botany, Zoology and Geology. Three scientists (PhDs) are employed to deal with monitoring and assessing different groups of fauna and flora, and with national and international projects.

The Forest and Pasture Research Institute carries out research on silviculture and genetic improvement, forest management and inventory, forest protection against diseases and fires, and pasture and medical plants. There are 64 employees in the Institute, including highly educated experts, technical and administrative staff. The Institute is engaged in five scientific research projects, dealing with the rehabilitation of degraded forests, land use and planning, forest road construction, genetic improvement of forest species, and monitoring of pests and diseases. Also, the Institute's specialists are developing a new concept of forest management, EIA expertise, and seminars on forest management within the scope of the Strategy for the Development of the Forestry and Pasture Sector (see the above item on *Forestry*).

Inspection

The Ministry of Environment and its 12 Regional Environmental Agencies are responsible for environmental and biodiversity inspection.

The Directorate of Forest Police is responsible for forest and protected area inspection, and five employees are engaged in this task.

At county level, there are 36 Forest District Directorates, with 1350 employees. Some of them are responsible for inspection, and the number of inspectors per county depends on the size of the forest management areas.

Since environmental inspection (the Ministry of Environment) also includes biodiversity protection, and the Ministry of Agriculture and Food (Forest Police) is responsible for protected areas, responsibilities between these two overlap and must be clearly redefined.

Both inspections lack equipment and staff, and neither is able to do its work properly.

Legislation

There is no specific law on biodiversity conservation and management. The 2002 Law on Environmental Protection deals with natural resources and requires environmental permits to be issued by the environmental authorities for listed activities that may have an impact on the environment (art. 34). They include a variety of activities such as the building of infrastructure, exploration and exploitation of soil, forests, wildlife and fish. The same law also states (art. 4) that, among the main strategic elements of environmental protection are the conservation of biological diversity specific to the country's natural biogeographical background; the ecological restoration of damaged areas; and the preservation of the ecological balance.

Otherwise, all topics related to biodiversity are fragmentary and mainly incorporated into other sectoral legislation.

Law No. 7223, of 13 October 1992, on Forestry and the Forestry Police Service regulates forest management and protection, defining State, municipal and private forests. It also deals with district forest enterprises, the protection of watersheds (requiring afforestation and the closing of areas to logging and grazing, where necessary), the management of fisheries in mountain water bodies, forest national parks, minor forest produce, the forest police service, and the protection against forest fires. The Ministry of Agriculture and Food is responsible for the application of this Law.

Provisions on protected areas are included in forest legislation. Decision No. 577, of 6 February 1993, under the 1992 Law on Forestry, No. 7223, defines the categories of protected areas, in accordance with the classification of the World Conservation Union (IUCN): scientific reserves, national parks, natural monuments, natural reserves, and protected forestry areas. The Biodiversity Strategy and Action Plan (1999) includes a new proposal for protected area network that meets the requirements of the Convention on Biological Diversity in terms of the size and management of protected areas. The Ministry of Agriculture and Food is responsible for the application of this instrument.

Recently, the *Law on Protected Areas, No. 8906 of 6 June 2002,* was adopted. The Law regulates the preservation, administration, management and the sustainable use of the protected areas. The classification of the protected areas is based on experience and contemporary legislation, especially the IUCN categories. For the first time in Albanian environmental legislation the concept of "buffer" zones has been introduced. An important article within the Law identifies the Ministry of the Environment as the only governmental body which has the right to make proposals for new protected areas to the Council of Ministers, after consultations with local authorities, the public and other relevant governmental bodies.

Law No. 7917, of 13 April 1995, on Pastures and Grazing, defines 'pastures and meadows' as all land covered by grass or shrubs and that neither belongs to the forest fund nor is agricultural land, and which is used for grazing livestock. They are classified as (1) State-owned pastures, to be managed by the State forestry administration, (2) pastures for general use, given by local authorities to local populations, and (3) private pastures. The Ministry of Agriculture and Food is responsible for the application of this Law.

Law No. 7908, of 5 April 1995, on Fisheries and Fish Farming regulates both marine and freshwater fisheries. The Ministry of Agriculture and Food is responsible for the application of this Law.

Law No. 7875, of 23 November 1994, on Hunting and Wildlife Protection deals with the wildlife management plans that must be based on scientific criteria. The Ministry of Agriculture and Food is responsible for the application of this Law.

Law No. 7662, of 1993 (amended in 1999), on the Plant Protection Service provides for the organization of the Service and for parasite control, pesticides and plant quarantine. The Ministry of Agriculture and Food is responsible for the application of this Law.

International agreements

Albania ratified the Convention concerning the Protection of the World Cultural and Natural Heritage (1972) in 1979. Four nature monuments were established in 1996. These are: Fir of Sotira, Blue Eye, Vlashaj, and Zhej, with a total surface of 4650 ha.

Albania ratified the Convention on Wetlands of International Importance especially as Waterfowl Habitat (Ramsar, 1971) in 1996. The Karavasta Lagoon was the first Ramsar site, although there are at least another five wetland sites in the coastal zone that meet the Ramsar criteria on bird protection. They are included in the draft proposal for a new (extended) protected area network in the National Strategy and Action Plan.

Albania ratified the Convention on the Conservation of European Wildlife and Natural Habitats (Bern, 1979) in 1998. The conservation of wild flora and fauna and their natural habitats, especially those species and habitats whose conservation requires the cooperation of several States, obliges Albania to develop cooperation mechanisms in border areas with Yugoslavia and Greece (especially lakes Prespa, Ohrid, and Shkodra and their surroundings).

Albania signed the Convention on Biological Diversity (Rio de Janeiro, 1992) in 1994. Its National Biodiversity Strategy and Action Plan was completed in 1999.

Albania ratified the Convention to Combat Desertification (Paris, 1994) in 1999. It is very important for the conservation of Albania's soils. Degraded forest and pastureland, and the inadequate use of agricultural land, expose these areas to erosion. The implementation of this Convention will also help Albania to solve its soil pollution problems (see Chapter 10).

Albania also ratified the Convention on the Conservation of Migratory Species of Wild Animals (Bonn, 1979) in 2000. Its implementation is closely connected with the protected area network and its management.

Albania is preparing to accede to the Convention on International Trade in Endangered Species of Fauna and Flora (CITES) (Washington, 1973). It is of particular importance to Albania as it can help establish control over the export of animals and animal products, and so decrease illegal hunting.

Objectives of nature conservation policy and biodiversity strategy

Albania completed its *Biodiversity Strategy and Action Plan* in 1999. It was developed by the former National Environmental Agency, in cooperation with the Institute of Biological Research and the Museum of Natural Sciences, and other national, district and local organizations. It was supported by GEF/World Bank. An Advisory Board supervised the work. The Biodiversity Strategy and Action Plan assesses the biodiversity status, threats, priorities and action plans, including reform and institutional strengthening, legislation, inter-sectoral cooperation, public interest, and international cooperation. Actions are prioritized according to the criteria of the Convention on Biological Diversity, thus providing the basis for achieving national biodiversity policy goals in accordance with international conservation and management standards. The first list of short-term priorities includes the protection of 80 species/taxa (42 vertebrate, 26 invertebrate, and 12 plant species), while the long-term priorities include the protection of 143 species/taxa (95 vertebrate, 31 invertebrate, and 17 plant species). The proposed protected area network would exceed 10 per cent of the territory, as required by the Convention on Biological Diversity.

The 1993 *National Environmental Action Plan (NEAP)* already outlined the threats to biodiversity and the appropriate social remedies. It served as the basis for further conservation and development documents. The report on Immediate Measures for the Implementation of the NEAP (2001) proposes measures for the mitigation of chemical soil pollution and a pilot scheme against deforestation (two projects on the management and afforestation of the Kune and Vaini natural reserves).

A Coastal Area Management Programme has been developed since the early 1990s. Many natural coastal habitats have been destroyed by excessive drainage and land reclamation for agriculture, currently abandoned for practical (unsuitable salt soils) or political reasons (landownership unclear). The Coastal Area Management Programme – biodiversity component (Final Report, 1996) deals with the conservation and protection of sites of ecological and aesthetic value. It integrates the

results and proposals of reports and studies produced in the framework of the Programme and the Mediterranean Environmental Technical Assistance Programme. The report includes: (i) a section on the legal and institutional framework; (ii) a definition of the coastal zone management units; (iii) a definition and description of the sites of interest; (iv) a diagnosis of the main environmental issues and threats affecting these sites; (v) a selection of the national priorities for conservation; and (vi) recommendations for action. The Coastal Area Management Programme has not yet been approved by the Council of Ministers (see Chapter 11).

Protected areas

The development of the protected area network started in 1940. The first protected areas were the Kune-Vain-Tale Hunting Reserve and the "Tomorri Mountain" National Park. In the 1960-1966 period, there were 6 national parks, and the hunting reserves comprised 15 forest and lagoon areas by 1970. In 1994, the protected area network was harmonized with the IUCN classification and enlarged. In 1999, Prespa National Lake and Lake Ohrid were designated as protected landscapes, bringing the areas under protection up to 5.8 per cent of the national territory. The categories and number of protected areas and their conservation objectives are shown in Table 8.6.

Protected areas are managed by the General Directorate of Forests and Pastures of the Ministry of Agriculture and Food. Only two or three protected areas have management plans that, according to the reported status, do not meet the requirements of the Convention on Biological Diversity. It is reported that the categories of the existing protected areas should be revised so as to introduce areas of the ecosystems that are underrepresented (or not represented at all), and to merge some existing ones to improve conservation management.

Expanding and strengthening the protected area network in accordance with the European Ecological Network (EECONET) is one of the main goals of the National Biodiversity Strategy and Action Plan (Annex B-1: Proposed Representative Network of Protected Areas – RNPA – for Albania).

Table 8.6: The protected area system

Category	Protected area Number	Protected area in ha	% of area protected	IUCN category	Main goals
Total	386	164,110	100		or 5.8% of Albania's territory
Strictly protected area	4	14,500	13	I	Scientific research, fauna protection
National park	12	25,890	24	II	Ecosystem protection, recreation/tourism
Monuments of nature	300	4,360	4	III	Protection of specific features
Managed areas	26	42,960	39	IV	Protection through management activities
Protected landscape	5	59,200	2	V	Landscape protection, recreation/tourism
Protected resource	4	18,245	17	VI	Sustainable use

Source: State of the Environment Report 1997-1998; and REC. Final Country Report, Strategic Environmental Analysis, Albania, 2001.

Monitoring and databases

CORINE Biotope Mapping was completed only for protected areas (less than 4 per cent of the territory). There is no system for biodiversity inventorying and monitoring. Some species are periodically observed according to the requirements of international conventions (Convention on Biological Diversity and Ramsar Convention). Biodiversity research and monitoring are priorities in the Biodiversity Strategy and Action Plan as immediate actions, as they are very insufficient. Short-term actions necessary for its implementation are training staff in the responsible institutions, establishing permanent sampling plots and CORINE Biotope Mapping.

Since the Action Plan does not include budgets, it is not possible to assess the necessary financing for the biodiversity inventory and monitoring.

8.4   Conclusions and Recommendations

Since 1998, Albania has done much to improve its nature conservation policy. First, the Committee for Environmental Protection (under the Ministry of Health and Environment) was transformed into the National Environmental Agency, which started establishing many important programmes and strategies. In the past three years it was recognized that the Agency was not strong enough to carry out its obligations fully. Therefore, the Ministry of Environment was established in 2001, as the government body responsible for nature conservation policy. At the same time, the Ministry of Agriculture and Food (more precisely the General Directorate for Forests and Pastures) retained responsibility for protected areas.

The division of responsibilities between the Ministry of Agriculture and Food and the Ministry of Environment for the management of the protected area network prevents any effective implementation of the national nature conservation policy, as defined in the Biodiversity Strategy and Action Plan. The Ministry of Environment should bear full responsibility for it with the assistance of the Ministry of Agriculture and Food and other government bodies, scientific institutions, and NGOs.

The Ministry of Environment has the mandate to implement the national nature conservation and biodiversity management policy. However, the Ministry is institutionally still too weak and does not have the adequate capacities to fulfil the requirements defined by the nature conservation legislation and related policies and strategic documents. At the same time, the Protected Area Directorate of the Ministry of Agriculture and Food, within the General Directorate for Forests and Pastures, has managed the protected areas since they were established, and is the only institution that has the required experience, personnel, organization and methodology.

Recently, the Law on Protected Areas was adopted. This law regulates the preservation, administration, management and the sustainable use of the protected areas. The law also identifies the Ministry of the Environment as the only governmental body which has the right to make proposals for new protected areas.

The designation and management of protected areas should take into consideration the interests of local authorities, the private sector and other stakeholders. This can be achieved by including them at an early stage into the planning and decision-making processes of protected area management, and enabling them to share the benefits and better accept the related constraints (on their activities, for instance). This process adds value by mitigating poverty and raising public awareness of biodiversity values.

Recommendation 8.1:
The Ministry of Environment should support the responsible authorities to establish management plans for protected areas under the new Law on Protected Areas, for example by financing studies and developing methodologies and procedures.

According to the Convention on Biological Diversity, each country should develop national strategies, plans or programmes for the conservation and sustainable use of biodiversity or adapt existing ones to reflect the measures set out in the Convention. It should integrate, as far as possible and appropriate, the conservation and sustainable use of biodiversity into relevant sectoral or cross-sectoral plans, programmes and policies. The country should also identify and monitor the biodiversity components that are important for its conservation and sustainable use, as well as the processes and activities that have or are likely to have significant adverse impacts on the conservation and sustainable use of biodiversity. In order to achieve this, the country should establish a system of protected areas, and regulate or manage biological resources important for biodiversity conservation whether within or outside protected areas.

Species are protected by two main tools: (a) specific measures on species management (e.g. bans on activities that damage or disturb them), and (b) conservation of their habitats. Therefore, the protection of particular flora and fauna species is an integral part of the ecosystem protection that is carried out, inter alia, by establishing a protected area network. Measures for the protection of particular species should be incorporated into the management plans of protected areas. All European countries have one law to regulate both species protection and protected areas (there do not seem to be any exceptions).

The Government has recently adopted a new Law on protected Areas. However, there remain other laws and draft laws relevant to nature protection. The preparation of a single consistent and coherent legal act on biodiversity conservation would help to clarify the respective competencies of the Ministry of Environment and the Ministry of Agriculture and Food.

Recommendation 8.2:
To achieve the goals of the Biodiversity Strategy and Action Plan and fulfil the obligations under the Convention on Biological Diversity, the Ministry of Environment should develop a legal act on biodiversity conservation.

Minor forest produce has been an important source of income to local Albanian populations in recent years. Medicinal and aromatic plants have been collected and exported to foreign markets. Studies done by international organizations and national scientific institutions indicate the economic importance of medicinal and aromatic plants to the country, and also emphasize the increasing threats to biodiversity. To prevent damage to species and ecosystem degradation, people who collect and cultivate medicinal plants should be educated and trained. The collection of those wild plants should gradually be replaced by their cultivation, while both should be regulated by adequate institutional and legal arrangements.

Recommendation 8.3:
The Ministry of Environment and the Ministry of Agriculture and Food should develop, as soon as possible, a proper institutional and legal framework for the medicinal and aromatic plant market to promote the cultivation of such plants. Their collection should be based on biodiversity conservation criteria and methods, and on a licensing system.

Forest degradation and forest loss have resulted, among other things, in increased soil erosion and changed water regimes. Poor soil quality, reduced aesthetic landscape values and biodiversity loss affect all sectors and the Albanian environment as a whole. Although reforestation is currently supported by international projects, a permanent national reforestation scheme, based on ensured financial contributions, should be established. The experience of some other countries in transition could be taken into account, such as that of the reforestation fund in Croatia. According to the Croatian Forest Code, each State or private company is obliged to pay 0.07 per cent of its total annual income to the reforestation fund, which is managed by the State Forest Enterprise. Recently, the control of the fund was discussed to make its management more transparent. Money from the fund should be available and accessible to any company or NGO proposing adequate reforestation programmes for priority areas. The fund should be administered by the General Directorate for Forests and Pastures. All stakeholders, including the local community, should keep an eye on its transparency.

Recommendation 8.4:
The Ministry of Agriculture and Food should establish a permanent national reforestation scheme and undertake actions to protect forests from legal cutting and fires, based on secured financial contributions.

At the moment the Karavasta Lagoon is the only Ramsar site of Albania. There are however at least five wetland sites in the coastal zone that meet RAMSAR criteria.

Recommendation 8.5:
The Ministry of Environment should take steps to include those sites that fulfil criteria of wetlands of international importance, to be included as RAMSAR sites and in the national network of protected areas.

PART III: SECTORAL INTEGRATION

Chapter 9

ENVIRONMENTAL INTEGRATION

9.1 Introduction

Under central planning, governments usually had rigid vertical structures and little coordination among the sectors. In addition, the economic sectors paid little attention to environmental issues, even though the interdependence between environmental problems and the activities of the various sectors of Albania's economy was apparent. Instead of being the subject of an integrated approach, the environment was viewed as a separate sector and given less priority than other critical national issues. Financial allocations from the State budget to the environment sector were very limited, totalling but 0.04 per cent of gross domestic product (GDP). The economic decline in the early 1990s eased the environmental pressure from large polluting sectors such as industry and agriculture. Since 1998, however, GDP has been growing at a steady rate of 7 to 8 per cent a year, increasing the potential pressure from economic sectors on the environment.

9.2 Environmental pressure

The sectors of the Albanian economy are mining, oil refining, transport, tourism, agriculture, energy, forestry and industry. Due to the economic decline, it is mainly transport, tourism and agriculture that are currently putting pressure on the environment.

Transport

Before 1989 there were only 2000 cars in Albania, as private car ownership was prohibited. This situation has changed rapidly and, in 1999, there were 99,000 cars. The fleet is generally old and uses diesel and leaded petrol, thereby polluting the air with NO_x, SO_x, CO_2, lead, and particulate matter. The expected further rise in the number of vehicles will increase these emissions. Albania's national road network is 3,221 km long, of which 677 km are part of the strategic north-south and east-west corridor routes. These routes are being upgraded with financial support from the Stability Pact. The environmental impacts from air, rail and water transport are relatively limited. Albania has a small international airport near Tirana and an international harbour in Durrës. The harbour will be upgraded with financial support from the World Bank. An environmental action plan is part of this development. The 447-km railway track is in serious condition and hardly used anymore. Due to the poor state of the rails the average speed of trains has been reduced to 35 km/h.

The Ministry of Transport and Telecommunications is the competent authority for all national transport developments, including infrastructure. The Ministry has appointed an environmental coordinator, who holds a technical position, low in the ministerial hierarchy. The coordinator works in the Road Safety sector, which falls under the Technical Directorate on Road Transport. Individual work plans have been made for air transport and railway transport, but there is so far no overall strategy for the transport sector.

Tourism

In 1997, 19,000 tourist arrivals were recorded – a decline of 58 per cent compared to 1993. According to the National Committee for Tourism, there were over 900,000 visitors in 2000, generating an income of over US$ 350 million. The Adriatic coast has great tourism potential, and Albania hopes that the tourism sector will benefit from infrastructure investments under the Stability Pact. Most tourism activities take place along the Ionian and Adriatic coastline.

Unfortunately, most development along the coastline has taken place without taking spatial planning, construction or environmental considerations into account. Few houses and hotels are connected to the sewage system and there are many illegal connections to the electricity grid and drinking water supply system. For example, approximately 1000 illegal constructions were erected in Durrës in 2000, most of them along the coastline.

The National Committee for Tourism developed a Tourism Strategy in 1993. This Strategy was approved but has never been implemented. In 2001, the National Committee was integrated into the Ministry of Territorial Adjustment and Tourism.

Agriculture

Agriculture is an important sector of Albania's economy, contributing 53 per cent of GDP in 1999. The main crops are barley, maize, potatoes, rice, sugar beet and wheat. About half the active population is employed in agriculture. Due to the economic decline, the use of fertilizers and pesticides has fallen drastically since 1990. According to the Albanian country office of the Regional Environmental Center for Central and Eastern Europe (REC), the actual use of fertilizers is below the optimum dose and does not pose any environmental problem. Fertilizer requirements are estimated to be 380,000 tons, while in 1998 only 125,000 tons were applied. If domestic production of pesticides resumes, an increase in their use would result in water and soil pollution unless good agricultural practices were applied (see Chapter 10). In 1998, 76 tons of pesticides were imported, 20 per cent less than in the previous year. The REC country office states furthermore that nearly 45 per cent of all pesticides in Albania are classified as hazardous chemicals. The disposal of pesticide packaging on landfills poses a risk to groundwater and soils.

Soil erosion is also a threat to the environment as many terraces in the mountains are not maintained and are overgrazed. One fifth of the country suffers from strong erosion (more than 30 tons/ha/year) and 70 per cent from medium erosion.

The Ministry of Agriculture and Food is responsible for the agricultural sector. The Ministry developed a "Green Strategy" to set environmental policies for forestry, agriculture, fisheries and aquaculture. The Strategy was approved by the Council of Ministers in December 1998. According to the Ministry, it is being implemented through the work programmes of the various directorates. The Ministry has a department of environmental protection within the General Directorate for Forests and Pastures.

Other sectors

Before the 1990s, the oil refinery, forestry, mining and other industrial sectors used to have a negative impact on Albania's environment. Because of the economic decline and the collapse of industrial output, their polluting effects have drastically

diminished and are not considered a priority concern. The most important environmental problems of these sectors are direct air, water and soil pollution caused by outdated and inefficient processes, the lack of sufficient abatement and treatment techniques and inappropriate waste handling. Another problem associated with industry is the pollution on abandoned sites (soil and water) and the lack of finance for cleaning them up (see Chapter 7).

Hydroelectric stations generate most of the electricity in Albania. Therefore, Albania has cleaner and more sustainable electricity than many other countries that use fossil fuels to generate electricity. The only operating thermopower station is a large contributor to the overall emissions of CO_2 and SO_2 in the country (see Chapter 5). The Ministry of Industry and Energy is supported by the National Energy Agency. The Agency advises the Minister and ensures the sound, safe and suitable development of energy production, supply and consumption taking into account environmental considerations.

The National Energy Agency developed a draft national strategy of energy in March 2000, which highlights the potential for significant energy savings in the household, service and industrial sectors. Household energy demand could decrease by 20 per cent and electricity demand by 35 per cent. No-cost measures in industry could result in a permanent reduction of 20 per cent in its energy demand. The strategy fails however to take environmental issues, such as pollution by the Fier thermoelectric station, into account. A task force established to develop an action plan to solve the electricity crisis does not include any representatives from the Ministry of Environment. A further increase in electricity demand is anticipated and a new hydropower station is being built in Bushati. In addition, a comparative feasibility study is under way for the rehabilitation of the Fier thermopower station and the development of a new thermopower station near Vlorë.

The energy, mining and industrial sectors all fall under the jurisdiction of the Ministry of Industry and Energy. There is no specific policy or strategy for the development of the mining sector or the industrial sector except the "Privatization Strategy for State-owned Companies in Important Primary Sectors". Environmental issues within the Ministry fall under the Technical Safety and Environment Section. This Section consists of two staff and is responsible for the monitoring of law enforcement and the implementation of government policies. In addition, it manages projects and supervises studies conducted by various institutions. A pollution report is provided annually to the Ministry of Environment. There is no mechanism within the Ministry of Industry of Energy to integrate environmental concerns into its activities. The environmental permit, issued by the Ministry of Environment, should in principle ensure this integration but it is inadequate.

Cross sectoral initiatives

In 1994, the National Environmental Action Plan (NEAP) was developed and approved. One of its priorities is the establishment of a comprehensive link between sectoral policies and the environment. Different measures were defined in order to develop sectoral policies related to the restructuring of the economy, privatization, the establishment of an environmental taxation system, and the development of the agricultural, transport, and energy sectors. For various reasons, such as weak institutional capacity and low political support, few measures have been implemented. Recently, the NEAP has been revised and updated with funding from the World Bank and PHARE. Inter-ministerial working groups have been set up to draft chapters of the new plan and there has been a large participation of civil society. The revised NEAP (adopted in 2002) identifies the main activities for the coming five to seven years and puts more emphasis on (i) greater intra-governmental cooperation, (ii) establishing environmental units in key ministries and municipalities, and (iii) strengthening the environmental impact assessment system.

Water management is a typical issue that requires a cross-sectoral approach. For this purpose, an independent National Water Council was established in Albania. The Prime Minister chairs the Council, and the Ministry of Agriculture and Food, the Ministry of Territorial Adjustment and Tourism, and the Ministry of Environment are represented. The Council developed a national water strategy in 1997, but it has still not been approved because of opposition from various ministries. In addition, the Council has too few staff and financial resources to execute its many water management tasks (see also Chapter 6).

Albania has also prepared a Strategy on Growth and Poverty Reduction. The Ministry of Environment has produced a chapter on Environment, Growth and Poverty Reduction, which sets out the short–, medium– and long-term priorities. The priorities mentioned in Strategy include the establishment of a national committee on sustainable development and the drawing-up of sustainable strategies for land use, rural and urban development, transport and monitoring. However, the Ministry of Environment was not part of the supervising Steering Committee, the Working Group in charge of drafting the Strategy or of any of the sectoral technical groups.

The Ministry of Environment and the Ministry of Territorial Adjustment and Tourism are drafting an agreement to define the responsibilities arising from waste management, urban planning, water management and environmental legislation. The agreement foresees wide-ranging cooperation. It would include joint inspections, joint work plans, information exchange and joint working groups to complete legislation.

Instruments for environmental integration

The most important instruments specifically aimed at environmental integration are environmental permits, environmental impact assessment and spatial planning (see Chapter 2).

Environmental impact assessment

Environmental impact assessment (EIA) is a legally binding instrument that identifies the environmental impacts of a proposed project in order to take them into consideration in the decision-making process. The 2002 framework Law on Environmental Protection requires both environmental impact assessment for all public and private projects that can have a significant impact on the environment, and strategic environmental assessment (SEA) for policies, plans and programmes on the development of transport, energy, tourism, industries, services, territory adjustment and economic and social development in general.

There are, however, no regulations that specify the contents and procedures yet in place either for environmental impact assessments or for strategic environmental assessment.

The 2002 Law on Environmental Protection stipulates that an environmental permit must be issued before an activity with possible effects on the environment may be developed. Consequently, all privatization requests should be accompanied by an EIA and an environmental permit. In addition to the lack of EIA regulations, the EIA capacity within the Ministry of Environment – including the Regional Environmental Agencies – is very limited. A draft law on environmental impact assessment has been prepared with funding from the World Bank. The draft law would ensure broader public participation. According to the 2002 Law on Environmental Protection, the permit applications require an Environmental Statement, but the relationship between an Environmental Statement and an EIA is not clear. Alternative site locations and mitigation measures as proposed in an EIA have not, up to now, to be included in an environmental permit.

Spatial planning

The National Council for Territorial Development is the highest independent decision-making body for territorial planning. It is headed by the Prime Minister and operates directly under the Council of Ministers. The Minister of Environment is part of this National Council. Its main task is to approve territorial plans exceeding 5000 ha for tourist zones and city centres. In addition, the 13 largest cities must develop a spatial 'master plan'. This master plan needs the approval of the Local Territorial Development Council. The Regional Environmental Agencies are part of the Local Territorial Development Councils. The master plans are still of a general nature and require further detailed plans. A developer must provide a detailed plan of the plot to be developed. This requires the approval of the municipality. For all other areas outside the 13 big cities, specific administrative structures named 'qarqeve' have been established. Their geographical areas coincide with the 13 prefectures. At the local level, the urban planning laws date back to 1986 and take account of neither private ownership nor the demographic changes of the past ten years. An EIA is compulsory before the approval of any spatial plan.

There is, however, no national spatial plan. Since 1996 various coastal zone management plans have been developed to encourage tourism and protect Albania's coastline. No EIA was carried out for the plans and, to date, the Albanian Government has not approved any of them (see Chapter 11).

9.3   Environmental integration and industrial privatization

Two major environmental issues play a role when privatizing industries. First, poorly defined responsibilities for financing the clean-up of polluted facilities could put entrepreneurs off privatization. These rehabilitation costs are often enormous. In its Post-Conflict Environmental Assessment, UNEP states that until the liability issue for past pollution is clarified, it will undoubtedly act as a disincentive to many potential investors in Albanian industry. Based on some recent privatizations, it appears that the State of Albania has accepted liability for the remediation of pre-existing environmental pollution.

The second issue is the need for investment in environmentally sound technologies. Many industries are equipped with outdated production processes. Abatement techniques are lacking. The valuation of the property will take this into account, but huge investments are nevertheless required to update and improve production processes to meet environmental standards. Foreign companies with experience with these techniques and management systems could set a welcome example to others.

The Ministry of Industry and Energy published its "Privatization Strategy for State-owned Companies in Important Primary Sectors" in December 1997. This Strategy does not incorporate any environmental issues. A privatization programme is being prepared for the remaining medium-sized enterprises and the strategic sectors. The National Agency for Privatization is responsible for the technical implementation of the privatization of 'non-strategic' enterprises. The Albanian Economic Development Agency is responsible for promoting investments and assisting national and international investors. In the organizations responsible for privatization, there is little awareness of the environment. Neither the National Agency for Privatization nor the General Directorate for

---

Box 9.1:   Immediate measures for the implementation of the National Environmental Action Plan

The World Bank started a programme on Immediate Measures for the Implementation of the NEAP, which was adopted by the Albanian Government in June 2001. According to the draft document of this US$ 200,000 programme, additional environmental units should be established, while existing units should be strengthened in various ministries, and mechanisms should be created to improve their cooperation with the Ministry of Environment. The role of various institutions and levels of government in the environmental management in Albania is also clearly defined.

Privatization for small and medium enterprises of the Ministry of Industry and Energy is aware of the requirements for environmental impact assessments when privatizing. Nor are other mechanisms in the privatization process that could help secure a better environmental performance, such as a deposit for environmental improvements or an environmental clause in the sales contract, applied.

Some concession agreements between the Albanian Government and private companies make specific reference to environmental standards, and environmental investments are part of the agreement. Under a concession agreement between the Ministry of Industry and Energy and an Italian joint-stock company, it was agreed that the concessionaire would operate "according to European Community norms". In addition, US$ 6 million would be invested in environmental protection over a period of six years. The concessionaire will present a project proposal for the environmental investments to the Ministry of Industry and Energy for approval.

The privatization of many State-owned properties proceeded faster than the restructuring of the banking system and the development of the capital markets. The financial system was therefore not able to meet the demands of new entrepreneurs. Privatizing the banking sector will have a twofold benefit: the non-effective part of the banking system can be eliminated and a lending capacity will be developed, through foreign private capital, to the benefit of the private sector in Albania. Currently, it is almost impossible to obtain a loan from an Albanian bank. Collaterals can be as high as 100 per cent and interest rates fluctuate between 12 and 22 per cent. Albanian banks do not include environmental requirements in their loan agreements, a practice that international banks are increasingly incorporating in theirs (see Box 9.2).

9.4   Challenges to environmental integration

The framework for environmental management in Albania is challenged by the low economic development and the internal crisis of the past years. The establishment of a Ministry of Environment, however, indicates that environment has moved up the political agenda. Environmental concerns are now represented at the highest decision-making level, the Council of Ministers. The tasks of the Minister of Environment will be to promote and integrate the environment into Albania's many other priorities. The establishment of a Ministry of Environment, the expected negotiations on an Agreement for Association and Stabilization with the European Union and closer participation in the UNECE 'Environment for Europe' process are clear indicators of the commitment of the Albanian Government to its environmental responsibilities.

Challenges at strategic level

Strategies to provide direction for the development of economic sectors have been developed only for tourism (1993) and agriculture and forestry (1998). A Privatization Strategy was also adopted in 1997. The energy sector has had a draft strategy since 2000. But none of these strategies have been truly implemented. It is clear that there has been little agreement on the development of the other sectors.

The Ministry of Environment has not been consulted in the development of any of the sectoral policy documents, and environmental concerns are rarely reflected in the few policy documents that do exist. For example, increasing energy efficiency is often regarded as the key to integrating environment and energy. While the draft energy strategy refers to energy savings and increased efficiency measures, the aim seems to be to manage the growing demand for electricity rather than to integrate user needs and environmental purposes, preserving fossil fuels and cutting emissions.

The fact that not all sectors have an agreed written direction for development does not mean that no economic development is taking place. For example, the energy sector is desperate to meet the growing demand for electricity, and is investigating for both upgrading existing or building new power stations (see above).

Box 9.2:   Environmental concerns and financial loans

In April 2001 the European Bank for Reconstruction and Development and the International Finance Corporation approved a nine-and-a-half-year loan of € 32 million to reconstruct the privately owned cement factory in Elbasan. After the two-year reconstruction, the annual production capacity will increase from the current 200,000 tons to 1 million tons. An environmental action plan requiring the approval of the Bank has been included in the loan agreement. The plan includes measures that could lead to a two-third cut in fuel consumption and a one-third cut in electricity consumption. In addition, major air emission reductions are foreseen to meet national and international (World Bank and EU) standards.

In the transport sector, no strategy has been agreed upon at government level. However, according to the Medium-term Expenditure Framework for 2001-2003, more than 90 per cent of the Ministry of Transport and Telecommunications' total budget of 11,705 million leks was allocated to the national road network, while only 5 per cent went to railway transport and only 2.5 per cent to marine transport and civil aviation. This expenditure pattern reveals an implicit choice to develop road transport above other means of transport.

There is no doubt that the energy and transport infrastructure needs to expand and improve if Albania is to develop. The lack of clear direction, however, does not contribute to the transparency of the Government's decision-making processes. Furthermore, environmental concerns are not incorporated in these decisions. The environmental implications of road, rail and air transport, as well as the impacts of hydropower and thermopower are numerous, but no strategic environmental analysis has been made so as to take a well-informed decision.

Institutional challenges

As part of the World-Bank-funded project Immediate Measures for the Implementation of the NEAP, the institutional capacity of the relevant line ministries was analysed. Based on this analysis recommendations were made to train staff and to expand the units' capacity by employing more staff. The report foresees among other things the strengthening of the environmental units of the Ministry of Industry and Energy, the Ministry of Transport and Telecommunications, the Ministry of Agriculture and Food and the Ministry of Territorial Adjustment and Tourism, by appointing additional staff to the environmental functions and redefining the responsibilities and tasks of the environmental units.

The technical safety and environmental protection section has been well positioned in the organizational structure of the Ministry of Industry and Energy. It is placed as a non-line function advising and reporting directly to the Vice-Minister. The section's work programme and specific project proposals need the approval of the Vice-Minister. Project proposals developed by the general directorates are not often submitted to the technical safety and environmental protection section for comments. Nor are tasks such as

environmental monitoring and compliance of projects carried out by directorates allocated to the section. In addition, the section is strained by severe budget limitations; in 2001 it had no separate budget and therefore no environmental projects were carried out. Since the section is not given the political clout and financial means required to fulfil its tasks, environmental considerations are not well integrated and coordinated in the Ministry.

Institutes working semi-independently from the line ministries are carrying out projects with environmental components. The Institute for Chemical Studies, for example, drew up a complete inventory of chemicals used, stored and disposed of in enterprises and government institutes. The Institute has also developed the draft law on the handling of chemicals but without any input from other ministries. Only when the draft law is finished will the relevant ministries be invited to provide comments before it goes to parliament for approval.

Early and sufficient participation of all relevant actors in the development of laws and policies is important for their approval and implementation. Insufficient participation could lead to an absence of any feeling of responsibility. For the integration of environmental concerns it is of the utmost importance that those involved feel responsible for their contribution to solving or mitigating the environmental impacts of their activities. The current situation whereby policy documents are 'parked', sometimes for years as in the case of the National Water Strategy, for approval by the Council of Ministers is counterproductive. The establishment of cross-sectoral working groups for the development of laws and policies that have an environmental impact could facilitate decision-making as all concerns could be incorporated at an early stage. Ultimately, the integration of environmental concerns could lead to the development of cross-sectoral policies and action programmes to tackle specific issues such as transport and environment, energy and environment, and health and environment.

The Directorate for Environmental Policy and Project Implementation and the Directorate for Environmental Legislation and Foreign Relations within the Ministry of Environment should be responsible for the analysis of sectoral policies. Their capacity and experience for strategic analysis need strengthening.

Challenges in the privatization process

In principle it should not make a difference whether a company is privately or publicly owned. According to the 2002 Law on Environmental Protection, an environmental permit is required for any activity with an impact on the environment, regardless of who is responsible for it. The environmental licence should provide an opportunity to limit the impacts of the company's activities, based on an environmental audit or environmental impact assessment. Currently, environmental concerns are not taken into consideration during privatization. The authorities responsible for privatization are not aware of any environmental requirements for industries.

The financial sector in Albania does not provide favourable conditions for loans, let alone for environmental investments. There are some cases, however, where environmental investments are secured through sales or concession agreements between the State and a private entrepreneur. The Ministry of Environment is not part of nor even consulted in these agreements. Due to the lack of sufficient national standards, some privatization agreements refer to World Bank standards and European Community standards. If the European Bank for Reconstruction and Development provides a loan for environmental investments, the Bank requires the company to prepare an environmental action plan for its approval. The Ministry of Environment has not been involved at all in specifying the contents of these environmental action plans, nor is their approval required. Therefore, it seems that international banks are filling the vacuum created by the Ministry of Environment's lack of capacity and currently these banks are playing an important role in the environmental performance of privatized companies.

9.5 Conclusions and recommendations

The basis for environmental integration is embedded in many parts of a government's institutional framework. A good permit system is part of the basis to protect the environment from the impacts of various economic activities. A permit should provide the 'environmental space' in which a company can operate. In other words, it should set limits, for instance, to the air pollutants, noise, waste and waste water produced. This would obviously require an extensive system of standards, preferably based on internationally accepted methods. In addition, the compliance and

enforcement of this permit system would need to be sufficient. Companies should be held accountable for their impact on the environment and especially their non-compliance with existing regulations. The current enforcement by the Regional Environmental Agencies is insufficient. The lack of respect for environmental requirements and environmental inspectors clearly limits the environmental performance of industry (see also Chapter 2).

Recommendation 9.1:
As a basis for environmental integration, the environmental permit system should be improved by developing clear procedures for conducting environmental impact assessment and linking the environmental impact assessment to environmental permits. In addition, existing environmental regulations should be better enforced (see recommendation 2.1).

The lack of strategies and directions for various economic sectors does not help to make the decision-making process transparent. The lack of direction and strategic choices leads to economically and environmentally inefficient allocations of staff, capital and facilities. The low environmental awareness in Albania is clearly reflected in the fact that environmental concerns are not incorporated in these decisions. Strategic environmental assessment is a helpful tool to identify the environmental impacts of various policy options. There is a clear need in Albania to develop its strategic environmental analysis capacity. However, taking the current capacity constraints of the Ministry of Environment into consideration, a stepwise approach is required. Setting environmental targets for the various sectors could form an appropriate first step to better integrating the environment into sectoral policies. The identification of the main environmental problems per sector should form the basis for target-setting, followed by the measures that should be taken to reach these targets.

Recommendations 9.2:
The line ministries, with the support of the Ministry of Environment, are encouraged to establish environmental targets in the preparation of their sectoral strategies and plans. An implementation plan – clearly defining actions, responsibilities, time frame and financing – should support the achievement of the environmental targets.

Most line ministries have appointed officials responsible for environmental concerns and communication with the Ministry of Environment.

Their capacity is however limited. As part of the 'Immediate Measures for Implementation of the National Environmental Action Plan,' recommendations were made to improve this capacity. In addition to increasing their number and redefining their responsibilities, the environment staff should be in a position to influence decision-making. Sufficient resources should be given in line with their responsibilities.

Recommendation 9.3:
The Government, in conformity with the report on 'Immediate Measures for Implementation of the NEAP', should establish environmental units within ministries. These units should be allocated sufficient resources.

Policies and laws are currently developed by individual ministries or agencies with little participation of other relevant ministries and actors. This situation could lead to a 'lack of ownership', hampering effective implementation. Furthermore, the incorporation of all concerns at an early stage could speed up the approval of policies by the Council of Ministers. Initiatives such as the proposed agreement between the Ministry of Environment and the Ministry of Territorial Adjustment and Tourism might provide a good framework for cooperation.

Recommendation 9.4:
To improve environmental integration and the decision-making process, the Council of Ministers should establish cross-sectoral or inter-ministerial working groups at the expert level for the development of laws and policies.

Currently, the Ministry of Environment does not play a role in the privatization process, which is predominantly carried out by the Ministry of Industry and Energy and rarely incorporates environmental concerns. Environmental action plans, such as those used by the European Bank for Reconstruction and Development, are a useful tool to ensure compliance by privatized enterprises.

Recommendation 9.5:
The Ministry of Environment should ensure that environmental impact assessments and environmental audits are part of the privatization process and that environmental investments and environmental clauses are included in the sales agreement.

Chapter 10

ENVIRONMENTAL CONCERNS IN AGRICULTURE AND SOIL PROTECTION

10.1 Conditions and activities in agriculture

Economics and production

Albania is predominantly an agricultural country and will remain so for a long time. In 2001, agriculture generated 54 per cent of GDP (compared to 40 per cent in 1990). By 1995, the sector had recovered its losses from the privatization process and begun a new period of growth. Since that time, the annual growth rate has been relatively steady at 4 to 5 per cent. It is estimated that domestic production meets 70 per cent of the population's food requirements. On the whole, agriculture is increasingly capable of providing food for the rural population, but agriculture remains to a large extent at a subsistence level and the country was, consequently, highly dependent on food imports during the 1990s.

The food trade balance is negative. The persistent negative agricultural trade balance represents a major component of the overall trade deficit, and it seems that the gap is widening, increasing the external debt, which is a source of great concern for the country. Albania exports watermelons and tomatoes to neighbouring Balkan countries. Medicinal plants and herbs account for 40 per cent of agricultural exports.

Agriculture is the main source of employment for 70 per cent (1998) of the labour force, and 59 per cent of the population lives in the rural areas. Part-time work on farms dominates (44 per cent of income comes from agriculture), but farmers are not registered as unemployed.

Migration was non-existent before the 1990s, but, from 1994 to 1999, a flow of rural-urban migration resulted in a decrease of 4.1 per cent in the rural population. In addition, some 500,000 Albanians, or 15 per cent of the active population, have emigrated, and approximately one quarter of all rural families have at least one member abroad.

Crops

The main crops are wheat, maize, vegetables and alfalfa. Average cereal production between 1992 and 1998 was 370,800 tons of wheat (average yields of 27 metric quintals/ha) and 191,300 tons of maize (28 metric quintals/ha). Seventy-one per cent of wheat production is for the growers' own consumption, but it is declining in favour of vegetables. Forty per cent of the farms no longer produce wheat. Vegetables are in general grown for own consumption or as a cash crop near the cities, often cultivated in plastic-sheet greenhouses. Forage crops, i.e. maize and alfalfa for cattle, are also increasingly grown even in the plains where more than half the arable land is used for forage. Maize and potato output remain the same (maize surface decreased by 24 per cent, but this was compensated by increasing yields). Industrial crops fell abruptly, including good tobacco, which used to be an Albanian specialty. In all districts, more fruit trees and grapevines have been planted.

Wheat is a strategic crop, as the Albanian diet (2961 kcal/day) is heavily based on bread (200 kg/year/person): in the poorest households, 75 per cent or more of income is spent on food, and half of that on bread or flour. Production has fallen to well below pre-transition levels, from 900,000 to 600,000 tons, and, in 1999, Albania had to import 50 per cent of its domestic cereal requirements, including most of the wheat needed for human consumption (200,000 tons/year).

Livestock

After the privatization of agriculture (1992-1993), livestock increased by 80 to 90 per cent. Small-scale farmers (2-3 cows, 10-20 sheep and goats) chose to increase their cattle because of the low capital requirements and the growing demand for livestock products. From 1994 to 1998, livestock provided 75 to 85 per cent of farmers' income and accounted for half the agricultural output (a third in the 1980s). Over the same period, milk production was the principal source of growth (+130 per cent) owing to the combination of an increased number of cows and higher milk yields (average now of 1700 kg/year), sold at a good price.

In 1995, the number of livestock peaked, with 840,000 head of cattle, and 4,130,000 head of sheep and goats. This was followed by a strong decrease (-12 per cent for cattle and -30 per cent for sheep and goats). One explanation is that people who abandoned land in the hilly and mountainous parts of the country in the 1997 crisis to move to the cities sold their cattle. In 1997, a survey by the Ministry of Agriculture and Food suggested that breeding stock has stabilized at a number that can easily be supported by the forage available. There is now a considerable potential for improving livestock production by better domestic breed rearing and selection and greater access to veterinary treatment.

Agro-processing

The agro-processing industry was one of the first to be privatized (1991-1992). The transition period led to a significant decline in production and the destruction of some of the 2000 units. Much of the sector collapsed. In 1997, around 300 plants still existed and beverage industries recovered so allowing a reduction in imports.

Albanian agriculture, which was once a monolithic State producer and marketing system, moved to near subsistence units. From 60 per cent (in the coastal areas) to 90 per cent (in the mountainous areas) of the produce is consumed by the farmers themselves. Agriculture is characterized by small plots and a diversification of crops and livestock, extensive farming and low productivity.

Agriculture suffers from a lack of capital and credit facilities (there are no credit schemes), a lack of marketing links (associations) and transport facilities. Roads are poor and scarce, and communities isolated. Mechanization is difficult to develop on small plots, and its availability is limited. The lack of wholesale structures, small-scale agro-processing plants, standardization and a good trading system is also a drawback. Consequently, imported products are pushing the local ones out of the domestic market.

Land redistribution and actual farming structures

Fragmentation of rural land is a big problem in Albania. According to the Law on Land and its

Distribution, the land of some 550 collective and State farms was distributed by the end of 1993, generating more than 400,000 family farms with an average size of 1.06 hectares; in the northern mountains the average is just over 0.5 hectares. Only 2 per cent of the farms have more than 2 hectares. After the crisis of 1997, the number of farms increased again by 58,000. In 1997, theoretically more than 97 per cent of the land was for private use. More than 100,000 hectares have remained under the administration of the municipalities (see Law No. 8312/1998) as "refused" land because it is barren, eroded or saline, or because ownership is not clear (Table 10.1).

Further fragmentation resulted from the fact that the redistribution took into consideration the quality of the land and its uses (i.e. arable land, olive groves, orchards and vineyards) to ensure that all families received equal allocations of all comparable land (Table 10.2). The resulting mosaic of small parcels (at least two to three per farm) may include plots too far from the homestead to be used efficiently. The land market is not functioning properly because the price of arable land is as high as that of land earmarked for construction. Parliament is debating a law that would restrict fragmentation (setting a minimal farm size), make consolidation compulsory in certain cases and promote voluntary consolidation through exemption from land tax. The Ministry of Agriculture and Food expects the farms to enlarge rapidly: by 2010, 10 per cent will have more than 8 hectares and 30 per cent 3 to 5 hectares.

10.2   Environmental concerns in agriculture

Land management and erosion

Albania is divided into four geo-climatic zones based on topography, climate, soils and vegetation: the south western coast; and the north western coast; and in the fertile coastal plains, the intermediate hilly region and the non-arable mountain zones.

According to the national soil classification system, the soil systems of Albania are divided into four belts. The hydrography of Albania is made up of six main hydrographical basins (see Figure 10.1). Arable irrigated land includes 417,000 hectares (of which 226,000 hectares are in the coastal plains) and non-irrigated arable land 285,000 hectares (see Table 10.2).

Table 10.1: Land distribution in 1998

	1000 ha	Nb of families	Status*)	Previous status *)
Cooperative land workers with private plot	426	365	ownership	Small holders previous collectivization
State land workers with no private plot	120	101	use	in communist time 1) reclaimed 2) confiscated
Cooperative or State land	130	Not distributed	Refused**)	in communist time 1) reclaimed 2) confiscated or 3) redistributed (3rd reform)

Source: AGOLLI Shkëlqim. Review of Albanian agriculture.

*) Europe-Asia Studies, vol. 50, No 1, 1998

**) Reasons: low fertility, lack of irrigation, distance from habitation, fear of paying taxes for not used land, property disputes.

Table 10.2: Land use

	1950		1990		1999	
	1000 ha	%	1000 ha	%	1000 ha	%
TOTAL	2,875	100	2,875	100	2,875	100
Forests	1,282	45	1,045	36	1,027	36
Pastures and meadows	816	28	417	15	446	15
Arable land	391	14	704	24	699	24
Other land or new soils	386	13	709	25	703	25

Source : National Environmental Agency: Overview of the Steps Undertaken in the Context of the Convention to Combat Desertification, 2001.

Albania is mainly a hilly and mountainous country where only a small percentage of land is considered appropriate for cultivation. During the Communist era with the objective of self-sufficiency in cereal production, much energy was expended on enlarging the stock of arable land by terracing vast expanses of hills and by draining swamps, deviating rivers and disturbing downstream ecosystems (lakes, wetlands). Between 1950 and 1990, arable land increased from 235,000 hectares to 703,000 hectares with the clearance of 468,000 hectares of forests and pastures. In Albania desertification results not so much from a lack of moisture but rather from degradation by human intervention, for instance, reclaimed soils that became saline or are barren due to erosion, and are then abandoned (see Figure 10.1).

Soil erosion is a serious problem in Albania. Although the country's mountainous topography (60 per cent of the territory) and weather patterns are natural causes of erosion, human activities (i.e. the dredging of rivers for construction materials, logging, overgrazing, the abandonment of terraced land, poorly designed terraces, roads and channels) are exacerbating the problem and decreasing agricultural soil productivity (see Table 10.3).

Much of the eroded sediments end up in the major rivers. The natural functions of the floodplains have been by-passed by the flood protection and land reclamation projects of the 1945-1980 period, with the result that sediment is carried to the sea rather than being deposited in the floodplains. The annual loss of soil has been estimated to be between 20 and 70 tons/ha, and may reach over 100 tons/ha in extreme cases. The rivers carry to the sea more than 60 million tons of solid materials with 1.2 million tons of humus as well as 162,000 tons of fertilizers. Flooding affects 40,000 hectares of land; eroded land along riverbanks is estimated at about 100,000 hectares; and 150,000 hectares are affected by landslides, but probably a good part of that land is not used for agriculture.

In general, the sensitivity of Albanian soils is not high, except in the areas with flysch soils, where erosion intensity is 1.5 mm/year compared to Albania's average of 0.3 mm/year. In the Osulli and Devolli upper basins, erosion is most acute because of the sparse vegetal cover (Mediterranean shrubs or deforested). Albania's vulnerability to erosion has been classified according to rainfall (see Figure 10.1 and Table 10.4).

Table 10.3: Agricultural land with restricted fertility (selected problems)

	1000 ha	% of territory
Deforestation	500.5	17.4
Overgrazing	1220.1	42.4
Accelerated erosion	35.9	12.5
Salinization	65.4	2.3
Chemical pollution	16.5	0.6
Landmines	7.4	0.3

Source: Options méditerranéennes, Série B, vol. 34, 1998.

Note: According to the table, it seems that most of the agricultural land is under stress.

The direct effect of deforestation in a climate with heavy winter rains is a lack of water retention in the topsoil, leading to more rapid water discharge and increased peak charges and flooding. The other consequence is the deposition of sediments in the reservoirs, reducing their retention and regulation capacity, as well as damage to irrigation works and canals, changing the course of the water and flooding. Flooding by mountain torrents tumbling from steep slopes to the plain is a frequent problem in Albania. Erosion and flash run-off from the surrounding upland areas may constitute a very severe problem for the watersheds and irrigation schemes, leading to excessive costs for flood control. Periodically removing the eroded material from these canals, reservoirs and drains is costly.

Spatial planning

One result of continued economic decline has been the internal migration of the population. With the end of restrictions on mobility, many people left Albania in search of better economic prospects elsewhere, but they also moved from the more economically depressed rural regions (the north-east) to the cities. One of the many impacts of this

migration has been the use of agricultural land to develop suburban areas around the major cities where vineyards, fruit trees and vegetables in greenhouses used to grow. Only very small-scale subsistence agriculture remains in those areas. In one of the most affected villages, 16.2 per cent of the good agricultural land was lost within four years, and the figure is expected to increase to 40.3 per cent in the near future.

Most of the construction has taken place illegally: 32 per cent of the population lives in illegal settlements, without planning permission. People also decide to build on their own property, without the necessary infrastructure and without the benefit of master plans. Buildings – especially small enterprises – are scattered along water pipes, electric lines and roads, using more land than necessary. This leads to the misuse of infrastructure and to environmental problems, such as the contamination of drinking-water wells by sewage, erosion of abandoned agricultural land and an alarming loss of and damage to green areas in the city and valuable landscapes outside. Another problem is deforestation and the intensive excavation of material from the rivers for building.

As Albania has little agricultural land per capita, the rapid urbanization invading enormous areas of very fertile farmland in the valleys is one of the biggest stresses on land. In the valleys, the land under construction is the most productive in the country from an agricultural perspective and needs to be protected for future generations in accordance with the governmental objectives of increased self-sufficiency and environmental protection. At the same time, the abandoned agricultural land on steep mountain slopes is creating serious problems of erosion and landslides due to the lack of terrace maintenance.

Table 10.4: Vulnerability to erosion

Zone	Regions	Rainfall (mm)	Erosion (tons/ha/year)	% of national territory
Zone A (high)	Shkodra, Tropoja, Saranda, Girokastra	> 2000	52	20
Zone B (medium)	Berat, Tirana, Durrës, Lushnja, Elbasan, Kruja	around 1500	37	70
Zone C (low)	Korça, Pogradec, Kolonja, Devoll, Librazhd, Dibra	< 1000	15	10

Source: State of the Environment Report, 1999; National Water Strategy, 1997 and Ministry of Environment. Overview of the Steps undertaken for Convention to Combat Desertification, 2001.

Figure 10.1: Soils affected by drought, erosion and other pressures

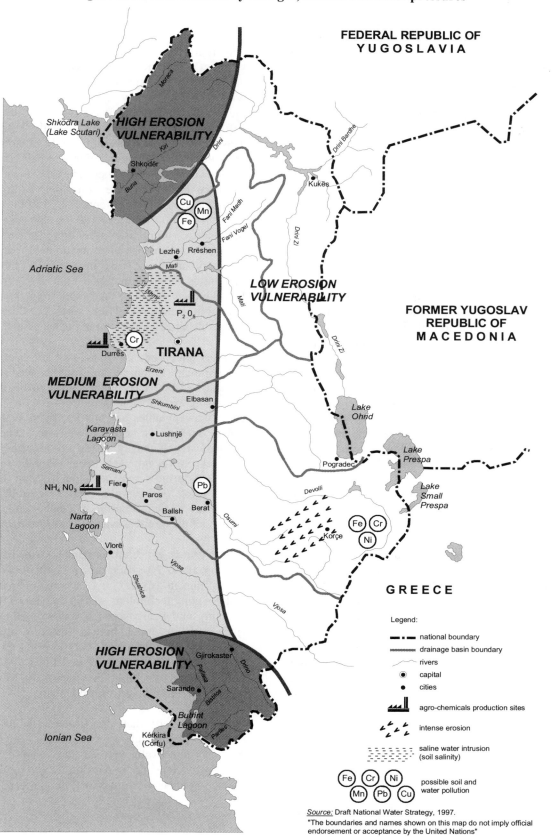

Source: Draft National Water Strategy, 1997.
"The boundaries and names shown on this map do not imply official endorsement or acceptance by the United Nations"

Irrigation and drainage

In Albania, irrigation relies mostly on surface water (see Chapter 6). About 60 per cent of the arable land is under irrigation, more than half in the coastal plains, accounting for some 80 per cent of the agricultural production. Irrigation offers the opportunity to produce two or three crops of vegetables per year. Winter crops such as wheat and fodder require only supplemental irrigation to compensate for irregular spring rainfall, but summer crops such as alfalfa, maize, fruits and vegetables need full irrigation.

Irrigation and reclamation were started on a larger scale in the mid-1930s. Massive investments between 1950 and 1975 increased the area under irrigation from 29,000 to 417,000 ha. Surface irrigation methods dominate, with 95 per cent either furrow-type or stripe-type systems. Water use efficiencies do not exceed 60 per cent. The development of irrigation was accompanied by drainage and reclamation of marshland below sea level and saline areas (280,000 ha, started in the mid-1930s), the building of 653 reservoirs or dams, 639 pumping stations, and flood protection works (865 km of dams on the coast and 300 km of channels in the hills directing waters to the sea). Most of the wetlands (an estimated 100,000 ha) in the extensive coastal plains have been drained to eradicate malaria and for agricultural purposes, and those remaining are estimated at 27,000 ha. Of the drained hectares, 75 per cent (206,000 ha) is drained by gravity with open drains. Drained and reclaimed areas form two thirds of the irrigated area.

Land distribution and social upheavals in 1991 resulted in substantial damage to the irrigation and drainage systems, and to the protection works. The lack of maintenance and of water supply to a multitude of farmers due to non-payment of user charges worsened the situation. In 1994, 114,000 hectares were inoperative and 153,000 hectares severely damaged, only 80,000 were operating normally. Missing or looted canal linings and inefficient irrigation methods resulted in 70 per cent losses, delivering only around 1,200 m³/ha. In any case, most of the irrigation schemes were designed before 1985 and do not meet the full crop water deficits (around 2,000 – 6,000 m³/ha, depending on the region and the crop, and even more for melons).

A number of projects are under way to repair the irrigation system. There are two projects supported by the Work Bank to rehabilitate the existing networks and to help establish approximately 700 new water users' associations. These local associations would be responsible for collecting irrigation fees and maintaining the pumping stations, irrigation and drainage stations, protection dams and works against erosion. The first project will rehabilitate the systems of seven districts along the coast (40 per cent of the total irrigable area in Lushnjë, Fier, Tirana, Durrës, Kavajë, Krujë, Laç). The second project is available only to farmers who are able to form an association and pay 10 per cent of the costs for another 75,000 hectares. The Ministry of Agriculture and Food estimates the overall rehabilitation potential at 315,000 hectares. Some 100,000 hectares will not be rehabilitated because of their low agronomic potential, and because the land has been abandoned, particularly the very small systems in the hills and in the mountains. The International Fund for Agricultural Development (IFAD) is supporting small-scale irrigation schemes. These are considered less profitable since more pumping is necessary.

Farmers have begun to pursue private groundwater development. Pumping the groundwater used to be marginal (1,000 ha), but it seems to be a rapidly increasing trend among farmers who want to cultivate vegetables and market them at attractive prices. This is especially true where the groundwater is easily extracted and the gravity channels have not yet been rehabilitated. This group of farmers may also get support from the Word Bank on condition that a feasibility study demonstrates that the project does not endanger the quality of the aquifer, especially regarding salinity.

Water use is expected to increase steadily in the coming 10 to 20 years, and probably reach about 1.4 million m³, even if it is accompanied by more water-saving technologies (drip irrigation). It seems that the total yearly surface water of all Albanian river basins is much higher than any imaginable future water requirements. The supply is ample and losses could be reduced by one third (400 m³/ha) with simple rehabilitation measures leading to significant agricultural improvements.

It is not likely that the irrigable land will be extended significantly in the near future. The projects aim exclusively at the rehabilitation of existing systems, not expansion to new areas. Their impact on the environment will not increase.

Water and soil pollution

Water quality

High amounts of nitrates, possibly of agricultural origin, have been found in the groundwater in the Semani and Vjosa basins. During the early transition process, agricultural water pollution decreased due to the strong reduction in the use of agrochemicals, but this trend has now been reversed. Fertilizer use increased by 36 per cent between 1994 and 1998 as a result of the rehabilitation of the irrigation networks, and today 70 to 75 per cent of farmers use fertilizers and 40 to 45 per cent use pesticides supplied by private dealers. This now poses an additional threat of agrochemical pollution to drainage water and groundwater.

Another source of negative impact on agriculture and the environment lies in the insufficient control of mining and industrial effluents, making the waters inappropriate for irrigation. In the past, there were areas, such as Matit, where a high content of metallic ions (Fe, Mn, Cu) was found, but the impact on irrigated agriculture was never fully assessed. Since 1991, however, the threat to agriculture of this kind of pollution has lessened as mining and associated activities have almost ceased. Measurements of irrigation waters started in 2000 at the Soil Science Institute on seven water sources at the entrance of the main irrigation system. These measurements show that there is currently no problem with heavy metals in the irrigation water, but the water of some districts (Thana, Kavajë) has a high salt content, which may cause salinization. Some of the water is even toxic for plants (Beden reservoir).

There is a growing demand for agrochemicals, leading to an increased interest in rehabilitating the factories for ammonium nitrate, super phosphates and pesticides production (see Figure 10.1), which were the core of the industrial structure. These industries were extremely polluting, and their reopening without new pollution control measures could cause serious problems.

Chemical pollution is a potential problem not only where the reuse of drainage water is an option (rare), but also where pollution may influence nitrate and pesticide levels in exploitable groundwater and cause the eutrophication of lakes and reservoirs. The foreseeable renewed take-off in Albanian agriculture may affect coastal wetlands by putting an increasing load in drainage water, leading in turn to the eutrophication of coastal lagoons. Drinking water could also be affected.

Soil pollution

After preliminary research and consultation with national environment experts, the United Nations Environment Programme investigated nine sites in Albania that appeared most likely to be environmental hot spots (see Chapter 7). The most urgent concern is the health of the people living on those sites and consuming contaminated water. Therefore, the analysis focused on the immediate effects on health and living conditions. The dissemination of pollution on larger agricultural lands has not yet been investigated. For instance, the cultivation of fresh vegetables and grazing on soils polluted with lead in the area surrounding the battery production facility in Berat has to be prohibited because of the high uptake by the plants. The transfer of chromium (in Durrës and Elbasan) to plants is limited, but grazing as direct uptake should be absolutely avoided.

Biodiversity

Between 1960 and 1980, agriculture had without doubt major impacts on biodiversity, with the intensification of agricultural practices, the extension of arable lands in swamps or pastures (see Table 10.2), and the improvement of pastures or terracing for the purpose of creating fruit tree plantations. In Albania, the major endangered ecosystems and habitats are not only the coastal areas, but also alpine pastures and meadows (see Chapter 8). Agriculture plays a vital role in the preservation and management of landscape and semi-natural habitats.

Pastures and meadows

Pastures cover 15 per cent of the territory and represent the main base for feeding sheep, goats and cattle. They are of the alpine and sub-alpine (60 per cent) and Mediterranean type and present a diversity of plant and animal communities. They are divided into winter and summer pastures according to the season they are grazed. (see Table 10.5).

Although animals are herded, there is no pasture management. The available pastures are not sufficient to cover the needs of the local herds and additional feed is harvested from trees. Overgrazing, particularly by goats near villages (20-30 per cent of the pastures), is frequent. Given the lack of management and of control, voluntary fires to burn weeds and regenerate plants are a problem as they are likely to set off forests fires (see Chapter 8).

The Albania Private Forestry Development Project, funded by the World Bank, is promoting integrated forest management and the decentralization of competences to 90 out of the 314 local communities (komunas) over a period of three years. This includes updating pasture registries, identifying damage and encouraging respect for management rules. Measures to regenerate the forests and the eroded land could include a grazing ban for a couple of years and simple works (fences, bushes, vetiver grass). More major works, such as watershed protection and land movement control could be financed by the Project. The main costs are due to the regeneration of forests. Pasture improvement may also include the creation of drinking points.

10.3   Policy objectives and management

Strategies

Albania's "Green Strategy", developed by the Ministry of Agriculture and Food and approved by the Council of Ministers in 1998, sets the following goals:
- To modernize and intensify agricultural practices and productivity to achieve food security and decrease the negative trade balance;
- To improve the welfare of farm families through agriculture and rural development with non-farm jobs, including jobs in agro-tourism;
- To penetrate export markets (fruit, grapes, citrus fruit, fresh and processed vegetables, olives); and

- To slow migration to the urban areas.

The Green Strategy of 1998 identifies a competitive agro-processing industry as the key to agriculture and rural development. The priorities are flour, pasta and bread production; the manufacture of oil and fats; and milk processing. The Strategy calls for their reactivation and support with credit lines, with the quality of the products ensured by the control of foodstuff through completion of the legal framework and technical assistance.

Overall, Albania is trying to move toward the gradual approximation of its agriculture to the standards of the European Union. In the present situation labour is abundant and agriculture is labour-intensive. The Green Strategy, however, does not address a number of environmental issues, including, for example, soil protection, erosion, chemical use or promotion of good agricultural practice. It does recognize principles of sustainable development, including the need for landscape conservation and biological diversity.

The new *Strategy on Growth and Poverty Reduction* addresses poverty alleviation in the rural areas. It does not integrate rural development and environmental concerns.

Table 10. 5: Pasture capacities

	Winter spring pastures up to 1000 m alt. 1000 ha	Summer pastures over 1000 m alt. 1000 ha	Total 1000 ha	In %
Total	**123**	**290**	**413**	
State	33	112	160	35
Municipal	78	163	245	58
Private	12	15	7	7
In %	29	71		100

Source: State of the environment report, 1997-1998.

Box 10.1:	The 1998-1999 Kosovo refugee wave and its immediate and lasting effects on Albania's rural environment

On the whole it is estimated that the Albanian Government and the international community were able to meet the needs of the refugees from Kosovo in 1998-1999 and take measures to ensure the preservation of Albania's environment so that the impacts were minimal, even though adverse environmental effects can be pointed out. Flat and well-drained locations were selected as campsites for quick, low-cost construction. A total of almost 500 hectares of good agricultural land was used, where now only gravel remains to a depth of 60 cm, requiring rehabilitation and hampering future agricultural use. The destruction of agricultural land – considered as the main environmental impact of the refugee camps – is likely to have significant economic impacts on the families that had farmed the land. Furthermore, a few camps were located inside or beside protected areas and resulted in the destruction of trees and sewage contamination as well as contamination of groundwater that provides drinking water to the region.

In addition, the dumping of solid packaging waste in illegal dump sites may have contaminated soil and groundwater in these areas, and adversely impacted local wild life. Waste water may also have contaminated groundwater and soils.

Agricultural practices are a major threat to biodiversity. In agriculture the main objectives in biodiversity conservation are: (i) to reduce erosion of the agricultural land, (ii) to protect autochthonous breeds and strengthen the National Seed Institute, which can conserve wild species and agricultural varieties both ex situ and in situ. The institutes for wheat and maize, with their experience in genetic resources research, could contribute with the production of elite breeds of local varieties adapted to the local soil and weather conditions, promoted through an efficient extension service.

Legislation

The new (2002) framework Law on Environmental Protection (art. 12) addresses the issue of soil protection, including land use activities for agriculture, livestock, and aquaculture, as well as non-agricultural activities (e.g., transport, exploitation of mineral and water resources, and depositing of substances and wastes into the soil). Persons who have used the soil are obligated to rehabilitate or restore it to its previous state.

The Law on Land and its Distribution (No. 7501/1991), in article 5, is primarily concerned with State measures to support peasant families who cannot get the necessary minimum income from agricultural land in the hilly and mountainous areas. Its main objectives are the development of incomes from agriculture and non-agricultural activities, the completion of property registration, the cultivation of barren land, the development of services to farmers, access to credits and support to processing units (see similar objectives in the Green

Strategy), and the development of infrastructure for drinking water, sewage systems, roads, health care and education. Environment is not an issue.

According to the Law on Land and its Distribution, the new owners of land may use it only for agricultural purposes. Enforcing this Law is the task of the local governments (art. 3), but they have so far been unable to do so. Those who break the Law should be deprived of the use of the land (art. 15) or suffer financial sanctions (art. 16). According to the Law on Urban Planning (No. 8405/1998) and the Regulation on Urban Planning, good agricultural land cannot be used for building (art. 6). Where there are violations, the construction police have the power to pull down illegal buildings, but this Law has also not been consistently enforced.

The Law on Water Resources (No. 8093/1996) and the Law on Irrigation and Drainage (No. 8518/1999) address water in the agricultural sector but do not include environmental issues associated with water management. A water protection law has been drafted. Should it be approved, it would control the use of soils to prevent erosion so that the washing away of agrochemicals is avoided; establish areas of sanitary protection to safeguard the quality of wells for drinking; and prohibit livestock activities and the use of fertilizers and pesticides in the adjacent areas.

Both the Law on Forestry (No. 7223/1992) and the Law on Pastures and Grazing (No. 7917/1995) contain provisions for grazing and grazing fees. The Law on the Leasing of State-owned Agricultural Land, Meadows, Pastures and Forests

---

Box 10.2:   The impact of mines on agriculture and rural safety

During the war in Kosovo, mines were placed at the border of Kosovo and in Albanian territory. The same areas were further affected by cluster bomblets (Rock Eye) dropped by NATO aeroplanes during the 1999 bombing campaign. The exact degree of the problem is difficult to quantify, but it is assumed to be both extensive and complex. From the point of view of land use, fields may be left uncultivated for fear of mines. In the districts of Tropojë, Has and Kukës, since 1998 there have been 17 deaths and 116 injuries (often amputation of a leg), i.e. 25 per cent of the total casualties due to mines and unexploded ordnance in Kosovo and Albania together. Mined areas were never recorded or mapped, but it is assumed that 74 km of the border (from Qerem to Shishtavec) on a width of more than 1 km (i.e. more than 7400 ha) are high-density nuisance minefields. The majority of the mine-affected areas are in remote and extremely poor rural communities. These areas are largely made up of land – if marginal from the agronomic point of view (pastures and meadows) – of vital importance to those communities as a prime resource for grazing livestock and harvesting wood and hay for the winter months. In addition many of the traditional tracks and paths linking remote communities together lead through mined areas.

Following the training and equipping of Albanian army teams, the majority of the cluster bomb sites (unexploded) have now been cleared, and work is continuing. Due to the high proportion of civilian mine casualties sustained since 1998 and the lack of national resources to effectively ease the problem in a remote and insecure region, the International Committee of the Red Cross has stared to recruit community-based clearance teams instructed by the network of the National Red Cross mines awareness instructors and coordinated by the Albanian Mine Action Executive.

(No. 8313/1998) stipulates leasing by auction (art. 15) with longer contracts. The Law on the Plant Protection Service (No. 7662/1993, amended by Law No. 8531/1999) is in accordance with EU regulation 91/414/EEC and deals with the quality control of all imported pesticides and their registration procedure by a State Commission of Registration, which includes members from the Ministry of Environment.

A comprehensive draft law on soil protection is currently under discussion. It contains general provisions on the protection and rehabilitation of eroded and polluted soils, defined as responsibilities of the Ministry of Environment. The Ministry of Agriculture and Food would be in charge of applying soil protection policies in the agricultural sector (arable land, forests and pastures) and organizing monitoring and protection on the local level (cadastre, land use, land evaluation, land protection, including erosion, degradation, pollution), in collaboration with the Soil Science Institute and the Geological Survey (data processing in a geographic information system (GIS)). The legal frame of action requires further clarification.

Institutional structures

The Ministry of Agriculture and Food is responsible for agriculture, forestry and fishing. Its responsibilities also include administering, protecting, studying and inventorying biodiversity. Within the Ministry, a permanent Project Environmental Management Unit has been established to integrate environmental issues into agricultural projects. To perform its task, the Unit can hire external experts and institutes and train government staff in environmental issues.

The Albania Private Forestry Development Project is experimenting with shared responsibility between the municipalities (or local governments), which would manage 60 per cent of the pastures (mainly winter pastures), and the State, which would retain 40 per cent (mainly summer pastures, which are ecologically more sensitive). Their privatization will remain marginal (< 10 per cent). In order to ensure their sustainable use, State supervision will be maintained, regardless of ownership. The General Directorate for Forests and Pastures has jurisdiction and will retain responsibility for both forests and pastures. The district forest directorates are responsible at the local level.

The Plant Protection Institute in Durrës carries out scientific work. There is a network of agricultural inspectors in the districts that provides information on disease outbreaks and chemical use. The Soil Science Institute performs research on all issues related to land and control of the quality of irrigation water, and it is equipped with a modern analytical laboratory. The Geological Survey carries out basic research in various fields of the earth sciences producing maps and data on natural resources (water, soil, underground resources) and their current use, as well as environmental threats (soil pollution, over-exploited materials). For the past three years, it has also been developing a database on GIS that should supply decision makers and other clients with digitalized data.

The Ministry of Agriculture and Food has developed a two-tier extension policy (2001). Larger farms in the plain will be served by private extension services on a fee basis, and information centres and extension workers provided by the State will support smaller farmers. In each of the 36 districts, there will be at least one information centre, and the country will be covered with 3000 public extension workers.

The Organic Agricultural Association was established in 1997. It is a member of the International Federation of Organic Farming and has local branches in Korçe, Pukë and Tepelenë. The main task of this Association is to organize inspections and certification according to international standards, advocating sustainable low input levels for agriculture in rural Albania, public awareness and lobbying. Organic farming is a governmental objective, but there is no legislation on organic farming.

10.4 Conclusions and recommendations

The rehabilitation of irrigation is a priority in order to enable farmers to increase their production and their income. Hence, the adjacent watershed stability, its conservation and management should be considered a primary prerequisite for all investments in irrigation rehabilitation.

In the agricultural sector, the use of water resources is determined only by the Law on Water Resources and the Law on Irrigation and Drainage. The proposed law on water protection is still only in draft form. The National Water Strategy of 1997 has never been adopted. It should provide the basis for action related to, inter alia, the rational and sustainable use of water resources for irrigation, establishing water charges for irrigation and a national water master plan. Such a strategy and a water master plan are urgently needed (see recommendation 1.1 and 6.6), as is the improvement of the legislation on water protection (see recommendation 1.2). In the meantime, given the lack of information on water resources and the intensity of their use, as is the case today, water use for irrigation is not rationalized and might be unsustainable in some parts of the country.

At the same time, there is a growing demand for agrochemicals, leading to an increased interest in rehabilitating the factories (ammonium nitrate, super phosphates, pesticides) that were the core of the industrial structure. These were extremely polluting and cannot be restarted without pollution control measures.

Chemical inputs are necessary to take full advantage of the irrigation potential. The problem should receive more attention, not only where the potential reuse of drainage water is an option (rare), but also where pollution may influence nitrate and pesticide levels in exploitable groundwater and cause eutrophication of lakes and reservoirs. Although agricultural pollution is currently low, the foreseeable take-off in agriculture may affect coastal wetlands by putting an increasing load in drainage water, leading in turn to the eutrophication of coastal lagoons (see Chapter 11).

Groundwater sources for drinking should be kept safe through the setting of sanitary protection perimeters, in which all activities are prohibited (20 m in the immediate protection area). Where this is not feasible, these activities, including the spreading of both agrochemicals and organic fertilizers and animal husbandry, should be strictly limited and combined with the cultivation of protective crops (300 m, extensive meadows in the adjacent protection area).

Recommendation 10.1:
(a) The Ministry of Environment should ensure that environmental impact assessments are carried out for all irrigation schemes and that they are included in the list of activities of the Law on Environmental Impact Assessment. These assessments need to look not only at the risks of salinization, but also at the pollution of drainage water by agrochemicals, the impact on groundwater and watershed stability;

(b) The Ministry of Agriculture and Food should establish an irrigation master plan giving priority to irrigation for the Semani and Erzeni-Ishmi river basins. The irrigation master plan should include water charges for irrigation;

(c) Ground water pumping should be subjected to the environmental permit system.

The Law on Land, the Law on Urban Planning and the Regulation on Urban Planning should establish guidelines for land use and land administration by local governments. Local governments should be given all necessary support to carry out their tasks under these laws. Public knowledge of the laws must be reinforced by media campaigns to prevent further illegal building.

In accordance with the rapid development of some cities, their suburbs must be the subject of new administrative boundaries and planning, and the land classified according to new criteria, pertinent to actual and future land use: housing, suburban agriculture, protected green spaces, corridors for infrastructure. In the rural municipalities, land-use categories also have to be designated to facilitate land-use planning and agricultural use (orchards, forestry). Territorial planning is essential to ensure the sustainable growth of the country.

Recommendation 10. 2:
(a) The National Council for Territorial Planning should draw up a master plan for land use for all Albania. A national land administration responsible for managing publicly owned land (State land) should be created with the authority to carry out transactions and oversee private transactions (control of property rights and leasing prices) for agricultural land;

(b) All municipalities, under the supervision of the National Council for Territorial Development, should urgently draw up spatial plans for land use, beginning with the rural municipalities located around large cities (Durrës, Tirana) which are subject to intense pressure from urbanization, in order to save the good agricultural land in these regions. After public hearings, those plans must be implemented very quickly.

The present forestry and pasture policy is relatively clear and sound, and if current sub-projects under the Albania Private Forestry Development Project of the World Bank are successful they could be replicated throughout the country, solving the main management problems and drastically reducing erosion in pastures.

Recommendation 10.3:
The Ministry of Agriculture and Food should promote sustainable management measures for wildlife protection and for pastures, including a moratorium on the use of systematic fertilization and weed-control chemicals.

A comprehensive draft law on soil protection is under discussion. It contains general provisions for the protection and rehabilitation of eroded and polluted soils. The Ministry of Agriculture and Food would be responsible for soil protection in the agricultural sector (arable land, forests and pastures) and for monitoring and protection on the local level in collaboration with the Soil Science Institute and the Geological Survey. The legal basis still needs further clarification. Taxes on agricultural land (as property) should be introduced. They should depend on soil quality, on distance from the market, means of transport and necessary investments in maintenance works.

There are two pilot projects under way to assess land erosion and land pollution, but in general, accurate indicators of soil degradation and scientific data are yet to be published and made available to decision makers. There is no national strategy to keep erosion under control and nothing is said about it in the Green Strategy.

Recommendation 10. 4:
(a) The Ministry of Agriculture and Food, through the Soil Science Institute, should collect and aggregate in a manner useful for decision makers all existing information about soil erosion and past soil pollution by mining and other industries so as to determine sound land use on the national level. Particular attention should be given to areas at high risk;

(b) The Ministry of Environment and the Ministry of Agriculture and Food should jointly finalize the draft law on soil protection and submit it to Parliament for adoption;

(c) The Ministry of Environment, in cooperation with line ministries and National Council for Territorial Planning, should develop a strategy and action plan to combat soil erosion.

The Law on the Plant Protection Service is in accordance with EU regulation 91/414/EEC and deals with the quality control of imported pesticides and their registration by a State Commission of Registration. The method used and advocated by the Ministry of Agriculture and Food for increasing yields includes better seeds, irrigation rehabilitation and the application of more fertilizers and pesticides. Indeed since 1993 the use of pesticides has been increasing annually. This puts particular emphasis on the role of the extension services, which should provide advice on the correct use of agrochemicals.

Recommendation 10.5:
The Ministry of Agriculture and Food needs to strengthen its extension services, particularly for small farmers. The extension information centres should promote organic farming and low-input farming and provide information on a range of critical issues, including, for example, agricultural waste management, sanitary measures and protection of waters.

With modest investments, at least in the coastal areas, agriculture can quickly start yielding much better results. This region is able to produce vegetables and fruit for food processing and export, and supply a growing market of increasing urban residents and tourists. It can be competitive on the national and international markets for Mediterranean produce, such as olive oil, wine, early vegetables and organically grown fruit. The international marketing of organic products such as sheep-milk cheese needs exploration and, for products from grazing animals, sustainable grazing patterns should be one of the criteria for obtaining a label. Collecting and cultivating medicinal and aromatic herbs, pine resin, mushrooms, forest fruits and berries, and willow for weaving are traditional activities based on an existing marketing network for export. It is considered as a diversification of rural income, but should be put under control (permits and monitoring system), because of the current unsustainable collecting practices. It is suggested that sustainable use should be certified (see also Chapter 8).

For exports of special agricultural products (as is already the case for honey or fresh herbs and will soon be for olive oil), certification is of the utmost importance and a law or regulation on organic farming should be passed without delay.

Recommendation 10.6:
The Government should take the necessary steps to establish certification procedures for organic farming meeting international eco-standards.

Chapter 11

COASTAL ZONE MANAGEMENT (INCLUDING TOURISM)

11.1 Current situation along the coast

Albania's coast is about 420 km long. Its exclusive economic zone covers about 12,000 km^2. The coast can be divided into two parts: the northern, Adriatic coast, and the southern, Ionian coast. They have very different geomorphologic features.

The Ionian coast, which runs southeast for 170 km from Cape Karabauruni to Stillo Island on the Greek border, is hilly, mostly steep mountains plunging into the sea, except for the Butrinti wetland in the south. This coastal zone has spectacular cliffs, grottoes, caves, hillsides, harbours, bays and some of the country's most intact natural areas.

The Adriatic coast, with a total length of about 250 km, is a low-lying alluvial plain 4 to 50 km wide. It comprises a series of small deltas and lagoons, which are formed by nine rivers: Buna, Drini, Mati, Ishmi, Erzeni, Darçi, Shkumbini, Semani and Vjose. Some of the deltas are still active and their shoreline shows dynamic changes in the vicinity of the river mouths. In the case of the Darçi River, however, the old delta is undergoing severe erosion at the river mouth as the sediment input to the coast has almost completely ceased. The low coast is interrupted at a number of locations by hills at a right angle to the coast forming capes. These divide the coast into a number of closed physiographic units of varying sizes.

This diverse and dynamic land-sea interface has been a corridor of intense interaction between natural systems and human activities for centuries. The rich diversity of coastal habitats and geomorphologic features has been providing an irreplaceable natural resource base for people since the Illyrian tribes first settled there over 3000 years ago. The alluvial plains and wetland areas of the northern coast have been considerably altered to support human settlement and activities, while the rugged character of the southern coast has so far

prevented intensive urbanization. Road access to most of the southern coast has long been undeveloped, with narrow, winding and intermittently unpaved roads at right angles to the shore. The former regime restricted boat access to most of the southern coast. The national road that runs parallel to the coastline has recently been upgraded and new segments are being constructed. There are only two harbours along the southern coastline: Sarandë, the larger one, near the Greek island of Corfu, and Porto Palermo, a small military port half way up the southern coast, now expanded for tourism. The northern coast benefits from the main traffic axis of Albania, consisting of a coastal road and railroad, which connects the northern and central regions. There are two harbours: Shengjin and Durrës, the latter being Albania's most important, and one international airport.

According to the preliminary results of the 2001 census, some 30 per cent of the total population lives in the coastal area, i.e. in the area that administratively belongs to the districts that have the coastline as one of their boundaries. However, another survey shows that about 97 per cent of the total population lives within 100 km from the coastline. Table 11.1 gives a more detailed overview of the development of the coastal population during the past decade. The population in the coastal districts has grown unevenly, but the general rule is that the northern districts have gained, while the most dynamic development occurred in coastal cities such as Durrës, Vlorë and Sarandë in the south.

11.2 Pressures on the coastal area

Now that the social and economic climate has been completely transformed, it is to be expected that development will put new pressure on the coastal environment. Unlike the degradation which was caused in the past by land reclamation, mining and industrial pollution, the present threats stem from urbanization, intensive resource exploitation and tourism.

Table 11.1: Coastal population, 1994 and 2001

persons

District	1994	2001
Laç	57,700	n.a.
Lezhë	69,822	68,218
Velipija Commune	7,708	n.a.
Durrës	157,132 *	182,988
Kanja	87,166 *	78,415
Lushnjë	132,195 *	144,351
Fier	203,517 *	200,154
Mallakastra	41,545 *	39,881
Vlorë	174,897 *	147,267
Himara Commune	9,119	n.a.
Sarandë	49,908	35,235

Sources: PAP/DMI, 1995. Albania CZM Plan and the census 2001.
*1989

Coastal urban development is driven by internal migration, exacerbated by the events in Kosovo, which drove many people from the north of the country to the coastal regions, especially the narrow coastal strip. Today, 41 per cent of the total population lives in towns. In 1994, in the coastal area, it was estimated to be around 39 per cent (Table 11.2). It is reasonable to expect that this figure is now at least equal or very close to the national average. Although the biggest cities are located inland (Tirana and Shkodër), the population of coastal cities, particularly Durrës, Vlorë and Sarandë, has increased over the past decade. Urbanization is speeded up by land privatization, as rural dwellers move from primarily mountainous and hilly areas to the coastal areas with better job opportunities and better living conditions. For instance, the coastal cities offer jobs in manufacturing, commerce and tourism (see also Chapter 10). The currently fast urbanization process is certainly having adverse effects on the natural resources and the environment around the main cities (squatter settlements), because in most cases it is not accompanied by planned housing development or the construction of appropriate infrastructure and services. As a consequence of the as yet undefined landownership, there is the growing phenomenon of illegal land possession and construction of houses, particularly in and around the big cities. There are illegally built houses even in public parks. In the rural areas, land privatization leads to more former workers of the State farms building farmhouses. These new homes are well built, but mostly along the roads and on the best agricultural land.

Table 11.2: Coastal urban population

Coastal region	Urban population 1994	% of total coastal population
North	46,100	36
Central *	310,600	39
South	20,900	35

Sources: Albanian Coastal Zone Management Plan, PAP/RAC, 1995; Coastal Zone Management Plan: the Region of Durresi-Vlora, PAP/RAC, 1996.
*1989

Tourism in Albania has a relatively high potential, but until now the Albanian coast has not been an important destination for international tourists. As Tables 11.3 and 11.4 show, it is still largely undeveloped with a small number of hotels, while the bars and restaurants are mainly located in cities, catering largely for the inhabitants, not for international tourists. Future trends will definitely change the structure of tourism. Today, 80 per cent of tourists are Albanians. Potential holiday destinations, especially along the coasts in the central and southern areas with beautiful landscapes and natural environment, will attract investors. Some modest capacities already exist in the area between Durrës and Kavajë. A number of hotels were built in Durrës, mainly by Albanian investors. However, some of the most attractive shores have already been spoiled by the development of human activities and settlements (Golemi beach) or are heavily polluted (Durrës beach). Coastal development is also characterized by the construction of secondary homes. Foreign investors, too, are becoming more active. A project to be developed in Lalëzit Bay by the Kuwait Investment Company ("MAK-Albania") has already been approved by the Government. Although there is a carrying-capacity assessment for tourism (prepared by UNEP-Mediterranean Action Programme, as part of Albania's coastal area management programme) which proposes that all major tourism development projects in Lalëzit Bay should take place behind the hills and at least 300 m from the coastline, this project will be developed approximately 100-150 m from the coastline. In addition, the Government, through the National Council for Territorial Planning, has approved four new tourist villages in Lalëzit Bay, also to be developed 150 m from the coastline. In the south, in the area of Ksamili, a large number of illegally constructed buildings are hampering the area's potential for sound tourism development. Recently the situation has been changing due to the action of the construction police in demolishing some illegal buildings. Such interventions have helped to prevent new illegal buildings all over the country, especially in the coastal area and the main coastal cities. Also, there are indications that tourist capacities could be developed on Sazani Island, practically the only Albanian island, which also has a high biodiversity potential. Since it is expected that pressure from tourism will grow (generated by domestic, as well as by international investors), it is of the utmost importance that both local and national authorities make all possible efforts to safeguard the environmental potential of the coastal area to secure the environmentally sound development of tourism and so guarantee long-term sustainability and the socio-economic security of the coastal population.

Fisheries, particularly commercial fisheries, are underdeveloped. Officially, the sector has about 3000 fishermen and other workers. The fleet is not modern; ships are usually second-hand and poorly maintained. Many fishermen work without a licence, but this is tolerated by the local authorities, who see this as a way to relieve poverty and social problems among the coastal communities. According to FAO (Table 11.5), the annual catch has dropped significantly in the past decade. However, unofficial data show that the real catch is double the one reported. The price is the most important factor in demand. Most of the catch is for the Albanian market; about 40 per cent of fish is exported, mainly to Greece and Italy. Domestic demand is increasing, especially for cheaper fish, whereas high-quality fish is exported. As far as aquaculture is concerned, the number of enterprises has dropped from 35 in 1990 to only 14 today. There are a few sites where sea bass and sea bream (in Sarandë and in Kavajë) are raised. The Ministry of Agriculture and Food, through its General Directorate for Fisheries, is trying to implement environmental measures in aquaculture, so as to reduce potential pollution from fish production. The Law on Fishing and Aquaculture contains provisions on environmental protection. To improve fishing practices, a few internationally financed projects are being implemented, such as those supported by Phare, AdriaMed and the World Bank. Among the main problems in coastal fisheries and aquaculture are the following:

- The inadequate application of the legislation abolishing dynamite fishing;
- Illegal fishing leading to overfishing (especially of sea bass and sea bream);
- Poor inspection (small boats cannot be controlled);
- The lack of appropriate fishing gear and fleet, and poor harbour infrastructure;
- The lack of stock assessments allowing for a sustainable management of the resource;
- The insufficient level of service for the boats due to the high operating cost of the fishing fleet, and the high price of fuel, nets and other equipment;
- Pollution problems facing lagoon fisheries, such as pesticides, over-exploitation and lack of dredging in the channels;
- The excessive, hence unsustainable, fishing of coastal waters; and
- Illegal and uncontrolled fishing by Italian fishermen.

Coastal agriculture. The central and northern coastal regions remain the country's most important agricultural areas. The coastal area has been strongly affected by migration flows, the main observed trends being urbanization within the districts (movement of the rural population to major urban centres) and the movement of people from other districts towards urban centres and coastal agricultural areas. Today about 58 per cent of the population lives on the coast. Before 1990, coastal agriculture was a big environment-related issue, with large wetlands being drained to provide land for agriculture. This policy had several negative consequences. First, valuable wetlands disappeared, reducing the biodiversity potential of the coastal area. Second, the reclaimed agricultural land was not as productive as expected because of the high salinization of the soil. Finally, complete new villages of high-rise flats were built for agricultural workers who were brought from elsewhere. Since this form of agriculture was not very productive, it soon ran into difficulty, creating a number of social, economic and environmental problems in the coastal region.

For any form of development, the provision of *environmental infrastructure* and services is vital. Unfortunately, except for harbours, railways and electric power plants, this has been completely neglected. Industrial and urban liquid and solid waste is discharged without any treatment, and there are critical shortages in the water supply.

Table 11.3: Structure of hotels, 2001

Type of hotel	Hotels	With restaurant	Rooms	Of which: Single rooms	Of which: Double rooms	Of which: Others	Beds
Total	130	106	2,218	631	1,425	162	3,954
** Hotels	72	53	694	117	466	111	1,376
*** Hotels	56	51	1,355	411	901	43	2,242
Other hotels	2	2	169	103	58	8	336

Source: INSTAT, Quarterly Bulletin of Statistics, 2001.

Table 11.4: Structure of bars and restaurants

Economic activity	Number	Number of places Restaurants	Number of places Café-bars
Total	4,687	40,557	124,619
Hotels	106	5,997	3,216
Restaurants	780	34,162	6,067
Café-bars	3,801	398	115,337

Source: INSTAT, Quarterly Bulletin of Statistics, 2001.

The water supply is constantly growing, but it cannot keep pace with rising demand, which is the result of improved living standards, the increased use of electrical equipment, improved sanitary conditions and sewerage systems. In urban areas about 80 per cent of the population has access to piped water. In the coastal area this figure is slightly higher than in the rest of the country (about 88-90 per cent). During the day running water is available in urban areas on an average only for two to three hours. Water use efficiency is low (about 50 per cent of Tirana's water is lost in the city's supply network). Conflicts over the use of water are likely, especially in the Durrës-Vlorë region. The water supply is already woefully inadequate, and the irrigation system is damaged and neglected, while agricultural development will require more water. Tourism is a great water consumer, requiring good-quality water.

Waste-water treatment is not available. Four major coastal cities with a resident population of 254,000 people, which significantly increases during the summer, are connected to a sewerage network, but the waste water is discharged untreated directly into the sea. Thousands of cubic metres of untreated waste water are discharged daily from the coastal cities into the sea (see Table 11.6). While the urban coastal areas are provided with sewerage systems, the suburban areas, which have recently become overpopulated as a result of uncontrolled migration, have almost no sewerage system. Similarly, the urbanized areas in the coastal zone, and particularly the newly built areas close to the beach, do not have any sewerage system in place, only septic tanks or simply sewage collectors. The existing sewerage systems are frequently damaged by the interruptions caused by the construction of new connections (often illegal) and overlooked, because new additions exceed their capacity. The waste-water treatment facilities that do exist were built as part of different industrial complexes, but they are no longer functional, because the industrial production facilities that they belong to have been closed down during the past ten years. A variety of projects are being considered for the construction of a sewerage network and waste-water treatment plants (see Chapter 6 for more details).

Resource extraction is another area where policies are unsatisfactory and exploitation could be considered unsustainable. Coastal forests are being cleared indiscriminately to clear land for coastal development, particularly in Lalëzit Bay and Golemi Beach. The deforestation is causing soil erosion in the coastal zone.

Table 11.5: Fish catch 1990-1997

(Mt)

Type of fish	1990	1992	1995	1997
Cephalopods	n.a.	n.a.	112	126
Crustaceans	45	15	30	22
Molluscs	4,624	357	300	104
Pelagic	4,661	251	353	102
Shellfish	4,669	372	442	252

Source: http://www.fao.org, Agriculture data, 2002.

Table 11.6: Pollution loads from cities, rivers and big industrial facilities into the sea

Hot spots	BOD ton/year	Total-N ton/year	Total-P ton/year	TSS ton/year	Type	Transboundary aspects*
Durrës	2,864	477	96	4,300	domestic	P, L, H,
Vlorë	2,628	438	88	3,942	domestic	P, L, H,
Drini river					domestic industrial	B, F
Mati river					domestic	B, F
Semani river					domestic	B, F
Skumbini river					domestic	B, F
Former PVC factory Vlora					industrial	P
Former chemical factory Durres					industrial	F, B, P

Source: UNEP. Identification of Priority Pollution Hot Spots and Sensitive Areas in the Mediterranean, 1997.
* Transboundary aspects
F- Fisheries
B- Biodiversity
L- Reduction in regional value of Mediterranean tourism
P- Public health
H- Habitats

Coastal erosion is a great problem in the northern and central coastal regions (the Adriatic coast), and in particular north of the city of Durrës. Sediment discharges from rivers are relatively large, which explains the very dynamic nature of the deltaic development of the coast, resulting in the rapid development of new coastal features, such as spits and lagoons. This also explains the significant coastal erosion which has been observed in recent decades as sediment input to the coast has declined due to several anthropogenic developments inland, including dam construction. There are four main causes of coastal erosion: (a) the reduction in sediment input, mainly that brought by rivers, into the coastal zone; (b) the reduction in the amount of sand in the coastal zone due to anthropogenic activities (sand extraction from the beaches and bottom of the sea although this is prohibited by

law); (c) the changing location of river mouths in deltaic systems, as a result of natural causes or anthropogenic effects; and (d) the alteration of the usual pattern of coastal currents and the associated sediment transport along and across the shoreline, due to man-made structures built along the coast.

11.3 Pollution "hot spots"

In 1997 the United Nations Environment Programme/Mediterranean Action Plan (UNEP/MAP) identified priority pollution "hot spots" and sensitive areas in all Mediterranean countries as part of the Strategic Action Programme in the Mediterranean, financed by the Global Environment Facility (GEF). Albania identified eight priority pollution "hot spots", four of them directly linked to waste-water discharges from cities (see Table 11.7).

Table 11.7: Municipal waste-water treatment facilities in the coastal zone

City	Permanent population (in thousands)	Population served (in thousands)	Waste-water treatment plant	Discharge of untreated waste water*
Durrës	120	135	No	DI
Lezhë	12	13	No	n.a.
Sarandë	12	15	No	n.a.
Vlorë	110	99	No	DI+SS

Source: UNEP. Municipal Wastewater Treatment Plants in Mediterranean Coastal Cities, 2000.
* Discharge of untreated waste water
DI- discharge directly into the sea
SS- discharge through many small submarine outfalls

Domestic pollution is dominant in the cities of Durrës and Vlorë, and in the Mati, Semani and Shkumbini rivers. In the Drini river the pollution is mixed, originating from both domestic and industrial sources. Industrial pollution is dominant in two areas where the former PVC factory in Vlorë and the former chemical factory in Durrës are located. These industrial sites are very close to the coast, and there is still evidence of continuing pollution, although the factories were closed some time ago. For instance, large deposits of hexavalent chromium compounds in Durrës pose a threat to the nearby Porto Romano area, while large amounts of mercury were found in Vlorë Bay. Apparently, some of these compounds are leaking into the nearby sea (see also Chapter 7).

In addition, three highly polluted but environmentally sensitive areas have been identified in Albania: Kuna-Vaini lagoons with domestic and industrial pollution; Karavasta lagoon with domestic pollution; and Narta lagoon with mixed pollution caused by agriculture and water extraction.

The Durrës area is the biggest "hot spot" on the Albanian coast, and is the most obvious example of what might happen if non-sustainable coastal development takes place. The city itself is a concentration of environmental problems, because of the near-total lack of environmental services. In addition, the nearby areas of Golemi Beach (south of Durrës), and Lalëzit Bay and Porto Romano (north of Durrës) should be singled out as sites with a high development potential which, due to the flawed implementation of industrial (Porto Romano) or tourism (Lalëzit Bay) policies, may disappear very soon.

11.4   Policy objectives and management

Soon after the liberalization process started in the early 1990s, the Adriatic and Ionian coastal regions' values were recognized as a major asset for Albania's development. Tourism was to be the driving engine. A number of *international coastal zone management programmes* were launched, financially supported by the World Bank, EBRD, UNEP and the European Union (EU).

In 1994-1995 the World Bank financed, through the Mediterranean Environmental Technical Assistance Programme, the preparation of the coastal zone management plans for northern (from the border with Montenegro to Durrës) and southern (from the Karaburuni Peninsula to the Greek border) coastal

regions. These plans were methodologically complementary with the UNEP/MAP Coastal Area Management Programme (CAMP), which concentrated on the central coastal region between Durrës and Vlorë (1993-1996). The major objective of these programmes was to integrate biodiversity protection, tourism development and institutional strengthening. All three coastal plans made a thorough analysis of the situation and gave valuable proposals for future development. But, above all, they were an opportunity for national experts to increase their expertise using some of the best international knowledge. Two obstacles stood in the way of the successful implementation of these projects:

- First, they did not involve as many stakeholders as they could have done (several NGOs, ministries and scientific institutions were not actively involved in the preparation of the plans). Later, it appeared that those that were not very much part of the process but which had great influence in the decision-making process had shown some resistance to implementing the plans;
- Second, the optimistic mood of the mid-1990s was suddenly crushed by the events in 1997 (see Chapter Introduction). That had very negative consequences for the coastal area's development, because many initiatives were interrupted or stopped, and no major international interest in tourism investment has been shown since then.

Parallel with the coastal zone management initiatives, EBRD was active in promoting the development of tourism, particularly of the private sector. It financed the preparation of Albania's first tourism strategy in 1992. It was to be followed by a detailed tourism study for the southern coastal region. Unfortunately, this initiative was also interrupted by the 1997 events. Now, the German Development Fund (GTZ) has prepared a new tourism strategy and EU has financed, through Phare, a number of projects focusing on biodiversity and wetland protection in the coastal area.

Following the sudden cessation of international support for coastal area management, Albania turned to its own resources and opportunities. In this respect, two initiatives should be singled out:

- The *National Biodiversity Strategy and Action Plan* was adopted in 2000. The Strategy proposes a network of 25 marine and coastal protected areas. Thirteen are lagoons, wetlands and estuaries, with a total area of 36,550 hectares. The remaining 12 are exquisite landscapes, with a total area of 64,300 hectares. Karavasta and Narta lagoons are coastal wetlands with a high biodiversity value, but only Karavasta has been designated as a Ramsar site under the Ramsar Convention. Albania is the country with the highest biodiversity loss in Europe, and coastal and marine sites are among the most endangered. The Strategy proposes a very ambitious programme but actual protection is lagging behind, and a number of wetlands in the coastal zone are still being used as sinks for waste water. Similarly, the coastal zone management plans that were mentioned above paid special attention to biodiversity protection and management, although at the time of their preparation Albania had not signed the international Convention on Biological Diversity nor adopted its National Biodiversity Strategy (see Chapter 8). However, these plans defined a number of environmentally sensitive areas and provided management guidelines for their protection and development.

- The former National Environmental Agency, now the Ministry of Environment, constantly insisted that the three above-mentioned coastal zone management plans should be adopted by the Government as its *strategy for the protection and management of Albania's coastal area*. This initiative faced opposition from the former Ministry of Territorial Adjustment and Tourism, which was responsible for physical planning. The guidelines provided by these plans apparently contradicted the policies for tourist development in the coastal area. Others, too, opposed the adoption of the plan, mainly on the grounds that there were already too many restrictions on development. However, the Ministry of Environment's initiative should be supported because the lack of plans is depriving the authorities of an instrument, even minimal, to curb the rampant illegal, and semi-legal, construction along the coast.

The issue of *legislation for coastal management* is addressed in a very discrete way. There is no law on coastal management. The most powerful piece of legislation regulating development in the coastal area is the Law on City Planning (1993, amended in 1998). It provides an entire hierarchy of planning interventions, many of which could be very useful if applied in the coastal area. This Law, however, does not define coastal strips, coastal zones or coastal areas and, consequently, does not provide management guidelines for them. Unfortunately, the technical capacity to apply this Law fully is not available. Other laws that indirectly touch upon coastal areas are:

- The Law on Environmental Protection (2002);
- The Law on Environmental Protection (1993, amended in 1998);
- The Law on the Development of Tourism Priority Zones (1993);
- The Law on Fishing and Fish Farming (1995);
- The Law on Water Resources (1996); and
- The Law on Water Supply and Sanitation Sector Regulation (1996).

Among the by-laws and regulations relevant to coastal development, the most important is the one that regulates the preparation of environmental impact assessments. It is now compulsory for most projects, including almost all construction in the coastal zone, to assess the environmental impact. There are two problems at the moment. First, there is a lack of qualified EIA experts, who are recruited on the consultancy market, which is still undeveloped. Second, although the Ministry of Environment, which is responsible for evaluating EIAs, has established a special department for their review, it cannot fully cope because it also lacks expertise and manpower (see Chapter 1 for more details on EIA).

The *lack of physical plans* is considered to be one of the major obstacles to sustainable coastal development. Physical plans for major investments and developments are being prepared by the National Institute for Physical Planning, but the local governments are also making some plans. According to the new Law on the Organization and Functioning of the Local Government, the local level prepares and approves local plans. The new Ministry of Territorial Adjustment and Tourism coordinates the local government and the National Institute to ensure compatibility among plans. There are two major problems: (i) the preparation of spatial plans is lagging behind the pace of construction; and (ii) the preparation and implementation of the infrastructure master plans is slower than the preparation of the physical plans for the same areas. This situation has led to illegal construction and to the inadequate provision of infrastructure, particularly where tourism development is planned. The scheme introduced in

Albania several years ago to compensate the previous owners of nationalized land whose land could not be returned to them poses special problems. In most cases, they were offered alternative land in the attractive coastal area. Most were given plots of up to 600 m², with the right to build up to three floors on up to 40 per cent of the plot. This right has been abused enormously, because it encouraged illegal housing particularly where there were no plans.

Albania is gradually signing and ratifying *international conventions*. Two that are closely related to coastal zone management are the Barcelona Convention for the Protection of Mediterranean Sea against Pollution (Albania acceded in 1990), and the Ramsar Convention on Wetlands of International Importance Especially as Waterfowl Habitat (acceded in 1995). Albania has benefited from both conventions. Karavasta – Divjaka lagoon has been designated a Ramsar site, while a number of programmes developed under the Barcelona Convention have also had their impact (Coastal Areas Management Programme, Mediterranean Pollution Monitoring and Research Programme, Strategic Action Programme). Albania has been rather slow in ratifying some of the protocols to the Barcelona Convention.

The institutional structure for coastal zone management is based, in practice, on the capacities of only two ministries: the Ministry of Environment and the Ministry of Territorial Adjustment and Tourism. An important feature of the Ministry of Environment is the existence of 12 Regional Environmental Agencies, which implement the environmental strategy, follow and implement preparatory procedures for environmental permits, and check compliance with the Law on Environmental Protection.

Especially important is the inter-ministerial Council for Territorial Planning. It is made up of the Prime Minister and representatives of the Ministry of Environment and the Ministry of Territorial Adjustment and Tourism, whose Department of Urban Planning and Urban Development acts as the Council's secretariat. All requests to the Council (studies and master plans; smaller plans go directly to local authorities for approval) go first to that Department. This gives the Ministry of Territorial Adjustment a real advantage when decisions are taken. The Council has a powerful role, because it

arbitrates when there are no plans or when larger projects contradict the plans and a compromise has to be found. Very often the Council's decisions go against the planning proposals.

In addition, protected area management is now under the General Directorate of Forests and Pastures, which is part of the Ministry of Agriculture and Food. The General Directorate of Fisheries within the same Ministry deals with fisheries.

There is no department in either Ministry dealing specifically with coastal management. The National Council for Territorial Planning deals only with planning, not with the wider issues of coastal management. In the Ministry of Environment, relations between the departments seem harmonious, but employees are overworked and do not have enough power. In the Ministry of Territorial Adjustment and Tourism, relations between departments are not so idyllic. For example, the Environmental Department, which is attached to the Urban Development and Planning Department, is often opposed to the decision taken by the Council because they do not respect basic environmental rules. The Regional Environmental Agencies often feel powerless when requested to act decisively, because they are understaffed, and there is no integration and coordination of work between the Ministry of Environment's Regional Agencies and those of other ministries (forestry, water, public works, for example). They also feel frustrated because decisions delegated to the regional level are often taken without consultation with the regional offices.

Economic instruments that might affect development in the coastal area are still rare (see more details in Chapter 2). Nevertheless, they will certainly play an important role in raising public awareness of environmental values. Some studies (financed by international funding sources) show that additional funds are needed for environmental purposes in the coastal area, especially for the water-supply and waste-water systems. Some funds have already been found (EU and the World Bank), but more are needed. Two environmental funds have been established: the first with earmarked money from the municipal waste charges, and the other with income generated by the State-owned forests and pastures.

Table 11.8: Environmental indicators of sea water quality

(mg/l)

Sampling points	Sampling date	pH	O2*	BOD	NH₄	NO₂	NO₃	PO₄	P total
Mati river mouth	10.11.98	7.8	10.2	1.5	0.10	0.001	0.18	0.03	0.25
200 m from the mouth	10.11.98	7.8	8.8	1.6	0.05	0.001	0.16	0.03	0.11
800 m from the mouth	10.11.98	7.3	11.7	1.5	0.02	0.001	0.27	0.03	0.10
Ishimi river mouth	11.11.98	7.5	8.4	6.0	1.20	0.060	0.55	0.08	0.50
200 m from the mouth	11.11.98	7.8	7.5	2.8	0.85	0.035	0.46	0.08	0.21
800 m from the mouth	11.11.98	8.0	8.0	2.6	0.51	0.030	0.50	0.10	0.25
Durres	13.11.98	8.2	6.7	6.5	1.20	0.200	0.20	0.06	1.79
Durres	13.11.98	8.5	8.5	4.5	0.30	0.025	0.12	0.03	0.33
Durres	13.11.98	8.3	9.0	3.2	0.10	0.003	0.10	0.04	0.06
Vlore	20.11.98	8.3	6.9	5.8	0.02	0.025	0.20	0.11	0.14
Vlore	20.11.98	8.5	8.5	3.2	0.02	0.001	0.22	0.05	0.11
Vlore	20.11.98	8.5	8.0	5.9	0.02	0.001	0.19	0.04	0.12
Semi river mouth	18.11.98	8.3	10.6	3.9	0.02	0.001	0.77	0.26	0.40
200 m from the mouth	18.11.98	8.3	9.8	3.5	0.02	0.001	0.66	0.13	0.39
800 m from the mouth	18.11.98	8.3	10.0	3.7	0.02	0.001	0.40	0.05	0.19

Source: State of the Environment Report, 1998.
Note: * dissolved oxygen

Ten different ministries and institutions are in charge of *monitoring* air, water and soil pollution, environmental radioactivity, transboundary pollution, biodiversity, soil erosion, and pollution caused by industrial and urban waste. The monitoring network has, however, proved unable to meet the requirements for the implementation of modern economic instruments. It is to be strengthened in the years to come in line with the monitoring strategy envisaged by the NEAP. The information collection system relies on three sources: the local administration; the Regional Environmental Agencies; and the regional and local offices of the different ministries and specialized State institutions. Table 11.8 illustrates the range of indicators that have been used in monitoring sea quality. The monitoring programme has been extensively supported by the UNEP/MAP Mediterranean Pollution Monitoring and Research Programme.

11.5 Conclusions and recommendations

Albania's coastal area is still its biggest development asset. In spite of intensive, albeit rather haphazard, development during the past decade, there are still pristine coastal sites that offer great potential, particularly for the development of tourism (Velipoja-Viluni Lagoon, Lalëzit Bay, Karaburuni Peninsula, Butrinti Lake). Significantly, all of these sites are relatively far from the major urban centres, although close enough to be affected by them in the future. At some locations, such as Velipoja-Viluni or Lalëzit Bay, decisions have already been taken to start with massive tourism development, which, unfortunately, largely disrespect the natural values of these sites as well as their carrying capacity for tourism. These two examples show what might happen to the coast if unregulated and haphazard development becomes predominant.

Pressures on the coastal area are extremely high. Rapid urban coastal development; tendencies towards short-term profit against long-term conservation of coastal resources; recent events that have forced the hinterland population, particularly from the mountainous regions, to migrate towards the coast and to find new livelihoods, very often at the expense of the coastal environment; compensation schemes for land that have absorbed large tracts of the valuable coastal land; the non-existence of coastal plans and very little or no respect for them even when they do exist; the legacy of the former regime's lack of respect for the environment resulting in the location of polluting industries in the most attractive coastal areas; a general lack of human and financial resources for coastal management and law enforcement, are only some of the problems that the Albanian authorities are facing today and which allow very little optimism about the future of the coastal region.

The lack of coordination, and even rivalry, among major actors in coastal management is almost legendary. There are not so many actors at the moment, but their number will certainly increase, as the elements of civil society start gaining in importance.

The starting point for the future of the Albanian coast is the new plan for integrated coastal zone management. A major bottleneck could be forcing the major stakeholders to commit themselves to implementing such a strategy. There are several other obstacles that could stand in the way of implementation:

- The poor respect for enforcement authorities, resulting in a low level of law enforcement. The responsible authorities are too badly equipped to be effective. They lack the manpower, political support and technical means to ensure respect for law enforcement;

- The lack of coordination and integration among institutions and authorities responsible for coastal management. They often compete among themselves and have different agendas with respect to coastal development;

- Coastal zone management is still not widely known, except in some institutional "pockets". There is little knowledge on its benefits, methods, tools and techniques, and on the procedures and stakeholders that need to be involved. Local action in coastal management is almost non-existent. This obstacle is hindering the implementation of a "bottom-up" approach to coastal management;

- Illegal housing along the coast is widespread. In some locations this will really create an obstacle to balanced development, because no authority will dare, despite some encouraging initiatives to destroy illegal buildings in major Albanian cities, demolish illegal houses on a large scale. But while illegal buildings are still there, the prospects for better development will be hindered, because they consume large portions of the most valuable coastal land;

- There is a benevolent attitude towards haphazard tourism development and unsustainable resource exploitation. The rationale is that these activities create jobs and help ease hardships in an unbearable social situation. This is certainly a short-sighted approach that could backfire;

- There is no developed monitoring system and a general lack of reliable data on marine and terrestrial ecosystems, as well as on pollution and other environmental problems;

- Public awareness on coastal environmental problems is generally very low;

- The use of economic instruments is underdeveloped.

Within the context of the new CZMP the existing regional plans for the north, central and south coastal areas should be updated. Moreover, a number of more detailed coastal projects could be developed for which international financing could then be sought (areas of Velipoja, Lalëzit Bay, Golemi Beach, Karavasta-Divjaka Lagoon, Karaburuni Peninsula, Porto Palermo, Lakes Xamili and Butrint).

The benefit of this recommendation is that it will provide the national authorities with a tool and a regulatory basis for the prevention of negative development along the coast, in particular urban sprawl and illegal construction, and better guide future development. The plans could also be considered as a strategy. They prioritize problems, concentrate on priorities and on the most relevant strategic axes (biodiversity protection, tourism development, institutional strengthening), provide a strategic framework for future development, include an action plan, and a financial estimate of the resources needed to create conditions for faster and more sustainable development (mainly for building the necessary physical infrastructure).

Regulatory instruments for coastal zone management should be prepared and adopted. They should define the exclusive economic zone, territorial waters, coastal waters, coastal strip, coastal zone, coastal area and coastal hinterland and that will have to provide management guidelines. The greatest emphasis should be on defining the narrow coastal strip, where the pressures are the highest and which creates most of the problems in the coastal waters. The public maritime domain will have to be defined and strict regulation will have to be proposed for it. The regulatory instruments will have to define development procedures for each of the segments of the coastal area, and in particular for the specific EIA in coastal areas.

Recommendation 11.1:
(a) The Government, together with the Ministry of Territorial Adjustment and Tourism, should stimulate implementation of the integrated coastal zone management plan for the entire coastal region. All necessary regulatory instruments to implement the plan should be adopted as soon as possible;

(b) To facilitate implementation, the Government should establish a special inter-ministerial coastal zone management committee, which consists of relevant ministries and local authorities.

A particularly difficult situation is that of the coastal cities, where a number of environmental problems are having a considerable negative impact on the surrounding areas. Untreated liquid waste and solid waste inadequately disposed of are a source of pollution that is spreading towards large nearby sections of the coastal marine and land area. Continuous coastal urbanization in the form of ribbon development is a feature that might freeze the future of these areas for a long period of time. Municipalities do not have the means to take strong action and to impose their development objectives. Too many developments in the coastal area were guided by unregulated private interest with very little respect for the law.

Recommendation 11.2
The Government should address the problem of illegal building along the coast, giving special attention to measures to eradicate existing illegal buildings along the coast.

Economic instruments for coastal management are implemented only marginally, and are of the simplest kind. The level of applicability in the Albanian context of more sophisticated economic instruments, such as effluent charges, product charges, a deposit-refund system, user charges for natural resources, payment for the change of use of natural areas, tariffs for obtaining an environmental licence, and non-compliance and administrative fines, should be assessed in more detail. It is expected that a gradual introduction of these instruments will make natural resource use more sustainable.

Improving the regular monitoring of beach water quality is crucial if Albania wants to tap some of the international tourism market. Thought should be given to having some beaches apply for the "Blue Flag". Special attention should be given to the enforcement of regulations and instruments.

The Ministry of Environment should be responsible for the development and implementation of these instruments. The role of the Regional Environmental Agencies' inspectors should be strengthened and their resources improved.

Recommendation 11.3:
The Ministry of Environment should develop and implement appropriate instruments to achieve the sustainable management of coastal resources.

Special importance should be given to the improvement of the monitoring systems, particularly regular monitoring of beach water quality.

The waste management plan will provide the strategy for waste management. It would consist of: an assessment of current pollution levels, a definition of "hot spots", the identification and prioritization of investments, and an action plan. The major problems with solid waste disposal and the lack of sanitary landfills will require urgent international support for building these sites. It also requires the active participation of local and regional authorities. They will be responsible for implementing the plan.

Recommendation 11.4:
The National Water Council, the Ministry of Territorial Adjustment and Tourism and the Ministry of Environment should work to improve waste-water treatment and solid waste management in large coastal cities, and prevent hazardous materials pollution, in order to reduce pollution from land-based sources.

In spite of diminishing resources, tourism is still considered to be one of the most important development potentials. The plan should identify the tourism development strategy, major stakeholders, potential investors, define the nature of the Albanian tourist product, and assess the carrying capacity for tourism in the most important locations along the coast, taking into consideration the existing and future development already approved.

The Ministry of Territorial Adjustment and Tourism should take the lead in implementing this recommendation in cooperation with the Ministry of Environment, the Ministry of Transport and Telecommunications, the Ministry of Culture, and the Ministry of Agriculture and Food (General Directorate of Forests and Pastures).

Recommendation 11.5:
The Ministry of Territorial Adjustment and Tourism, assisted by the Ministry of Environment, should implement the sustainable tourism development plan, including the preparation of carrying-capacity assessments for the most attractive tourist locations.

Chapter 12

HUMAN HEALTH AND THE ENVIRONMENT

12.1 Overall health status and environmental conditions

Population development

The census in 2000 showed that the total population of Albania is 3,985,039 (Table 12.1). The district of Tirana has 627,204 inhabitants, followed by Elbasan (264,877), Fier (254,123), Durrës (245,134), Shkodër (233,140) and Vlorë (214,313). Albania's population is younger than that of other European countries (average age 28.6). One third (33 per cent) is under 14, some 40 per cent are under 18, and almost half (49 per cent) under 25. During the past ten years, average annual population growth has been 1.9 per cent, but it is now declining. Since 1992, it is estimated that more than 300,000 people have left the country. However, the present more stable situation has probably encouraged some emigrants to return to Albania since the actual population is more than the estimated one. Most Albanian emigrants are between 19 and 40 years of age.

The rapid urbanization of the population is of growing concern. The urban/rural ratio of the population has changed, with the urban population of the ten major urban centres accounting for 36 per cent of the total population in 1999 compared to 20 per cent in 1990. The Tirana region has seen a population increase of 30 per cent due to internal migration mainly from places with poor economic opportunities, for instance rural areas in the mountainous north. The population in Tirana, Durrës and Fier has doubled over the past ten years. The population is expected to fall slightly (-0.3 per cent) in rural areas because of the significant levels of migration to urban areas. Population growth in urban areas is expected to be 3.8 per cent and, as a result of migration, urban populations are expected to increase by 10 per cent over a ten-year period, resulting in 55 per cent of the population living in urban areas by the year 2009.

In 1998, the birth rate was 17.6/1000 while the death rate was 5.1/1000. Life expectancy at birth has reached an average of 75 years, which is higher than the average in Central Europe (72 years), but three years less than the EU average (78.1 years). Women's life expectancy is seven years longer than men's.

Selected trends of mortality

After falling to a minimum of 761.5 deaths per 100,000 population in 1994, standardized death rates increased again to 878.4 in 1998 (Table 12.2). This rate is lower than in Central and Eastern Europe but above the EU averages. The male death rate from all causes, at 1210 per 100,000, is significantly higher than that of women. In 1998, the highest death rates were observed in Pukë, Pogradec, Devoll and Delvinë.

Death from infectious diseases drastically decreased from 9.53/100,000 in 1994 to 2.95/100,000 in 1998. The leading cause in 1994 was infectious intestinal diseases. Incidences of tuberculosis decreased from 81/100,000 to 21/100,000, as did the mortality rates (SDR 2.9/100,000 in 1987 versus 1.1/100,000 in 1998).

In parallel with the decrease in the birth rate, non-standardized infant mortality rates fell from 30.9 per 1000 live births in 1992 to 14.7 in 1999, still more than twice the EU average (5.5) (Figure 12.1). The leading causes of infant mortality are acute respiratory infections, congenital anomalies, diarrhoea and infectious diseases. Although interregional differences in infant mortality have decreased over the past few years, there is still almost a two-fold difference between the regions. In 1998 the highest infant mortality rates were observed in Kuçovë (33.5), Laç (32.9), Malsi E Madhe (27.1), Mallakaster (25.1) and Elbasan (22.4).

Albania's average maternal mortality rate is high (around 27.5 per 100,000 live births in 1997). The northern regions, such as Tropojë, Has and Kukës, have the highest rates with 282, 135 and 105 per 100,000 live births. Lack of access to good health care in mountainous rural areas is the biggest contributing factor.

Table 12.1: Demographic indicators 1994-2000

Indicators	1994	1995	1996	1997	1998	1999	2000
Population (estimated)	3,202,031	3,248,836	3,283,000	3,324,317	3,354,300	3,373,445	3,114,000
Population census*	..	..	..	..	..	..	3,985,039
% population aged 0-14 years	33.4	33.0	33.0	33.0	32.6	..	..
Ratio of births to deaths	6.9	6.5	5.7	4.8	3.49	..	..
Live births per 1000 population	22.5	22.2	20.8	18.6	18.0	17.2	..
Urban population (%)	37.0	37.0	..	37.9	38.3	41.0	..
Literacy rate (%)	85.0	85.0	..	85.0	83.5	..	..
Crude death rate	4.7	5.0	5.1	4.8	4.9	..	..

Source: WHO. Health For All Database, January 2001 and census.

Table 12.2: Standardized death rates for the most important causes of death and their share per 100,000 population

	Albania (1997)	EU average (1997)	Central and East European average (1997)
All causes	878.43 (100%)	690.47 (100%)	1097.98 (100%)
SDR, diseases of the circulatory system	405.09 (46%)	270.11 (39%)	595.5 (54%)
SDR cerebrovascular diseases	153.97	68.67	146.53
SDR ischaemic heart disease	90.91	109.35	181.7
SDR, malignant neoplasms	115.4 (13%)	187.89 (27%)	204.65 (18%)
SDR trachea/bronchitis/lung cancer	32.59	38.25	46.2
SDR malignant neoplasm female breast	7.37	29.01	23.95
SDR, diseases of the respiratory system	65.33 (7%)	56.85 (8%)	53.45 (4%)
SDR, external cause, injury and poisoning	93.38 (11%)	41.27 (5%)	72.54 (6%)

Source: WHO. Health For All Database, January 2001.

Selected trends in morbidity

Respiratory diseases are the main cause of hospital discharges, followed by gastrointestinal diseases. The districts of Mat and Lushnjë, Has, Përmet, Shkodër and Tirana have the highest incidence per 100,000 (1,447, 1,440, 1,322, 1,295, 1,220, 1,148, respectively). Infectious and parasitic diseases in general decreased from 1,069/100,000 in 1989 to 488/100,000 in 1998, still above the EU average of 322/100,000 in 1997.

Hospital discharges for injury and poisoning increased in 1993 (517/100,000) and in 1997 (539/100,000) as a result of the civil unrest. They were, however, significantly lower than the EU average (1,640/100,000) in 1998.

Although the overall infectious diseases reported seem to be decreasing, some diseases are showing abnormal increases or increasing trends, such as brucellosis, transmitted through unpasteurized milk. The incidence of viral hepatitis is still very high, and after a decline in 1996 and 1997, it is on the increase again. The distinction between hepatitis A and other forms is mainly based on clinical symptoms.

12.2 Environmental conditions associated with health risks

Air pollution

Air emissions from stationary sources have decreased sharply, dropping in 1998 to 45 per cent of their 1989 level. Today the main air polluter is mobile sources. In 1998 transport contributed 15.2 per cent of the total air pollution against only 1.4 per cent in 1989. This pattern is more remarkable in Tirana, where, according to a recent study, traffic-related emissions contribute approximately 65 per cent of the total air pollution.

Prior to 1990, the two main pollutants were SO_2 and soot, and the concentration of sulphur in fossil fuels was three to five times higher than in other European countries. Furthermore, the inefficiency of burning processes, mainly in industry, led to high pollution levels. Technically, when the soot/SO_2 ratio in the exhaust of a burning fuel in atmospheric air is higher than 1, the efficiency of the burning process is low, resulting in the injection of large quantities of unburned carbon particles into the atmosphere. Monitoring in Tirana has shown that this ratio was 2.25 during the 1976-1980 period, 3.88 during 1981-1994 and currently it is constantly over 3.

SO_2 levels were particularly high in the towns of Laç and Rubik, in the north of the country near to copper-smelting plants. Up to 1990, both towns had annual concentrations of SO_2 varying between 200-450 mg/m^3 (WHO guiding value is 0.05 mg/m^3, annual). At the end of the 1980s, a small village near Laç was evacuated due to the constant high SO_2 exposure.

Particularly high concentrations of total suspended particles (TSP) (ranging from 200 to 350 µg/m^3) and black smoke (ranging from 50 to 200 µg/m^3) were measured in 2000 in Tirana, Fier, Elbasan, Durrës and Vlorë. In Tirana PM_{10} was also measured, resulting in an average of 150 µg/m^3 in 1997 and 1998.

It is difficult to attribute morbidity or mortality to air pollution emissions, as no health impacts or exposure assessments were available. There was a steady decrease in the second half of the 1990s in both morbidity and mortality related to respiratory disease. In Tirana in particular the incidence of respiratory diseases is 10-15 per cent higher than the country's average, which may also be related to higher levels of air pollution, mainly dust and particulate matter.

Using the methodology of the WHO project "Health Impact Assessment of Air Pollution in the WHO European Region", it was estimated that, in Tirana, between 15 and 42 deaths annually may be attributed to O_3 exposure, of which 6-19 are due to cardiovascular and 1-5 due to respiratory diseases.

Indoor air quality

In Albania there are no studies on exposure to indoor air pollutants. Assumptions can only be made based on the change of heating and cooking fuels. At the beginning of the 1990s, kerosene was widely used for cooking while wood and coal were used for heating. Nowadays more and more electricity is used for cooking and heating.

The Institute of Public Health has recently conducted a study assessing the increase of smoking among Albanians. The results show that 66 per cent of schoolchildren have family members who smoke. Data on tobacco consumption show that in 1999 the consumption of cigarettes was 22.5 per cent higher than in 1980 (Table 12.3). Though the quantity of cigarettes smoked per person in Albania remains substantially lower than in the EU and other Central and East European countries, the rate of increase is much higher than in these countries.

The number of cases of smoking-related diseases followed the same trend, up from 261.2/100,000 in 1987 to 324.6/100,000 in 1997. This marks an increase of 24.3 per cent, compared to a 19 per cent decrease on average in EU countries and 2 per cent on average in other Central and East European countries.

Table 12.3: Changes in tobacco consumption (cigarettes/person/year) during the period 1980-2000

Country	1980	1985	1990	1995	1999	Change (%) in 1999 compared to 1980
Albania	786	721	822	923	963	22.50
EU average	1,964	1,852	1,799	1,616	1,651	-15.90
Central and East European average	2,127	2,094	2,128	2,248	2,128	0.00

Source: National Institute of Public Health, 2001.

Drinking water, waste water and health

The determinant factors of drinking water quality and associated health problems can be summarized as follows:

- The use of untreated surface water in rural areas: 0.1 per cent of the population uses untreated surface water. Around the Semani River, some communities still use untreated river water by digging holes close to the river;

- The contamination of drinking water in the supply system due to irregular water supply and low water pressure, illegal connections to the pipes, cracks in the old pipes and cross contamination from waste water;

- Waste water from hospitals and industries (with some exceptions) also flows into the pipes or directly into rivers. In rural areas household latrines are common and ultimately all the waste water is directly discharged into rivers;

- Uncontrolled and irregular chlorination in rural areas. Disinfection with calcium or sodium hypochlorite is often irregular and approximate. Furthermore, not all chlorination plants are working; enterprises often lack the money to buy calcium or sodium hypochlorite;

- The lack of respect for sanitary protection perimeters. An investigation of domestic wells showed that 73 per cent were bacteriologically contaminated; and

- The inconsistent and irregular sampling of drinking water. Although the Ministry of Health, through the Institute of Public Health and the regional directorates, is in charge of regular drinking water measurements in 36 districts, there is no clearly regulated framework. However, measurements focus on a few parameters and are not clearly defined by population, territory and risk parameters.

As a result, gastroenteritis is a recurrent problem. In 2000, the districts with the highest incidence of gastroenteritis were Kavajë (324/100,000), Gramsh (262/100,000), Librazhd (273/100,000) and Has (264/100000). The incidence of gastroenteritis has been decreasing since 1994, following the cholera epidemics when drastic measures were taken in high-risk areas (Table 12.4).

Bathing waters and the development of tourism

No standardized regular monitoring of bathing water is carried out in Albania. Between 1993 and

Table 12.4: Quality of drinking water, 1997-1999

	1997	1998	1999
Total samples	76,340	138,439	150,000
Outside norms (%)	5.73	5.88	6.53
Seriously contaminated (5)	0.39	0.43	0.50

Source: National Institute of Public Health, 2001.

1997 samples were taken from the beaches of Durrës, Sarandë, Vlorë, Shengui, Himara, Borci and Shkodër (UNEP/GRID project) during the summer twice a month. At that time, the most polluted beaches were Vlorë and Sarandë, whereas measurements carried out in 2001 showed the beach of Durrës as having very high levels of microbiological contamination. This is particularly worrying since in 1993 the Council of Ministers approved several decisions and laws for the development of coastal tourism (see Chapter 11). However, there are a number of environmental health concerns that hinder appropriate tourist development:

- High sea water pollution due to direct discharges of waste water from polluted rivers and households (see Chapter 6);

- The large volume of waste from construction or dumps (see Chapter 7);

- Nature and landscape damage caused by the extraction of raw materials like sand, gravel, stone, and clay (see Chapter 8); and

- The exploitation of toxic raw materials like oil, iron, zinc.

Food Safety

At this moment, food quality control is probably one of the most serious agricultural, environmental and health problems in Albania. Two thirds of a normal rural family's income derives from agriculture, with more and more cash income deriving from the sale of the livestock products, the milk, vegetables, fruits and grapes they produce. As in many East European countries, food illegally sold on the streets, especially milk and meat products, is a major income-earner for many families, in particular in the countryside. There is no legal provision or any other instrument available to block the illegal sales on the streets. Moreover, given the precarious economic situation, selling food on the streets is the only means of income for many families. The country is registering an increase in brucellosis, transmitted either through contact with animal tissue or through the ingestion of contaminated milk and derivates. The high numbers indicate a serious lack of meat and diary control (Table 12.5).

The Ministry of Health summarized the problem as follows:

- Animals are butchered in private homes usually without veterinary control;
- There are no slaughterhouses with appropriate hygienic, sanitary and veterinary conditions;
- Control is insufficient or incomplete in butcher shops;
- In many districts, particularly in urban areas, food products are traded illegally on the street;
- Food products are traded illegally across the border.

The 1995 Law on Food, No. 7941, regulates the conditions for the production, processing, storage, distribution, control and marketing of foodstuffs for human consumption, in order to protect the health of consumers. Until 1995, inspectorates in the districts carried out food control under the jurisdiction of the Ministry of Health. At present, the main responsibility lies with the Ministry of Agriculture, although the responsibility of the different inspectorates is not well defined at the regional and subregional level. The 36 inspectorates in the districts mainly control food imports, food processing and foodstuffs sold in official markets. The directorates are also responsible for licensing. However, there are 12 well-equipped regional laboratories of public health under the responsibility of the State Sanitary Inspectorate, and two more are planned. Penalties, which range from 5,000 to 500,000 leks to banning the activities, are issued if the food products breach the 1989 norms and standards. Disputes are settled by the National Food Research Institute.

The Ministry of Health's sanitary-epidemiological stations are also in charge of food product analysis. They do so mainly in public places such as restaurants, bars, kindergartens and markets. The veterinary service is in charge of analysing all dairy and animal products, from growth to consumption. In 1999, veterinary inspectors took 14,500 food samples and carried out related chemical and bacteriological analyses: as a result some products were forbidden (mostly salami, meat and condensed milk) and others simply eliminated.

There are problems with enforcement mechanisms and, in particular, with both the collection of fines and the implementation of administrative measures. This is true for a number of legal instruments, including the Law on Food.

Albania is part of the Codex Alimentarius system. However, so far only labelling has been legally approved by the Government. To date, there are 16 approved labels in Albania. In 1994 the National Food Board was set up, mainly to discuss regulations and strengthen inter-ministerial collaboration. So far, the Board has met once every two years.

Recent studies by the Institute of Public Health showed that 55 out of 61 retail market sites had permits from the local authorities, but only 14 met basic hygiene and sanitary conditions. In some districts, like Durrës, Gjirokastër and Sarandë, permits for food products for public consumption are issued without adequate tests. Fraud in the production and trading of food products, especially with regard to alcoholic and soft drinks, milk and dairy products, and oils, is also a matter of concern given the potentially costly consequences for public health; specific fraud is particularly prevalent in imported products, especially regarding expiry dates.

Table 12.5: The dynamics of some communicable diseases during 1990–1999, Number of cases

Diseases	1990	1991	1992	1993	1994	1995	1996	1997	1998	1999
Gastrointestinal infections	216,288	130,413	85,803	79,024	66,458	51,992	47,197	44,360	47,252	53,073
Toxic infections	1,309	619	543	1,079	1,323	745	696	742	1,173	1,186
Shigellosis	3,264	1,789	1,188	1,410	1,939	1,268	1,062	1,038	835	817
Salmonellosis	2,602	1,369	800	835	937	816	853	549	749	392
Typhus	94	102	140	59	109	54	67	34	40	7
Cholera	..	..	..	..	678	..	..	..	..	..
Brucellosis	37	17	62	29	117	172	149	155	523	458
Hepatitis	11,291	6,814	4,576	5,271	7,508	3,975	2,035	1,829	3,477	4,489

Source: National Institute of Public Health, 2001; Ministry of Health, 2001.

Solid Waste

During the past decade the production of waste has doubled to 0.7 kg/day/person. During 1998, Albania generated some 520,000 tons of urban waste; the main cities accounted for 44 per cent of the total. Tirana alone produced 116,000 tons, i.e. 22 per cent of the total. The amount of inert material in urban waste is about 12 per cent. Only 55 per cent of Albanians have access to rubbish removal services. In cities supplied with cast containers, some are damaged. In these conditions, urban solid waste is merely left on the road, frequented by dogs, cats and rodents (i.e. the main vectors for infectious diseases). Solid waste is usually stored in uncontrolled landfills regardless of its origin (see Chapter 7 for more details about solid waste management).

Health care waste

The daily production of hospital waste in the seven main cities has been estimated at 7.3 tons/day. Hospital waste is composed of non-risk waste, which can be stored in containers and transported to landfills, and risk waste. In Albania, risk waste such as infectious materials (e.g. gauze, used cotton, bandages, rubber gloves, syringes and placentas) is simply stored in plastic containers and also taken to landfills. All hospitals in the country are dependent on municipal structures for waste management (i.e. none has a separate system for disposing of medical waste). Even in landfills hospital waste is not separated from household waste. Risk and non-risk health care waste is often stored in open containers in the courtyard of the hospitals. Health care waste from private surgeries too is dumped in municipal waste containers (see also Chapter 7).

The project "Development of a health care waste management plan for Tirana/Albania" was initiated in December 1998 to bring current management policy and practice in line with international standards and regulations endorsed by WHO. The project assessment showed that unspecified hazardous health care waste is burned in crematoriums located near the various health institutions. Until 1998, these systems were somewhat primitive and relied on firewood as a primary source of fuel. Because of the low ceilings and inadequacies with the flue-gas cleaning system, smoke was widely dispersed and spread to the surrounding hospital wards. Due to the low level of awareness among the hospital staff about the risks associated with exposure, ash and residue from the

crematoriums were removed by hand using little or no protective measures.

Only the University Hospital in Tirana has an incinerator. An assessment by WHO has shown that there are problems with the installation and lack of ancillary equipment. There are concerns that the flue gas emitted from the incinerator contains dust and noxious gases. Despite the protective measures taken to minimize the risks associated with the use of this device, significant amounts of smoke are dispersed in the surrounding area.

The Institute for the Treatment of Pneumonia has its own incinerator. This device has a capacity of 4.5-10 kg/h and is located in the basement of the Institute. Problems identified here include defects with the loading feeder and the steam cylinder. Untreated particulate matter and smoke are emitted from the chimney, which is only one metre above the roof of the Institute.

The second principal method of health care waste treatment is disinfection. There are currently four main disinfecting points at the Technical University Hospital of Tirana in the Paediatrics, Neurology, Oncology and Internal Disease departments. These units sterilize equipment using steam/vapour pressure, which is not always appropriate for plastic containers and syringes. Moreover, there is considerable ignorance about the risks associated with health care waste. Record-keeping has been weak and inconsistent, so it has proved almost impossible to monitor and assess the effectiveness of current methods. This, in turn, has added to the ignorance of the hospital staff about the current situation.

The ignorance among the hospital staff of the health and environmental risks associated not only with untreated health care waste but also with the by-products (smoke, gas and particulate matter) from the incinerators is alarming. The sanitary personnel were found to have been largely unaware of the risks of infection and were not equipped with even the most basic protective measures - gloves, masks, special hermetic waste containers. Few studies have been conducted in the hospitals to determine the rate of accidents caused during waste removal and treatment.

Albania lacks a general law on waste management. The 2002 Law on Environmental Protection and Decision No. 26 of the Council of Ministers on hazardous waste and residues contain some articles banning hazardous waste imports for destruction and disposal, but they do not provide the basis for a sound and specific health care waste legal framework development. The definitions of waste and hazardous waste in such legal acts are not consistent with EU directives. In the meantime, the environmental legal framework does not include any definition of health care waste or any of its categories.

The Environmental Centre for Administration and Technology's project outlines the need to develop and adopt such a law and introduce the European Waste Catalogue. The main principles (prevention, reduction, recycling before disposal, value-based principle, producer responsibility principle, duty of care, precautionary principle and proximity principle) of good waste management should be included in the primary legislation. Besides these basic principles of waste management, the duty for waste producers to keep records on waste production, to plan and forecast waste production and to indicate the methods of disposal several years in advance should be established on the same level of legislation.

When such a general legal basis exists, the legal framework can be completed by developing some legal and regulatory acts or governmental orders related to the classification and categorization of health care waste, and technical standards for its packaging, labelling and transport, which are necessary administrative structures for sound health care waste management at hospitals at the district and national level. In this regard, scientific institutes or other bodies under the Ministry of Health's authority can prepare different guidelines based on those of WHO or other advanced experience in the field.

Another option, based more on the experience of other countries in the area with economies in transition, is to develop and adopt a self-standing specific law (enacted by parliament) on the management of health care waste. Such a law can provide for:

- Institutional and administrative structures at national, district and hospital levels;
- Basic waste management principles;
- Technical requirements for transport and labelling;
- Final treatment and disposal;
- Definitions and categorization fully consistent with the EU approach; and
- Licensing system.

Storage of hazardous chemicals including pesticides

The closure of many industrial plants over the past 12 years has led to many sites where hazardous compounds have just been left abandoned. The recent UNEP assessment has drawn the attention of the international community to this problem.

The country also inherited considerable stocks of pesticides (most of them expired) from the centralized economy. They had inappropriate structures, quality and conservation conditions, which posed a serious threat to human health, animals and the environment. For these reasons, two projects were initiated to tackle the following problems:

- The disposal of low-risk pesticides with the financial support of the Government; and
- The treatment and disposal, financed by the EU, of pesticides in the agricultural system. Hazardous waste would be exported for disposal.

Both projects are in the implementation phase.

At present, fertilizer application is estimated to be 30-40 kg per ha. This is related to decreasing domestic production, the rising prices of fertilizers and a lack of knowledge and information among farmers as to their appropriate use.

Procedures for the registration, import, conservation, trading, use, disposal, and the banning of pesticides are determined by the Law on the Plant Protection Service, No. 7662 of 1993, amended by Law No. 8531 of 1999 and related implementing legislation. Since 1993, the State Pesticide Commission, as approved by the Minister of Agriculture and Food, has become operational. Its mandate stems from Council of Ministers Decision No. 548, dated 6 December 1993, article 3 on the regulations for pesticides used in agriculture.

Pesticide registration requires a permit for the import and use of pesticides in the country, following review by some scientific institutions and the State Pesticide Commission as to their effectiveness, impact on human health, animals and the environment, and possible secondary effects. To date, approximately 83 pesticides have been registered for use. The classification of pesticides, according to toxicity, is based on WHO guidelines.

Table 12.6: Hazardous storage sites and potential health effects

Hazardous sites	Hazardous substances	Possible health effects	Measures
Chemical plant Durrës	Chlorobenzene; Lindane; Chromium	Neurophysiological disorders; genotoxicity and carcinogenicity	Strictly prohibit access to the plant; resettle residents; immediately store chemicals in a secure site; retrospective assessment of possible health effects
Chlor-alkali and PVC in Vlorë	Mercury	Neurological and urinary disorders	Strictly prohibit access to the plants; resettle residents; assess population exposure and health effects
Marize oil fields in Patos	Oil in the Gjanice river-possible contamination of local wells		Monitor private wells downstream; if contaminated, provide drinking water to the population affected; assess possible health effects
Oil refinery in Ballsh	Oil in Gjanice river-possible contamination of local wells		Monitor private wells downstream; if contaminated, provide drinking water to the population affected; assess possible health effects
Waste disposal in Sharra	Waste-water pollution of the Erzenit river – dioxin and furan air pollution	Health effects depend on the type of waste-water pollution	Strictly prohibit access to the plants; monitor air and water quality; develop management strategy for the landfill; workers should take protective measures
Nitrate fertilizer Plant in Fier	Arsenic	Chronic signs include dermal lesions, peripheral neuropathy, skin cancer, peripheral vascular diseases	Assess soil and surface waters; remove the arsenite and arsenate solutions and the contaminated soil
Metallurgical Complex in Elbasan	Solid waste containing heavy metals	Depends on the heavy metals present	Monitoring and assessment of chemical and microbiological parameters of the drinking water and private wells; air quality monitoring
Copper Factory in Rubik	Copper	Liver cirrhosis in Wilson disease; newborn babies are particularly sensitive	Assess the health effects, assess water quality downstream; prevent further groundwater pollution
Phosphate fertilizer factory in Laç	Arsenic and copper	Arsenic: chronic signs include dermal lesions, peripheral neuropathy, skin cancer, peripheral vascular diseases; Liver cirrhosis in those prone to it; newborn babies are particularly sensitive	Assess the health effects, assess water quality downstream; prevent further groundwater pollution

During 1992, 1996 and 1997, outbreaks of lead intoxication occurred in some rural zones as a result of the use of flour ground in old flour mills, repaired with lead. About 3000 individuals living in those zones were exposed to this pollutant in varying doses. Lead intoxication symptoms include headaches, muscle tremor, kidney damage, loss of memory, gastrointestinal problems and others. No information was available on what happened to

these people, as there was no post-monitoring of these outbreaks.

Ionizing radiation

Until the late 1980s, the problem of radon exposure was considered only within the framework of the occupational exposure of miners mining uranium and other minerals like coal bauxite, polymetals, and phosphorites in the early 1990s, the Geological Survey assessed the potential risk posed by radon in the Albanian western plain. This study, conducted on 5 per cent of the country's territory, showed that there was a risk due to the soil's high radon concentration.

Following this study, a group of houses investigated in Tirana were found to have average radon levels of 150 Bq/m^3 (WHO guiding value: 100 Bq/m^3). Houses located in a high-risk zone (in Dajti national park) had disturbing levels ranging from 1000 to 4000 Bq/m^3. The study was limited to measuring the level of radon and mapping the radon risk in the area under study. Subsequently, two areas close to Shkodër and Tirana were found to have high Bq levels. However, there have been no attempts to assess the potential health impacts in high-risk areas.

The protection of the population from different types of ionizing radiation is the responsibility of the State Commission for Radiation Protection at the Ministry of Health. The Radiation Protection Office is the executive body of the State Commission for Radiation Protection and acts as an inspectorate. It controls the implementation of the relevant legislation, inspects facilities and installations, drafts the regulations and standards for radiation protection, prepares the licences for the Commission regarding each subject and applies fines on behalf of the Commission. The Commission is headed by the Minister of Health. By law at least 50 per cent of its members should be radiation protection experts, a requirement that is far from fulfilled. The Commission ensures the implementation of the Law on Protection from Ionizing Radiations and other regulations concerning the protection of the population from radiation (see also Chapter 5).

Noise

Noise, mainly industrial, was studied in Albania from the early 1970s to the late 1980s. Ten thousand workers were estimated to be exposed to higher levels of noise than admissible for professional exposure (85 dB). Today the levels of exposure to industrial noise are estimated to be 10 per cent of those recorded at the end of the 1980s. During the past 10 years noise from traffic has increased. Buildings do not have special insulation. A survey performed at busy roads in Tirana showed that levels varied from 60 to 90 dB. Political, economic and social changes have created

opportunities for private activities with uncontrolled noise levels, which have mostly developed within the residential areas. It is important to stress that no standards or admissible levels exist for noise in residential areas.

Occupational health

Exposure to chemical and physical hazards in the workplace has changed dramatically during the past 10 years. Prior to 1990, a number of large heavy industry plants, including mining, metallurgy, chemical, and fertilizer plants, were operating near and around all the big cities. After the collapse of State industry in the early 1990s, the country's economy witnessed a rapid decline in industrial production and the closure of almost all the large industrial facilities.

These developments also affected the occupational health services and the monitoring of the health status in the workplace. Prior to 1990, all enterprises had a doctor.

The first regulation on occupational hygiene dates back to 1975. This regulation set various standards for workplace safety. The list of indices under consideration was updated in 1980. In 1993 a set of new regulations that addressed various occupational hygiene issues was introduced, but there is no law to regulate safety norms in the workplace. The basic legislation on occupational health is represented by:

- The Labour Code;
- The Law on the State Health Inspectorate;
- The Law on Social Insurance; and
- The Law on Health Insurance.

The responsibility for monitoring occupational health and hygiene at the workplace lies with the State Health Inspectorate. However, there is no well-defined monitoring programme; the health inspectors in the districts and the Occupational Hygiene Section in the Institute of Public Health intervene mostly in emergencies or accidents. The latter is responsible for monitoring the indoor environment of industrial facilities, through specialized laboratories at the Institute of Public Health, and for drafting national occupational standards. The Labour Inspectorate is also responsible for occupational health and conditions at the workplace, but the respective responsibility of each is not clear.

Table 12.7: Concentration of lead in flour in some areas

ppb

Years	Number	Minimum	Maximum	Average
1992	40	10.00	72.50	42.97
1996	25	1.84	550.00	93.92
1997	18	0.00	1253.44	258.38

Source : National Institute of Public Health and Ministry of Health, 1999.

12.3 Environmental health policy and management

Policy commitments relevant to environmental health

The Government approved the National Environmental Health Action Plan (NEHAP) in 1999. It was developed with the support of WHO and the participation of a large working group which, in addition to the Ministry of Health, included the Ministry of Public Works and Transport (now the Ministry of Transport and Telecommunications), the Ministry of Tourism (now the Ministry of Territorial Adjustment and Tourism), the Ministry of Agriculture and Food, the Ministry of Public Economy and Privatization (now the Ministry of Industry and Energy), the National Environmental Agency (now the Ministry of Environment) and non-governmental organizations.

However, when the NEHAP was drafted, the Ministry of Environment did not yet exist and was not included in the distribution of tasks. Furthermore, the NEHAP has an exhaustive list of objectives and actions, but it is not clear how these actions could be taken, who is responsible and who will fund them. Another problem is that it is not yet clear how the new health care reform will consider, fund and implement environment and health actions. There is a need to consider the NEHAP recommendations when restructuring the Ministry of Environment, and to develop a feasible plan of environment and health interventions within the health care reform.

Legal instruments and institutions

The Ministry of Health is the main financing source and provider of health care services. A national policy for the health care sector was produced in 1993, but it has not been updated. The World Bank, in collaboration with the WHO, is currently developing a new health care strategy. It is not clear what role the Institute of Public Health will have in the new health care strategy.

Within the current Albanian system, the Institute of Public Health provides technical and scientific assistance to the Ministry and is responsible for the technical guidance of the inspectors of the Primary Health Care Directorates at the district level. The network comprises 106 health inspectors and 170 deputy health inspectors, depending on the size of the district state health inspectorates. These inspectors report both to the Ministry of Health and to the Institute of Public Health. Their activities are based on Law No. 7643 on the State Health Inspectorate, which came into force on 2 December 1992 and the Law on Communicable Diseases, dated 1993. Several sectoral laws define many of the inspectorates' activities, which include controlling drinking water, waste water, solid waste, air pollution, food hygiene, hygiene in the workplace and at school.

Four major sources of problems have been detected in the work of the public health inspectorates:

- Difficult collaboration with the elected local bodies that bear the executive responsibility for the elimination of the identified problems;
- Difficulties in collecting fines and insufficient support to enforce penalties;
- Lack of coordination among inspectorates, for instance food, veterinary and labour inspectorates; and
- One management problem for the health inspectors is that the Institute of Public Health provides technical direction, but the public health care unit within the Ministry of Health provides operational direction and funding for the inspectors. The administrative hierarchy is as follows: Service Sector of the State Health Inspectorate – Department of Primary Health Care (District) – Department of Public Health (District) – Department of Primary Health Care at the Ministry of Health.

The Institute of Public Health has seven departments: microbiology, hygiene, epidemiology, health promotion, education, bio-statistics and health policies. It is also in charge of epidemiological surveillance and collects statistics on the incidence of diseases. However, the processed data do not make for agile decision-making in the development of public health policies. Better information through the efficient functioning of a modern reporting system would make it possible to analyse potential risk – the basis for the successful protection of consumer health. An infectious disease alert system has been set up. If there is an outbreak, the Institute investigates it and tries to solve the problem, with direct feedback to the Ministry of Health.

Congruent with the political stance of the country, two main features of the public health system financing in Albania in recent decades need to be mentioned:

- The main source of funds was the government budget;
- The system was characterized by severe under-funding, which can be identified as the direct cause for difficult conditions and low-quality health services.

At present government and municipal budgets remain the basic sources of health care funding (approximately 60-70 per cent), followed by contributions to the Health Insurance Institute (a further fifth of the total). Official co-payments amount to some 3-5 per cent of official funding. External aid also accounts for a considerable proportion of health care revenue (in 1992 and 1993, this amounted to over one third of the country's health revenue; by 1999 it was estimated at 70 per cent of total health care financing).

One of the major gaps in the legal provisions is that there is no formal development of health impact assessment because strategic environmental assessment and environmental impact assessment laws are still being drafted (Chapter 1). There is no law on outdoor and indoor air quality to set standards in compliance with WHO air quality guidelines.

Environmental health monitoring and information systems

The Albanian system of monitoring air, water, waste and environment in general is very basic. It is mainly a responsive but not an evaluative system. In most cases it does not respect European legislation, in particular with regard to the frequency, the methodology and the types of indicators selected (see Chapter 4). Biological monitoring is almost non-existent due to the impossibility of conducting analyses in time and space. Therefore it is impossible to develop epidemiological studies at present.

Figure 12.1 is a flowchart of the Ministry of Health's flow of information.

Air quality

The Institute of Public Health is responsible for monitoring air quality in urban areas. The monitoring network consists of 13 sampling sites in seven major cities: Tirana, Shkodër, Durrës, Elbasan, Fier, Vlorë and Korçe. The most extensive monitoring is carried out in Tirana, through six sampling points selected for spatial distribution and population exposure. Based on preliminary screening, Korçe has been selected as the reference of a "clean" location. In the other cities, there is only one sampling point in the centre of the cities.

The Institute of Hydrometeorology also monitors air quality through its own network. More details about air monitoring and the respective tasks of the two institutes are described in Chapter 5.

Radiation

Standards for radiation have been reviewed during the past two years. Two types of standards on occupational and population radiation are currently in force (see Box 12.2).

Drinking water

Twenty-seven district laboratories are supposed to monitor chlorine in the drinking water and the cleanliness of drinking water, and to monitor surface waters and bathing waters. Residual chlorine is analysed in 27 districts, in 5-20 sampling points five days a week. The results are sent once a month to the Ministry of Health, the Ministry of Territorial Adjustment and Tourism and the Ministry of Local Government and Decentralization on official forms. Cleanliness is based on the measurement of six basic indicators: ammonia, nitrites, nitrates, organic matter, chlorites and phosphates. The complete pollution check includes 13 indicators altogether, but very few laboratories are able to carry it out due to the lack of equipment and reagents. Only eight laboratories carry out the sampling of surface water based on eight indicators: ammonia, nitrites, nitrates, total phosphorus, COD, BOD_5, turbidity and total alkalinity. There are altogether 32 sampling points in the rivers. Bathing water is monitored in the areas of Shengjin, Durrës, Vlorë and Sarandë. The following chemical indexes are monitored: salinity, turbidity and suspended matter. The Department of Environment and Health reports the monitoring results to the Director of the Institute of Public Health, who then forwards them to the Ministry of Health. The results are also reported to the Ministry of Environment and other organizations with which the Institute has specific arrangements. Upon approval by the Director of the Institute of Public Health, the results are published in the Institute's bulletin, the medical journal and the journals of the Academy of Sciences.

There was no information available on waste, waste water or other types of monitoring. It seems that waste is monitored only if there are problems.

As outlined in the flowchart, monitoring information is transmitted from the district public health directorates to the Institute of Public Health and then to the Ministry of Health and the Ministry of Statistics. No data flow has so far been foreseen for the Ministry of Environment. The Institute of Public Health has recently started making available a biennial bulletin with the results of its assessments. Otherwise no information is made available to the public.

Table 12.8: Albanian standards for drinking water quality (1998) compared to WHO Water Quality Guidelines

Indicator	Albanian standard	Maximum permitted level	WHO Guidelines
Total coliforms	0	0	Must not be detectable
Coli-index	0	0	Must not be detectable
Faecal coliforms	0	0	
Colifagi			
Parasites (Cysts, larvae, amoebae, helminths, eggs)			
Boron	0.3 mg/l	1 mg/l	0.3 mg/l
Cadmium	0.003 mg/l	0.005 mg/l	0.003 mg/l
Molybdenum			0.07mg/l
Arsenic	0.01 mg/l	0.05 mg/l	0.005 mg/l
Nickel	0.02 mg/l	0.05 mg/l	0.02 mg/l
NO3	25 mg/l	50 mg/l	50 mg/l
NO2	0	0.05 mg/l	3
Mercury	0	0.001 mg/l	0.001 mg/l
Lead	0	0.05 mg/l	0.01 mg/l
Selenium	0	0.01 mg/l	0.01 mg/l
Fluoride	0.7 mg/l	1.5 mg/l	1.5 mg/l
Chromium	0	0.05 mg/l	00.5 mg/l
Phenols	0	0.5 mg/l	
BOD			
Polianilini			
Taste	No. dilution = 0	No. dilution = 2	-
Odour	No. dilution = 0	No. dilution = 2	-
Colour	1 mg/l Pt/Co	20 mg/l Pt/Co	-
Ph	6.5 – 8.5	9.5	-
General Mineralization	700 mg/l	1200 mg/l	
Fe	0.05 mg/l	0.3 mg/l	-
Hardness	10 – 15 °T	20 °T	-
Manganese	0.02 mg/l	0.05 mg/l	0.5 mg/l
Cu	0.1 mg/l	1 mg/l	2 mg/l
PO4	0.4 mg/l	2.5 mg/l	
SO4	25 mg/l	250 mg/l	500 mg/l
Chlorine	25 mg/l	200 mg/l	
Surfactants	0	0	
Zinc	0.1 mg/l	3 mg/l	3.0 mg
Oil	0		

Source: National Institute of Public Health, 2001.

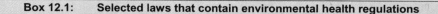

Box 12.1:   Selected laws that contain environmental health regulations

In addition to the environmental laws listed in boxes 1.1 and 1.2, the following are relevant:

- Law No. 7643, of 2 December 1992, on the State Health Inspectorate, amended by Law No. 7904, of 8 March 1995, covers a wide range of public health issues extending to the assessment of the health and environmental state, through the establishment of a State Health Inspectorate;
- Law No. 7941, of 31 May 1995, on Food defines the conditions for the production, processing, storage, distribution, control and marketing of foodstuffs for human consumption, aimed at protecting the health of consumers;
- Law No. 8109, of 28 March 1996, amending Law No. 7738, of 21 July 1993, on Health Care;
- Law No. 8094, of 31 March 1996, on public waste removal. Its intention is to protect the urban environment from waste and to organize the public waste removal services;
- Regulation 145 on drinking water quality water supply;
- Law No. 8484, of 10 May 1999, amending Law No. 7761, of 1 October 1993, on the prevention and treatment of communicable diseases;
- Law of 1995 on Protection from Ionizing Radiations;
- 1998 Rules for working with radioactive materials and other sources of ionizing and non-ionizing radiation.

(See Chapter 1 for additional legislation)

Figure 12.1: Information Flow in the Ministry of Health and its Institutes

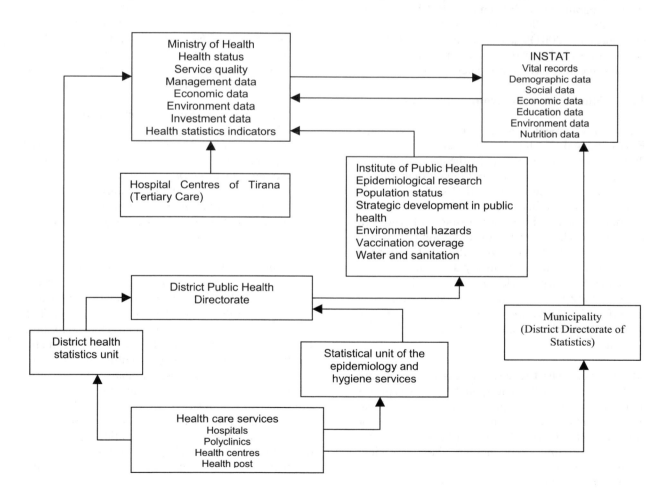

Box 12.2:   Radiation standards in Albania, 2000-2001

1)   Occupational

• Effective dose does not exceed 20 mSv/year (calculated as an average of five consecutive years)
• Effective annual dose does not exceed 50 mSv
• Equivalent annual dose does not exceed 150 mSv on the iris
• Equivalent annual dose does not exceed 500 mSv on the skin and limbs

2)   Population exposure

• Effective annual dose does not exceed 1 mSv
• In specific cases, effective annual dose does not exceed 5 mSv on condition that during the next five consecutive years the dose should not exceed more than 1 mSv/year
• Equivalent annual dose does not exceed 15 mSv on the iris
• Equivalent annual dose does not exceed 50 mSv on the skin

Professional education in environmental health

Training courses for health inspectors have started in cooperation with the *Ecole Polytechnique Fédérale de Lausanne* (1995 – 1996), under the Phare Programme (1999), under the WHO – FAO cooperation (2000-2001), under UNICEF cooperation (2001) and under INTEREC II cooperation (2001). Around 90 per cent of district health inspectors have participated so far.

12.4   Conclusions and recommendations

The Government approved the National Environmental Health Action Plan (NEHAP) in 2001. It was developed with the support of the World Health Organization and the participation of a number of ministries. The NEHAP makes many recommendations, but it is not clear how these can be implemented, who is responsible and who will fund them. The Ministry of Environment, which was established when the NEHAP had already been completed, has not been closely associated with it. Both the Ministry of Health and the Ministry of Environment now need to work together to review the NEHAP, clarify the tasks and the responsible bodies for implementation, and put the Plan in motion.

At local and district levels, health inspectorates are responsible for tasks that span both environment and health, while inspectors of the regional environmental offices are also responsible for environment. The coordination of their tasks is not always optimum, and neither has sufficient capacity. Low salaries and better opportunities in other countries have led to a massive emigration of specialized staff. In order to allow for efficient and effective performance of tasks, better coordination between the different inspectorates is essential.

Recommendation 12.1:
(a) The Ministry of Environment and the Ministry of Health should tighten their intersectoral cooperation in the implementation of environmental health policy and work jointly at a more concrete definition of the tasks to be undertaken and the measures needed to accomplish those tasks;

(b) The Ministry of Environment and the Ministry of Health, within the context of health care reform, should review the roles and organization of their inspectorates and ensure the coordination and efficient use of scarce resources. Working conditions should be improved and more attention given to institutional memory and appropriate training for all inspectors.

The context of the current health care reform demands an assessment of the organization of the Institute of Public Health and the regional networks together with their management and products. The same is true for public health and hygiene activities. Particular attention should be given to management, the motivation of staff, opportunities for capacity-building and the assignment of specific responsibilities within the legal and institutional framework. The Institute of Public Health could serve as the reference institution with regard to evidence-based research, the collection and analysis of environment and health monitoring information, licensing, outbreak investigation and capacity-building.

Recommendation 12.2:
The Ministry of Health should clarify and assess the respective roles of the institutions within the Ministry and subordinated institutions involved in environmental and health activities, and they should be given adequate consideration within the health care reform framework.

One of the major gaps in the legal framework for health and environment is the lack of health impact assessment, because strategic environmental assessment and environmental impact assessment laws are still being drafted (Chapter 1).

Recommendation 12.3:
The Ministry of Health should develop a methodology for health aspects within Environmental Impact Assessment.

There are severe temporal and spatial gaps in the current health and environment information system. Information about the environment is often insufficient since the Albanian system of monitoring air, water and waste is mainly responsive, not evaluative. In most cases it does not respect European legislation with regard to frequency, methodology and types of indicators selected. Finally, the information flow is unidirectional, from the bottom up, without feedback. A new information system is under development, but as long as the spatial and temporal data collection on environment and health cannot be assured, the information system will continue to be insufficient.

Recommendation 12.4:
The Ministry of Health, in cooperation with the Ministry of Environment, should develop an environmental health information system and good spatial and temporal coverage.

Air quality is of increasing concern in the big cities, in Tirana in particular. At present, the source of the problem is not so much active industrial facilities as older sites that have ceased to operate. At the same time, transport has become a more significant source of air pollution. The growing use of old, poorly maintained passenger cars and the use of diesel fuel have dramatically worsened air quality in urban areas (see also Chapter 5). However, the real impact of the present urban air pollution on public health is not known.

Recommendation 12.5:
(a) The Ministry of Health should promote studies to clarify the health impacts of pollution, with a special focus on urban centres and hotspot areas;

(b) The Ministries of Transport, Health and Environment should undertake actions to implement the World Health Organization's Charter on Transport, Environment and Health. The Ministries should also give consideration to the WHO-UNECE Transport, Health and Environment Pan European Programme.

Health care waste presents a risk to human health. Urgent measures have to be taken in hospitals to reduce the risks to human health that exist with the current handling of hospital waste. Professional conduct should be expected from every health worker to achieve good hygiene in hospitals to control infections. This includes proper management of health care waste. For this purpose, a national policy should be developed to establish good conduct guidelines for all medical staff (in private practice as well as in hospitals). In the hospitals, every medical department should be encouraged to adopt the WHO "three-container segregation system"; that is, segregating general waste, infectious waste and sharp waste.

To improve waste-related hygiene in medical areas, health care waste management staff needs to be provided with training and such equipment as coloured containers, storage bins and trolleys to transport waste. Local independent suppliers of waste containers and equipment should be encouraged to supply affordable waste handling equipment of proper quality. This will require the allocation of additional resources to health care waste management. Since these measures are costly, a stepwise strategy is suggested.

Recommendation 12.6:
(a) The Ministry of Health should improve the management of health care waste by:
- *Drawing up a national policy on health care waste management;*
- *Deciding on a set of minimum standards for health care waste management to be applied in each hospital;*

- *Giving the medical staff clear responsibilities for health care waste management in their department;*

(b) The Ministry of Health and the Ministry of Environment should improve and stimulate the separate collection of medical waste at all hospitals and treat it or incinerate it. To this end hospitals must receive additional funds from the regular budget. (see recommendation 7.7)

The quality of drinking water is another major concern for the health of Albanians. Leakages in the water distribution system, irregular water supply, low water pressure and cross contamination through waste water, uncontrolled and irregular chlorination, the lack of respect for sanitary protection areas, the inconsistent and irregular sampling of drinking water for quality, all pose a severe risk to human health. Appropriate measures should be taken for a more rational management and protection of water resources (see the recommendations contained in Chapter 6) and a better knowledge of the situation of Albanian water through the development of water monitoring (see Recommendation 4.1).

The environmental hot spots require urgent action from the Government. All sites represent a risk to human health. The sites need to be ranked by health risk in order to implement urgent action, e.g. forced evacuation of the population from the Durrës plant (see Chapter 7 and recommendation 7.3)

ANNEXES

ANNEX I
SELECTED ECONOMIC AND
ENVIRONMENTAL DATA

Albania: Selected economic data

	1995	2000
TOTAL AREA (1 000 km^2)	28.7	28.7
POPULATION		
Total population, (100 000 inh.)	32.4	34.0
% change (1995-2000)	..	4.9
Population density, (inh./km^2)	113.0	118.3
GROSS DOMESTIC PRODUCT		
GDP, (billion US$)	2476.5	3916.1
% change (1995-2000)	..	58.1
per capita, (US$ 1000/cap.)	737.8	1094.4
INDUSTRY		
Value added in industry (% of GDP)	11.7	11.9
Industrial production - % change (1995-2000)		1.7
AGRICULTURE		
Value added in agriculture (% of GDP)	54.5	52.6
ENERGY SUPPLY		
Total supply, (M toe)	..	..
% change (1995-2000)	..	..
Energy intensity, (Toe/US$ 1000)	..	..
% change (1995-2000)	..	..
Structure of energy supply, (%)		
Solid fuels	..	101.0
Oil	..	97.8
Gas	..	66.7
Nuclear	..	..
Hydro,etc.	..	93.2
ROAD TRANSPORT		
Road traffic volumes		
-billion veh.-km	..	..
- % change (1995-2000)	..	..
- per capita (1 000 veh.-km/cap.)	..	..
Road vehicle stock,	..	..
- 10 000 vehicles	10.5*	18.6
- % change (1995-2000)	..	..
- per capita (veh./100 inh.)	3*	5

Source: UNECE and National Statistics
.. = not available.   - = nil or negligible.
Note: * 1999

Albania: Selected environmental data

	1995	2000
LAND		
Total area (1 000 km^2)	28,748	28,748
Major protected areas (% of total area)	3.8	5.8
Nitrogenous fertilizer use (t/km^2 arable land)	..	..
FOREST		
Forest area (% of land area)	36	35
Use of forest resources (harvest/growth)	..	..
Tropical wood imports (US$/cap.)	..	..
THREATENED SPECIES		
Mammals (% of species known)	..	56
Birds (% of species known)	..	31
Fish (% of species known)	..	..
WATER		
Water withdrawal (million m3/year)		228
Fish catches (% of world catches)	..	..
Public waste water treatment	..	..
(% of population served)	..	..
AIR		
Emissions of sulphur oxides (kg/cap.)	..	..
" (kg/US$ 1000 GDP)	..	..
Emissions of nitrogen oxides (kg/cap.)	..	..
" (kg/US$ 1000 GDP)	..	..
Emissions of carbon dioxide (t/cap.)	..	..
" (ton/US$ 1000 GDP)	..	..
WASTE GENERATED		
Industrial waste (kg/US$ 1000 GDP)	..	..
Municipal waste (kg/cap.)	0.8*	0.7
Nuclear waste (ton/Mtoe of TPES)	..	..
NOISE		
Population exposed to leq > 65 dB (A)	..	..
(million inh.)		

Source: UNECE and National Statistics
.. = not available.   - = nil or negligible.
Note: * 1996

ANNEX II
SELECTED MULTILATERAL AND
BILATERAL AGREEMENTS

Worldwide agreements		
as of December 2001		**Albania**
1949 (GENEVA) Convention on Road Traffic	y	
1957 (BRUSSELS) International Convention on Limitation of Liability of Owners of Sea-going Ships	y	
1958 (GENEVA) Convention on Fishing and Conservation of Living Resources of the High Seas	y	
1960 (GENEVA) Convention concerning the Protection of Workers against Ionizing Radiations	y	
1963 (VIENNA) Convention on Civil Liability for Nuclear Damage	y	
1997 (VIENNA) Protocol to Amend the 1963 Vienna Convention on Civil Liability for Nuclear Damage	y	
1963 (MOSCOW) Treaty Banning Nuclear Weapon Tests in the Atmosphere, in Outer Space and under Water	y	
1969 (BRUSSELS) Convention on Civil Liability for Oil Pollution Damage	y	
1976 (LONDON) Protocol	y	
1969 (BRUSSELS) Convention relating to Intervention on the High Seas in Cases of Oil Pollution Casualties	y	
1971 (RAMSAR) Convention on Wetlands of International Importance especially as Waterfowl Habitat	y	R
1982 (PARIS) Amendment	y	
1987 (REGINA) Amendments	y	
1971 (GENEVA) Convention on Protection against Hazards from Benzene (ILO 136)	y	
1971 (BRUSSELS) Convention on the Establishment of an International Fund for Compensation for Oil Pollution Damage	y	
1971 (LONDON, MOSCOW, WASHINGTON) Treaty on the Prohibition of the Emplacement of Nuclear Weapons and Other Weapons of Mass Destruction on the Sea-bed and the Ocean Floor and in the Subsoil thereof		
1972 (PARIS) Convention on the Protection of the World Cultural and Natural Heritage	y	R
1972 (LONDON) Convention on the Prevention of Marine Pollution by Dumping of Wastes and Other Matter	y	
1978 Amendments (incineration)	y	
1980 Amendments (list of substances)	y	
1972 (GENEVA) International Convention for Safe Containers	y	
1973 (WASHINGTON) Convention on International Trade in Endangered Species of Wild Fauna and Flora	y	
1983 (GABORONE) Amendment	y	
1973 (LONDON) Convention for the Prevention of Pollution from Ships (MARPOL)	y	
1978 (LONDON) Protocol (segregated balast)	y	
1978 (LONDON) Annex III on Hazardous Substances carried in packaged form	y	
1978 (LONDON) Annex IV on Sewage		
1978 (LONDON) Annex V on Garbage	y	

y = in force; S = signed; R = ratified; D = denounced.

Selected bilateral and multilateral agreements (continued)

Worldwide agreements

as of December 2001		Albania	
1974	(GENEVA) Convention on Prevention and Control of Occupational Hazards caused by Carcinogenic Substances and Agents (ILO 139)	y	
1977	(GENEVA) Convention on Protection of Workers against Occupational Hazards from Air Pollution, Noise and Vibration (ILO 148)	y	
1979	(BONN) Convention on the Conservation of Migratory Species of Wild Animals	y	R
	1991 (LONDON) Agreement Conservation of Bats in Europe (EUROBATS)	y	R
	1992 (NEW YORK) Agreement on the Conservation of Small Cetaceans of the Baltic and North Seas (ASCOBANS)	y	
	1995 (THE HAGUE) African/Eurasian Migratory Waterbird Agreement (AEWA)	y	R
	1996 (MONACO) Agreement on the Conservation of Cetaceans of the Black Sea, Mediterranean Sea and Contiguous		R
1982	(MONTEGO BAY) Convention on the Law of the Sea	y	
	1994 (NEW YORK) Agreement Related to the Implementation of Part XI of the Convention	y	
	1994 (NEW YORK) Agreement for the Implementation of the Provisions of the United Nations Convention on the Law of the Sea of 10 December 1982 relating to the Conservation and Management of Straddling Fish Stocks and Highly Migratory Fish Stocks		
1985	(VIENNA) Convention for the Protection of the Ozone Layer	y	R
	1987 (MONTREAL) Protocol on Substances that Deplete the Ozone Layer	y	R
	1990 (LONDON) Amendment to Protocol	y	
	1992 (COPENHAGEN) Amendment to Protocol	y	
	1997 (MONTREAL) Amendment to Protocol		
1986	(VIENNA) Convention on Early Notification of a Nuclear Accident	y	
1986	(VIENNA) Convention on Assistance in the Case of a Nuclear Accident or Radiological Emergency	y	
1989	(BASEL) Convention on the Control of Transboundary Movements of Hazardous Wastes and their Disposal	y	R
	1995 Ban Amendment		
	1999 (BASEL) Protocol on Liability and Compensation		
1990	(LONDON) Convention on Oil Pollution Preparedness, Response and Cooperation	y	
1992	(RIO) Convention on Biological Diversity	y	R
	2000 (CARTAGENA) Protocol on Biosafety		
1992	(NEW YORK) Framework Convention on Climate Change	y	R
	1997 (KYOTO) Protocol		
1994	(VIENNA) Convention on Nuclear Safety	y	
1994	(PARIS) Convention to Combat Desertification	y	R
1997	(VIENNA) Joint Convention on the Safety of Spent Fuel Management and on the Safety of Radioactive Waste Management		
1997	(VIENNA) Convention on Supplementary Compensation for Nuclear Damage		
1998	(ROTTERDAM) Convention on the Prior Informed Consent Procedure for Certain Hazardous Chemicals and Pesticides in International Trade		
2001	(STOCKHOLM) Convention on Persistent Organic Chemicals		S

y = in force; S = signed; R = ratified; D = denounced.

Selected bilareral and multilateral agreements *(continued)*

Regional and subregional agreements

as of December 2001		Albania
1950 (PARIS) International Convention for the Protection of Birds	y	
1957 (GENEVA) European Agreement - International Carriage of Dangerous Goods by Road (ADR)	y	
1958 (GENEVA) Agreement - Adoption of Uniform Conditions of Approval and Reciprocal Recognition of Approval for Motor Vehicle Equipment and Parts.	y	
1968 (PARIS) European Convention - Protection of Animals during International Transport	y	
1979 (STRASBOURG) Additional Protocol	y	
1969 (LONDON) European Convention - Protection of the Archeological Heritage	y	
1976 (BARCELONA) Convention for the Protection of the Mediterranean Sea against Pollution	y	R
1976 (BARCELONA) Dumping Protocol	y	
1976 (BARCELONA) Emergency Protocol	y	
1980 (ATHENS) Land-based Sources Protocol	y	
1982 (GENEVA) Specially Protected Areas Protocol	y	
1994 (MADRID) Offshore Protocol		
1995 (BARCELONA) Specially Protected Areas and Biodiversity Protocol	y	
1996 (IZMIR) Hazardous Wastes Protocol		
1979 (BERN) Convention on the Conservation of European Wildlife and Natural Habitats	y	R
1979 (GENEVA) Convention on Long-range Transboundary Air Pollution	y	
1984 (GENEVA) Protocol - Financing of Co-operative Programme (EMEP)	y	
1985 (HELSINKI) Protocol - Reduction of Sulphur Emissions by 30%	y	
1988 (SOFIA) Protocol - Control of Emissions of Nitrogen Oxides	y	
1991 (GENEVA) Protocol - Volatile Organic Compounds	y	
1994 (OSLO) Protocol - Further Reduction of Sulphur Emissions	y	
1998 (AARHUS) Protocol on Heavy Metals		
1998 (AARHUS) Protocol on Persistent Organic Pollutants		
1999 (GOTHENBURG) Protocol to Abate Acidification, Eutrophication and Ground-level Ozone		
1991 (ESPOO) Convention on Environmental Impact Assessment in a Transboundary Context	y	R
1992 (HELSINKI) Convention on the Protection and Use of Transboundary Waters and International Lakes	y	R
1999 (LONDON) Protocol on Water and Health		
1992 (HELSINKI) Convention on the Transboundary Effects of Industrial Accidents	y	R
1993 (OSLO and LUGANO) Convention - Civil Liability for Damage from Activities Dangerous for the Environment		
1994 (LISBON) Energy Charter Treaty		
1994 (LISBON) Protocol on Energy Efficiency and Related Aspects		
1998 (AARHUS) Convention on Access to Information, Public Participation in Decision-making and Access to Justice in Environmental Matters	y	S

y = in force; **S** = signed; **R** = ratified; **D** = denounced.

SOURCES

Personal authors

1. Den Hexter, Hermans, H. Hulst, E., "Health Care Legislation in Central and Eastern Europe. A problem-oriented method of legal analysis of health care systems in central and eastern Europe. The Albanian example", Review of Central and East European Law, No. 2, 1997, pp. 117-132.
2. Fremuth, W. et al. Albania. Guide to its Natural Treasures. ECAT-Tirana. Tirana, Albania 2000.
3. Fremuth, W. et al. Assessment of the Sustainable Use of Medicinal Plants from the Ohrid and Prespa Region. ECAT-Tirana. Tirana, Albania 1999.
4. Gace Arian et al. Albania National Coastal Biodiversity Report: Regional GEF Project Proposal, "Conservation of wetlands and coastal ecosystems in the Mediterranean Region". December 1996.
5. Habili Dalip et al. Ecological Survey of Selected High Forest of Albania. March 1995.
6. Hetzer, A. "Dokumentation: Neues in der albanischen Literatur". Südosteuropa Mitteilungen. Jahrgang 37, Heft 2. 1997.
7. Koca, Arriana. Biodiversity.
8. Lemel, H. "Rural Land Privatisation and Distribution in Albania: Evidence from the Field", Europe-Asia Studies, Vol. 50, No. 1, 1998, pp. 121-140.
9. Lipsius, S. "Albanien - Dauerkrise oder Neubeginn?", Sudosteuropa Mitteilungen, No. 4, 1997. pp. 247-276.
10. Mappes-Niediek, N. "Von Albanien nach Rumanien, Unruhen und Umbruche in Sudosteuropa", Blatter fur deutsche und internationale Politik, April 1997, pp. 472-480.
11. Swetzer A. EPR Country Profile: "Albania" (Draft), ECE/ENHS Internal Papers, 5 July 1996.
12. Vangjeli J., B. Ruci, A. Mullaj, Libri I Kuq. Akademia E Shkencave, Instituti I Kërkimeve Biologjike. Tirana, 1995.

Material from Albania:

13. Accademia delle Scienze di Albania. Università Politecnica di Tirana. La Gestione delle Georisorse: Il Contributo allo Sviluppo e le Internazioni con l'ambiante. Seminario italo-albanese, Tirana 17-18 ottobre 2000. Albania, 2001.
14. Albanian Forestry Project. An Ecological Survey of Albanian Selected High Forests. http://pages.albaniaonline.net/forestry/docs%20HTML/Ecolsur.htm
15. Albanian Forestry Project. Institutional and Organizational Profile of the Project. http://pages.albaniaonline.net/forestry/docs%20HTML/inst-prof.htm
16. INSTAT. Albania in figures, 1996.
17. INSTAT. Causes of Deaths for the Year 1998. Tirana, 2000.
18. INSTAT. Causes of Deaths for the Years 1994-1997. Tirana, 1999.
19. INSTAT. General Results of Annual Structural Survey of Economic Enterprises. Year 1997. Tirane, 2000.
20. INSTAT. General Results of Annual Structural Survey of Economic Enterprises. Year 1998. Tirane, 2000.
21. INSTAT. General Results of Annual Structural Survey of Economic Enterprises. Year 1999. Tirane, 2001.
22. INSTAT. Social Indicators Yearbook 1999. Tirane, 1999.
23. Law on EIA. (Draft). NEAP, 2001.
24. Ministria e Mjedisit. 4° Incontro Seminariale. La cooperazione italo-albanese per la valorizzazione della biodiversità. Tirana, 22-23 Ottobre 2001.
25. Ministry of Health and the Environment of Albania. Data on Nature and Land use, extract from the Ecological Survey, working document, 1996.
26. Ministry of Tourism of Albania/EBRD. Albania: Investing in Tourism, Tirana.
27. Ministry of Tourism of Albania/European Bank for Reconstruction and Development. Albania Tourism Guidelines, November 1992.
28. National Environmental Agency. Air Quality Data. Received 26 July 2001.
29. National Environmental Agency. Overview of the Steps Undertaken in the Context of the Convention to Combat Desertification. Received 26 July 2001.
30. Njësia e Vlerësimit Mjedisor të Projektit të Pyjeve. Udhëzues për Vlerësimin Mjedisor të Punimeve në rrygët Pyjore. Albania, 1999.
31. Preliminary text of draft Law on Soil Management, Protection and Rehabilitation. NEAP, 2001.
32. Preliminary text of Law on Water Quality Protection. NEAP, 2001.
33. Republic of Albania. Council of Ministers. "Duties and Objectives for the Management of the Forest Environment", under the Decision "On the approval of the National Environmental Action Plan", 31.01.94.
34. Republic of Albania. Council of Ministers. Decision no. 26, 31 January 1994. On Hazardous Wastes and Residues.
35. Republic of Albania. Council of Ministers. Decision on "The duties of the Ministries, Institutions, Legal and Physical Persons for Environmental Monitoring and Control", No. 541, 25.09.95.
36. Republic of Albania. Council of Ministers. Growth and Poverty Reduction Strategy (First Draft). Tirana, Albania 2001.

37. Republic of Albania. Council of Ministers. Ministry of Construction, Housing and Territory Regulation. Decision No. 321. On "The coastal bordering line from river Buna to the Cape of Stillos", 20.07.92.
38. Republic of Albania. Council of Ministers. Ministry of Tourism of Albania: Decision No. 88, 21.01.1993. "For the approval of priority tourism development areas, Implementing the Law No. 7665, For the Priority Tourism Development Area, 21.03.93.
39. Republic of Albania. Law no. 7491, 29 April 1991, On Land.
40. Republic of Albania. Law no. 7664, 2 January 1993, On Environmental Protection.
41. Republic of Albania. Law no. 7917, 13. April 1995, On the Pastures and Meadows.
42. Republic of Albania. Law no. 8093, 21 March 1996, On Water Resources.
43. Republic of Albania. Law no. 8102, 28 March, 1996. On the Regulatory Framework of the Water Supply Sector and the Sector of the Drainage and Processing of Contaminated Water.
44. Republic of Albania. Law no. 8318, 15 April 1998, On Leasing the Agricultural Land, Forest Land, Meadows and Pastures, which are State Property.
45. Republic of Albania. Law no. 8364, 2 July, 1998, On some amendments and changes to Law no. 7664 On Environmental Protection.
46. Republic of Albania. Law no. 8405, 17 September 1998. On Urban Planning.
47. Republic of Albania. Law no.7693, 20 April 1993, On City Planning.
48. Republic of Albania. Law on City Planning, no. 7693, 6 April 1993.
49. Republic of Albania. Law on Organization and Function of Local Governments, No 8652, 31.07.2000.
50. Republic of Albania. Law on Priority Tourism Development Zones, Tirana, 21.01.93
51. Republic of Albania. Lists of Administrative bodies responsible for environmental protection, monitoring, and public access to environmental information, including Annex I, Organizational Chart. Environmental Monitoring Network.
52. Republic of Albania. Ministry of Agriculture and Food. The Strategy of Agricultural Development in Albania (The Green Strategy). Tirana, Albania 1998.
53. Republic of Albania. Ministry of Health and Environment Protection. Report on the environmental situation in Albania, National Environmental Action Plan. July 1993.
54. Republic of Albania. Ministry of Health and Environment Protection. Environmental Status Report 1993-1994. CEP, 1995.
55. Republic of Albania. Ministry of Health. Committee on Environmental Protection: Analyses of the Environmental Health Situation in Albania. Tirana, Albania, May 1998.
56. Republic of Albania. Ministry of Health. National Environmental Health Action Plan. Tirana, Albania July 1998.
57. Republic of Albania. Ministry of Public Economy and Privatisation. National Energy Strategy. Tirana, Albania, March 2000.
58. Republic of Albania. Ministry of Public Economy and Privatization. Privatization Strategy of State Owned Companies in Primary Importance Sectors. Tirana, Albania December 1997.
59. Republic of Albania. National Report for United Nations Conference on Human Settlements - HABITAT II Istanbul, 3-14 June 1996. Tirana 1996.
60. Republic of Albania. State of the Environment Report 1993-1994. Tirana, Albania 1995.
61. Republic of Albania. State of the Environment Report 1997-1998. Tirana, Albania October 1999.
62. Republic of Albania. The National Environmental Action Plan. Tirana, Albania July 1993.
63. Republic of Albania. The Strategy for the Development of the Forestry and Pasture Sector in Albania. Tirana, Albania.
64. Republic of Albania. Updated National Environmental Action Plan 2001. Draft.
65. Republika Shqipërisë. Ministria e Mjedisit. Report Për gjendjen e Mjedisit 1999-200. Tirane, Tetor 2001.

Regional and international institutions:

66. Aegis. European Environment Protection Newsletter, Volume I, Issue 4, article entitled: Global funds marshalled to upgrade hydroelectric power plants in Albania, Dec./Jan. 1995.
67. Albania Private Forestry Development Program. Fourth Annual Report, October 1 through December 31, 1999. http://www.ee-environment.net/docs/apfdp4yrreport.html
68. Albania REC. Doors to Democracy: Current Trends in Public Participation in Environmental Decision making in Central and Eastern Europe. Chapter 1: Budapest, Hungary June 1998.
69. Albania. REC. Status of Public Participation Practices in Environmental Decision making in Central and Eastern Europe. Country Report, Budapest, Hungary September 1995.
70. CCET. Politiques, marchés et échanges agricoles dans les pays en transition, Suivi et Evaluation 1996.
71. Centre Naturopa. Naturopa Newsletter. Special issue on Albania: Environmental Protection and Nature Conservation in Albania, 1996.
72. Commission of the European Union & Government of the Republic of Albania. Phare Programme. National Water Strategy for Albania. Final Report. Tirana, Albania, February 1997.
73. Commission of the European Union & Republic of Albania. EU Phare Programme. National Waste Management Plan for Albania. Tirana, Albania 1996.
74. East European Constitutional Review. "Albania". Volume 7, No 3, 1998.
75. ECAT. Environmental Centres for Administration and Technology, Newsletter, ECAT-Tirana, June-September 1996.
76. ECAT. The Environment Centre for Administration and Technology. Strategic Plan for Health Care Waste management in the Tirana Region. Draft, July 2000, Tirana.
77. ECAT-Tirana. Institutional Strengthening and Project Preparation. Tirana, Albania.
78. ECAT-Tirana. Organisation of the Urban Waste Management in 6 main Municipalities of Albania. Tirana, Albania 1998.
79. ECAT-Tirana. Strategic Plan for Health Care Waste Management in the Tirana Region. Tirana, Albania, June 2001.
80. EIU. Albania: Country Profile 1995-96 + Country Report, first and second quarter 1996.
81. European Conference of Ministers of Transport, Council of Ministers. Report on Transport in Albania. CEMT/CM(96)18, 24 April 1996.

82. European Union. "Albanian wetlands face serious challenges" and "Albanian water sector challenges government", two articles from "Green Phare No 1", November/December 1996.
83. FAO. Special Relief Operations Service TCOR: The Republic of Albania, Impact of the Kosovo Crisis on Albanian and the Environment. TCP/ALB/8924.Tirana, Albania, September 1999.
84. Global Environmental Facility & National Environmental Agency. The Biodiversity Strategy and Action Plan for Albania. 1999.
85. IEA. Recent Energy Developments in Central and Eastern Europe, "Albania", IEA/NMC(96)24, 07/10/96.
86. IUCN. East European Programme. Environmental Status Report: 1990, Volume Two: Albania, Bulgaria, Romania, Yugoslavia.
87. IUCN. East European Programme. Protected areas in Eastern and Central Europe and the USSR, an interim Review, 1990.
88. MedWet. ECAT-Tirana. Conservation and Wise Use of Wetlands in the Mediterranean Basin. Focus on the Kune-Vaini Lagoon, Lezhe, Albania. Technical Reports. Tirana, Albania. April 1998.
89. MedWet. Final Technical Report. February 1998.
90. National Environmental Agency & IBRD. Lake Ohrid Conservation Project, Mid-term Report. Tirana-Pogradec, Albania 2001.
91. OECD/CCET. Directorate for Food, Agriculture and Fisheries. Ad Hoc Group on East/West Economic Relations in Agriculture: Agricultural Trade, Income and Rural Development Policies in Albania. CCET/AGR/EW/EG(96)77, 23 September 1996.
92. Oxford Analytica Brief. Albania. Economic Dependency, April 27, 1998.
93. PHARE Programme mission in Albania (in connection with the Ministry of Tourism of Albania). Potential Development of Tourism in Albania, Environment and Institutional Aspects, 19 May -10 June 1992.
94. REC. A Strategic Environmental Analysis of Albania. Tirana, Albania, June 2000.
95. REC. Assessment of the Environmental Impact of Military Activity during Yugoslavia Conflict, June 1999.
96. REC. Beyond Boundaries. The International Dimensions of Public Participation for the Countries of Central and Eastern Europe. Part II: Case Examples from Central and Eastern Europe - Albania, p.83-87, Budapest, Hungary September 1996.
97. REC. Environmental Needs Assessment in Ten Countries. Albania. 1994.
98. REC. Manual on Public Participation in Environmental Decisionmaking. Current Practice and Future Possibilities in Central and Eastern Europe. P. 117-130.
99. REC. Media Source Directory. A Journalist's Guide to Environmental Contacts in Central and Eastern Europe. Szentendre, Hungary 1999.
100. REC. Nature, Landscape and Biodiversity Conservation in Albania. Tirana, Albania 1997.
101. REC. NGO Community in Pogradec, Albania. A Need Assessment of NGOs in Progradec Region. Tirana, Albania 1999.
102. REC. NGO Directory. A Directory of Environmental NGOs in Central and Eastern Europe. Overview Albania, p.30-41. Szentendre, Hungary December 1997.
103. REC. Problems, Progress and Possibilities. A Needs Assessment of Environmental NGOs in Central and Eastern Europe. Chapter 6: Country Reports - Albania, p.33-34. Szentendre, Hungary, April 1997.
104. REC. The Regional Environmental Center for Central and Eastern Europe. Newsletter "The Bulletin". "Local beat: Albania", Autumn 1996, Volume 6, No. 3.
105. REC. The Regional Environmental Center for Central and Eastern Europe. Newsletter "The Bulletin". "Awakening awareness", Autumn 1996, Volume 6, No. 3.
106. REC. The Regional Environmental Center for Central and Eastern Europe. Status of National Environmental Action Programs in Central and Eastern Europe, Case Study of Albania, May 1995.
107. The World Bank Group. Immediate Measures for the Implementation of the National Environmental Action Plan Albania Part I (Final Report) and Part II (Appendices). Washington D.C., United States of America 2001.
108. The World Bank. Albania Environmental Strategy Study. Report No. 11784-ALB, June 11, 1993.
109. The World Bank. Immediate Measures for the Implementation of the National Environmental Action Plan – Albania. Preliminary text of the draft law: Soil Protection and Preservation from Pollution, Erosion and other Adverse Natural Events; Final Report, part 2 Appendices, Doc. No. 99-508-H2 Rev. 1, Washington, D.C. USA June 2001.
110. The World Bank. Immediate Measures for the Implementation of the National Environmental Action Plan – Albania. 'Establishing an Environment Impact Assessment Procedure'. Final Report, part 2 Appendices, Doc. No. 99-508-H2 Rev. 1, Washington, D.C. USA June 2001.
111. The World Bank. Immediate Measures for the Implementation of the National Environmental Action Plan – Albania. 'Environmental Impact Assessment'. Final Report, part 2 Appendices, Doc. No. 99-508-H2 Rev. 1, Washington, D.C. USA June 2001.
112. The World Bank. Staff Appraisal Report. Albania, Irrigation Rehabilitation Project; report No. 12609-ALB, July 20, 1994.
113. The World Bank. Staff Appraisal Report. Albania, Power Loss Reduction Project; report No. 12779-ALB, December 7, 1994.
114. UNDP. Albanian Human Development Report 2000. Tirana, Albania 2000.
115. UNDP. Human Development Report Albania 1998. Tirana, Albania 1998.
116. UNDP. Human Development Report, Albania 1995, Tirana, Albania.
117. UNDP/ECE. Albania. National Report on Technological Requirements for the abatement of SO2 and NOx Emissions from Stationary Sources. ECE/UNDP/AP/15/R.4. 27 August 1990.
118. UNECE Trade Division. Albanian National report for joint EFc/timber committee session 9-13 October 2000.
119. UNECE/FAO. Forest and Forest Products Country Profile: "Albania", 1994.
120. UNEP. Feasibility Study for Urgent Risk Reduction at Hot Spots in Albania. UNEP/DEPI/Balkans Unit, Geneva, August 2001.
121. UNEP. Implications of climate change for the Albanian coast, MAP Technical Reports Series No 98, Athens, 1996.
122. UNEP. Post-Conflict Environmental Assessment – Albania. Geneva, Switzerland 2000.
123. UNEP. Report on the presentation of the results of the coastal areas management programme (CAMP) for Albania, UNEP (OCA) MED WG.113/2, Athens, 1996.
124. UNEP. The Kosovo Conflict - Consequences for the Environment and Human Settlements; Post-Conflict Environmental Assessment - Albania. Geneva, Switzerland 2000.
125. UNEP/Blue Plan Regional Activity Centre. "Albania", Mediterranean Country Profiles, Institutions, Environment, Development, June 1995.

126. UNEP/Blue Plan Regional Activity Centre. Systemic and Prospective Analysis for Mediterranean Sustainable Development, Activities and Outputs. April 1995.
127. UNEP/CAMP (Coastal Area Management Programme). Specially Protected Areas Rapport Albania. Tirana, Albania.
128. UNEP/CAMP. SPA report: "Specially Protected Areas".
129. UNEP/MAP. United Nations Environment Programme -Mediterranean Action Plan. Albania, Coastal Area Management Programme (CAMP). Conservation and Wise Use of Lagoons and Coastal Wetlands, Phase I Report. 5-9 December, 1994.
130. UNEP/World Conservation Monitoring Centre. National Assessment of Implementation of the Convention on Biological Diversity, "Albania". 16 August 2000.
131. UNEP-MAP and Dobbin Milus International. Albania Coastal Zone Management Plan. Final Report- Phase One. Priority Actions Programme, Split, Croatia and Vienna, Virginia, United States of America 1995.
132. UNEP-MAP and Dobbin Milus International. Albania Coastal Zone Management Plan. Final Report- Phase Two. Priority Actions Programme, Split, Croatia and Vienna, Virginia, United States of America 1995.
133. UNEP-MAP and Dobbin Milus International. Albania Coastal Zone Management Plan. Executive Summary, Split, Croatia and Vienna, Virginia, USA.
134. UNEP-MAP. Coastal Area Management Programme. The Region of Durres-Vlore Coastal Profile. CAMP/1993/AL/ICAM-CP, Priority Actions Programme. Split, Croatia 1994.
135. UNEP-MAP. The Region of Durresi-Vlora. Coastal Zone Management Plan. Priority Actions Programme. Split, Croatia 1996.
136. UNICEF. Children and Women of Albania, A situation Analysis. 1995.

Internet Addresses:

Ministries and government institutions:

137. Bank of Albania: http://www.bankofalbania.org/pages/epara/topic.htm
138. Department of Information - Council of Ministers: http://depinf.gov.al/english/default1.htm
139. Homepage of Albanian Parliament: http://www.parlament.al/english/eng-ver.html
140. Ministry of Economic Cooperation and Trade: http://www.mbet.gov.al/
141. Ministry of Foreign Affairs: http://www.mfa.gov.al/
142. Ministry of Information: http://mininf.gov.al/
143. Ministry of Labour and Social Affairs: http://www.molsa.gov.al/
144. National Environmental Agency: http://www.nea.gov.al/
145. Presidency: http://www.president.al/
146. Securities Commission: http://www.asc.gov.al/

Other sites:

147. Albania Forestry Project: http://pages.albaniaonline.net/forestry/
148. Albania News: http://www.albanianews.com/
149. Albanian Legal Information Initiative: http://pbosnia.kentlaw.edu/projects/albania/
150. Albanian Resource Centre: http://www.albania.co.uk/
151. Amnesty International: http://web.amnesty.org/ai.nsf/countries/albania
152. Australasian Legal Information Institute - Links to Albanian Laws on the Internet: http://www.austlii.edu.au/links/2387.html
153. CIA - Chief of State and Cabinet Members: http://www.cia.gov/cia/publications/chiefs/chiefs1.html
154. CIA World Factbook: http://www.cia.gov/cia/publications/factbook/geos/al.html
155. CIPE - The Center for the International Private Enterprise - Economic Reform in Albania: Working Paper 1994: http://www.cipe.org/wp/alb.html
156. Commission on Sustainable Development: http://www.un.org/esa/sustdev/csd.htm
157. Compton's Encyclopedia Online: http://www.comptons.com/encyclopedia/
158. Democratic Party of Albania: http://www.dpalbania.org/english/main/site2.html
159. EBRD - Albania and the EBRD: http://www.ebrd.com/english/opera/
160. EFERN (European Forest Ecosystem Research Network): EFERN Database-Experts, http://ifff.boku.ac.at/efern/
161. Elections in Albania: http://www.agora.it/elections/election/albania.htm
162. ENS- Environment News Service: http://ens.lycos.com/ens/sep2000/2000L-09-11-01.html
163. Environment and Natural Resources Information Network: http://www.grida.no/enrin/index.htm
164. European Bank for Reconstruction and Development (EBRD): Projects and Investments: http://www.ebrd.com/english/index.htm
165. European Investment Bank (EIB): Financing activities of EIB: http://www.eib.org/loans.htm
166. Faculty of Natural Sciences: http://www.gsf.de/UNEP/albfns.html
167. Forests and Pastures Research Institute (IKPK): http://www.gsf.de/UNEP/albikpk.html
168. GEF - Country Programme Strategies: Albania: http://www.undp.org/sgp/download/cps.htm
169. GEF - Small Grant Programme: Projects List Albania: http://www.undp.org/sgp/cty/EUROPE/ALBANIA/ov.htm
170. Governments on the WWW – Albania: http://www.gksoft.com/govt/en/al.html
171. GRID Arendal: http://www.grida.no/index.htm
172. Hutchinson Encyclopedia: http://ebooks.whsmithonline.co.uk/encyclopedia/02/C0000002.htm
173. IFES - Albanian Parliamentary Elections: http://www.ifes.org/albania/index.htm
174. IMF - Albania and the IMF: http://www.imf.org/external/country/ALB/index.htm
175. Institute for Policy and Legal Studies: http://www.ipls.org/

176. Institute of Chemical Technology: http://www.gsf.de/UNEP/albict.html
177. Institute of Hydrometeorology (IHM): http://www.gsf.de/UNEP/albih.html
178. Library of Congress - Country Study published 1992: http://lcweb2.loc.gov/frd/cs/altoc.html
179. Microsoft Encarta: http://encarta.msn.com/find/Concise.asp?ti=0276F000
180. OECD - Albania and the OECD Agricultural, trade and environmental issues: http://www.oecd.org/sge/ccnm/programs/albania/albania.htm
181. OECD – Environment: http://www.oecd.org/env
182. OECD - Investment Guide Albania: http://www.oecd.org/sge/ccnm/pubs/cpuz0904/present.htm
183. Pace University - Albanian Environmental Laws: http://www.pace.edu/lawschool/env/albanian.html
184. PHARE, search for details of EU external aid projects: http://europa.eu.int/comm/europeaid/cgi/frame12.pl
185. Political Resources - Albania Albanian political party homepage links. http://www.politicalresources.net/albania.htm
186. REC - Albanian Legislation: http://www.rec.org/REC/Databases/EcoLegis/ecolegisdbs.htm
187. REC - Basic Environmental Country Information Albania: http://www.rec.org/REC/Databases/GovDir/PDFs/Albania.pdf
188. REC - Country Report Albania: http://www.rec.org/REC/Publications/CountryReports/Albania.PDF
189. REC - Manual on Public: http://www.rec.org/REC/Publications/PPManual/Albania.html
190. REC - Status of NEAP in Albania 1995: http://www.rec.org/REC/Publications/NEAPstatus/FeeBased/Albania.html
191. REReP - The Regional Environmental Reconstruction Program for South East Europe: http://www.rec.org/REC/Programs/REREP/
192. Russian and East European Network Information Center - Basic Country Information Lots of links (about 50) on different subjects from culture to associations and religion. http://reenic.utexas.edu/reenic/countries/albania.html
193. SEERECON - Economic and Reconstruction and development in South East Europe: http://www.seerecon.org/
194. SIGMA - Center of Government Profile: http://www.oecd.org/puma/sigmaweb/acts/cogprofiles/alb-cog.htm
195. SIGMA - Political Background: http://www.oecd.org/puma/sigmaweb/profiles/albania-r/alb-toc.htm
196. Soros Open Society Foundation: http://www.soros.al/osfa/soros/english/english.html
197. Stability Pact: http://www.stabilitypact.org/
198. State Supreme Audit Control: http://pages.albaniaonline.net/klsh/englishh.htm
199. The European Union for Coastal Conservation: Albania: http://www.eucc.nl/eucc/index.htm
200. The World Conservation Union: http://www.iucn.org/
201. UN/DESA - Sustainable Development Country Profile Agenda 21: http://www.un.org/esa/earthsummit/alban-cp.htm
202. UNDP - UNDP Regional Office Albania: http://www.undp.org.al/
203. UNEP – Balkans: http://balkans.unep.ch/
204. UNEP - Mediterranean Action Programme: http://www.unepmap.gr/
205. UNEP - National Environmental Outlook: http://www.unep.net/profile/index.cfm?tab=100&countrycode=AL&submit=Go
206. UNEP - Post Conflict Environmental Assessment: http://balkans.unep.ch/albania/reports/report.html
207. UNEP - Regional Activity Centre for Specially Protected Areas: http://www.rac.spa.org
208. UNEP / DTIE (Paris): Division of Technology, Industry, and Economics: http://www.uneptie.org
209. UNEP/GRID - Environmental Information Systems in Albania: http://www.grida.no/enrin/htmls/albania/albania.htm
210. UNEP/MAP - The Mediterranean Action Plan: http://www.unepmap.gr/
211. USAID - Interim Report Supporting Implementation of the legal and regulatory framework for Albania's Water Supply, waste water, and solid waste sectors: http://www.usaid.gov/regions/europe_eurasia/local_gov/pdf_docs/interim.pdf
212. USAID: http://www.usaid.gov/
213. World Bank – Albania: http://www.worldbank.org/html/extdr/regions.htm
214. World Bank - Second Irrigation and Drainage Rehabilitation Project: http://www.worldbank.org/pics/pid/al43178.txt
215. World Environment: http://www.worldenvironment.com/

Conventions and programmes:

216. Bern Convention: http://www.nature.coe.int/english/cadres/berne.htm
217. Bonn Convention (Convention on Migratory Species): http://www.wcmc.org.uk/cms/
218. Convention on Biological Diversity: http://www.biodiv.org/
219. RAMSAR Convention: http://www.ramsar.org/
220. REC: http://www.rec.org/Default.shtml
221. UNECE Helsinki Convention (Convention on the Protection and Use of Transboundary Watercourses and International Lakes): http://www.unece.org/env/water/wel

DATE DUE

Demco, Inc. 38-293